JAPAN'S WORLD WAR II LEGACY

*To Barbara and Penny
with love
Hiroko 裕子 Feb. 2016*

Japan's World War II Legacy

HIROKO SHERWIN

QUARTET

First published in 2015 by
Quartet Books Limited
A member of the Namara Group
27 Goodge Street, London W1T 2LD

A catalogue record for this book
is available from the British Library

ISBN   978 0 7043 7402 7

Typeset by Antony Gray
Printed and bound in Great Britain by
T J International Ltd, Padstow, Cornwall

To my husband, Jimmy

Contents

Introduction

The Asia Pacific campaigns of World War II lasted from 1941 until 1945. But Japan's war had begun ten years earlier with the conquest of Manchuria in 1931 and had continued with the invasion of a wide expanse of China, which left the Japanese Army in a quagmire. When the Japanese advanced deep into Southeast Asia, America imposed an oil embargo on Japan. It was insane for a small nation to start a war against the United States, a country with five hundred times more oil and twenty times more steel, but they did. On 15 August 1945, when Japan surrendered, the country stood dazed at ground zero, exhausted and devastated after fifteen years of war.

I was eight when the war ended. The first thought I had on that day was that now I could return to Nagoya. With Japan spending all of its resources on the military, Nagoya had been a grey city, and life there had been austere; the only toys I can remember my mother buying for me were paper balloons and a bamboo flute from a toy-stand during a festival. My sister and I amused ourselves by folding newspapers like origami, making beanbags we juggled and creating puzzles. But Nagoya was where I had grown up.

The reason our family had left Nagoya was that soon after I began elementary school, American B-29 bombers had started to visit the sky. They dropped incendiary bombs and turned the city into a sea of fire. Every time a siren blew, I dashed into a shelter in our garden with my family and squatted in a pitch-dark cave as primitive as that of any prehistoric man. Mud slid down the cave walls as the bombs shook the earth. Once I peeped through a crack in the wooden flap of the cave and saw a swarm of winged creatures like locusts approaching at great speed, their glaring eyes blinking in the dark. They were dropping hundreds of spear-headed demons of death onto thousands of houses.

Then a deafening thud lifted me off the ground. I saw the upper half of a big house across the street slide into the ground as if it were molten lava. Millions of sparks showered on the neighbourhood, lighting it up as if it were day. The next morning my best friend Misa was missing. I saw one of her red boots in a pile of debris.

Soon afterwards, my mother took her youngest three children – my older sister, myself and a younger brother – to a village in Gifu, leaving my father behind. He worked for an electric power company. My two elder brothers made bombs in an arms factory instead of going to high school.

We rented two rooms of a farmer's house, which stood at the foot of a small mountain. In front of the house was a rice field that extended to a clear river where we swam in the summer. It could have been an idyllic life for a city child like me, but I was always hungry and sick from lack of nutrition. My sister, brother and I picked edible weeds and ferns on the mountain for my mother to cook. We went to the rice field and caught grasshoppers, which my mother marinated with soy sauce and roasted on a hibachi stove. This was our daily supper. Although we lived on a farm, the farmers said they had to send all their rice, eggs and chickens off to soldiers on the battlefield. The rationed food the government gave us was ground powder, a dubious mixture of ingredients that never agreed with my stomach.

My mother was too proud to beg the neighbouring farmers for food. But when she saw us as thin as skeletons, a bald spot on my sister's head and other signs of malnutrition, she finally took her best kimono out of her chest of drawers and visited a rich farmer in the village. She, a daughter of a baron and former Minister of War, bowed deeply down to her knees half a dozen times before the farmer gave her a bag of rice in exchange for the kimono.

At school my classmates talked about me as 'that city girl' and laughed at my accent. Although I eventually became fluent in the local dialect and made a few good friends, I still missed my former life.

One afternoon in August 1945, an old man with a long goatee and a bamboo stick walked to the square in the centre of the village. I could tell that he was no villager because he spoke with a different accent. His face twisted in agony as he said, 'Doomsday has come. A terrible thing happened in Hiroshima. Satan ignited his magic lamp and lit up the whole sky. Then a monstrous mushroom sprouted – the most virulent mushroom that has ever grown on earth. As it sputtered its poison, the whole city turned into an inferno, burning hundreds of thousands of people, blackening and peeling their skin as if they were potatoes, blowing eyes out of their sockets, wrenching off heads, limbs and hearts. All the buildings collapsed and the city turned into a grave of burnt bodies. The river was flooded with the dead.' He walked away in the direction of the train station from which he had come, leaning on his stick. The war ended eight days later.

After the war, we returned to Nagoya. The city was even greyer than before, with burnt houses piled up in a vast wasteland. We cleaned up the debris in the backyard and sowed tomato and eggplant seeds.

My school had burnt down and my friends had scattered. At a makeshift school with a tin roof, we used brushes dipped in sumi ink to blot out all the sentences in our textbook that glorified the Emperor and praised the courageous soldiers who fought a holy war. Now teachers lavished praise on America instead of the Emperor. It was strange that the Emperor, who had been a god, was suddenly a man, and that the Americans we used to call green-eyed monsters were heroes. It was humiliating to see in the newspaper the picture of a frail-looking man with sloping shoulders standing timidly next to the pipe-smoking MacArthur, who towered over him. This was the Emperor for whom millions of our men fought and died. This was the man in whose name they had killed millions of enemies.

The soldiers and sailors who returned from the war abroad were not given a hero's welcome. I remember a man with one leg in an old hospital gown who stood on crutches at a street corner, bowing his head. By his side was a small post saying, 'a disabled veteran'. The upside-down rusty iron helmet in front of him had only a few coins in it. People passed by hurriedly, pretending not to see him or his helmet.

The scars of the war faded from the facades of cities and the soldiers kept memories of the war hidden deep down in their chests. At school children read textbooks in which inconvenient facts were minimised. The stories they heard from their parents and grandparents were about the bombings of Tokyo, Hiroshima, and Nagasaki. That fostered a victim mentality amongst the post-war generation.

I never learned the history of the war at school in Japan. In 1960 I went to the United States and attended graduate school at Harvard. One day the four walls of our history classroom were covered by posters which said in Chinese, 'Don't forget the Nanjing Massacre. Down with the Japanese, the Devils from the East! They killed 200,000 Chinese civilians.' That day I went to the library and learned about the massacre for the first time.

This marked the beginning of my soul-searching. Why did no teacher at school ever teach us about the Nanjing Massacre, or about the war itself? Why was our nation so insane as to fight a war that it had almost no chance of winning? Why did Japanese, who were ordinarily gentle and rational people, turn into inhuman demons on the battlefield? Was there anything in our national character that pushed us to cruelty? Or do all men turn into animals when the circumstances warrant?

My journey was slow. At one point I traced my paternal grandfather's life which coincided with modern Japan's rise, and wrote a generational novel covering the period from 1865 to 1945.[1] The early Meiji men like him worked hard to help build a modern nation, but the country turned fascist and advanced along the road to war.

My husband's work took us from America to England in 1999. Soon after arriving, I met some old men who were not as friendly as the normally kind British. They turned out to be former POWs who had worked on the Thai-Burma Railway. I am ashamed to say that I had no knowledge of this camp or any other. No one in Japan had ever mentioned the POW camps to me.

A neighbour allowed me to read the diary his father had kept during his POW days. People introduced me to former prisoners they knew. I wrote a book about them in Japanese,[2] thinking that their stories should be heard by my countrymen. Most of the Japanese who read the book said that it was the first time they had learned about the POWs and their suffering.

1 Sherwin, Hiroko, *Eight Million Gods and Demons*, Plume, Penguin Group, 2001
2 Sherwin, Hiroko, *Even So I Lived* (Soredemo Bokuwa Ikinuita), Nashinoki-sha, Tokyo, 2009

The collective image of Japanese soldiers which emerged from their former enemies' accounts was one of cruelty. They were possessed by their fanatical adoration of the Emperor. But I did not want to believe that every one of them was inhuman. If they had been, what had made them so?

I had read stories of the Russo-Japanese War (1904–5) in which men in the Japanese army helped wounded enemy soldiers, sailors rescued Russian seamen drifting in the ocean, and prison guards treated POWs like important guests. What happened to such conduct in World War II?

After I finished the book on the Allied POWs, I turned my attention to the Japanese soldiers. From 2011 through 2014 I flew to Japan several times to interview veterans. Most of them were in their nineties. Their sense that they had little time left prompted them to speak the truth about the war. One of them said, 'Soon there will be a day when no one will be able to bear witness to the war. That's why I'll tell you my story, even if it means exposing my deepest regrets and shame.'

It is one thing to reflect on the dark side of history by myself and quite another to translate the soldiers' words into English and expose an ugly part of my country's history to the wider world. But I kept telling myself that what happened in the war was part of world history and had to be shared by everyone. We owe the truth to the memory of those who died or suffered because of the war.

Part One of this book tells the stories of former soldiers. I am enormously grateful to those who were willing to meet me. They were often introduced to me by young men and women who had done interviews with them for historical research or for archival records. Each former soldier I met had a special story to tell, but unfortunately, I could not include all the interviews I had. Most of the stories chosen here were told by low-ranking soldiers and junior officers. I met a few high-ranking officers, but in the end their testimony was not included because they tended to be protective of the role they had played in the war.

The soldiers who appear in this book are student soldiers, boy volunteers, *Tokko* crew, POW guards and those who fought in China, the Philippines and New Guinea. I wanted to learn from the veterans what they saw and experienced in the War. I did not intend to write an all-inclusive history book. Therefore, certain theatres of the war such as Okinawa are not covered.

The interviews with the old veterans answered my question: Why did the Japanese wage an inhumanely savage war? The answer, or at least what I thought it was, is explained in depth in the Preface to Part Two: 'From War to Post-war.' What I can say here is that former soldiers – not only those who committed atrocities, but also those who just did their duty and saw their comrades die on the battlefield – have lived with deep guilt and sadness. Without exception, all the former soldiers I interviewed hope that their nation will never fight another war.

During the interviews with veterans, I kept wondering what their children had done about the dark legacy of their fathers' war. Just as their fathers had no choice but to fight the war, it was inevitable for the next generation to face the aftermath of the war. How did they cope with it? Did the nation reflect on the war and mourn for it sufficiently?

In Part Two I tried to find this out. Japan, as a nation, did not engage in soul-searching as the Germans did after their war. The emperor never apologised to the millions who had fought the War for him, and died for him. No Japanese prime minister knelt before a foreign victims' memorial, as Willy Brandt had done. There was no formal apology issued to the world until the 1990s. Lack of national mourning and of any truthful education about the War may explain the recent rise of nationalism under Prime Minister Abe's government.

But I met many people who had done soul-searching about their fathers' war and mourned for it as if it had been their own. They made efforts of reconciliation with former enemies. They travelled overseas and apologised to their victims' families and friends. Some founded organisations that attempted to help the victims of the War. Others expressed their sadness about it in literature, art and the theatre.

On 15 August 2015, Prime Minister Abe gave an address on the 70th Anniversary of the War, saying that Japan had inflicted 'immeasurable damage and suffering' when 'it took the wrong course and advanced along the road to war.' Although the address was carefully composed under the advice of an advisory panel, at least he said: 'I express my feelings of profound grief and my eternal, sincere condolences.'

Preface to Part One

> I cry for you, Brother,
>   don't you dare lay down your life,
> You, the youngest child in our family,
>   thus cherished all the more –
> Mother and Father didn't educate you
>   to wield weapons and to murder; they didn't
> bring you up, to the age of twenty-four,
>   so that you could kill, or be killed yourself.
>
>   Yosano Akiko, translated by Arthur Binard[3]

Yosano Akiko dedicated this poem to her brother, who was then a soldier in the Imperial Army at Port Arthur in the Russo-Japanese War. The soldiers there were rumored to be volunteering for suicide missions in the protracted assault on the fortress. Yosano went on to ask, 'What is it to you whether / the walls of Port Arthur tumble or they stand?'

In the third stanza, she was even more outspoken:

> Don't you dare lay down your life.
>   The Emperor himself doesn't go
> to fight at the front; others
>   spill out their blood there.
> If His Majesty be indeed just
>   and magnanimous, surely he won't wish
> his subjects to die like beasts,
>   nor would he call such barbarity 'glory'.

---

3 Yosano, Akiko, 'Kimi Shinitamou Kotonakare' (Don't Lay down Your Life), published in *Famous Japanaese Poems Shine in English*, Misuzu Shobo, Tokyo, Japan, pp. 76–9

This forty-line poem was published in the September 1904 issue of a literary magazine, *the Myojo*. Yosano, a liberated woman, was well-known for her colourful romantic poems. This poem, which she sent to her brother, was written as a plea rather than a political protest, but liberal-minded women and men embraced it passionately after it was published. Although it enraged the militarists, the authorities did not imprison her, nor did they ban publication. Twenty-five years later, anyone attempting to publish such a poem in Japan would have been punished for high treason.

Before the 1920s, people in Japan enjoyed relatively free speech and democracy. Vigorous thought control began in 1925, under the Public Peace Preservation Law. The police rounded up thousands of socialists as well as anyone who revealed signs of being anti-Emperor or anti-government. Intellectuals, scholars, writers and religious leaders had to publicly renounce their former beliefs, or go into hiding.

In 1929, the Depression brought a downturn in the previously booming Japanese economy. Nationalists in the Japanese Army saw Manchuria, in the north-east of China, not only as the key to pushing back Russia and expanding into China, but also as the source of desperately needed food, coal, and iron.

On 18 September 1931, Japanese Army personnel detonated a small quantity of dynamite near a railroad owned by Japan's South Manchuria Railway, near Mukden. After accusing Chinese dissidents of the act, the Army 'responded' with a full invasion that led to the occupation of Manchuria. There, Japan established the puppet state of Manchuko. The international community soon became aware of Japan's ruse, which led to Japan's diplomatic isolation from the League of Nations.

Intermittent fighting in northern China followed. In the summer of 1937, as Japanese troops carried out military training manoeuvres in the vicinity of the Marco Polo Bridge where Chinese troops happened to be, they exchanged fire. The exact cause of this incident still remains a mystery. The skirmish quickly escalated into a full-scale campaign which continued until 1945, merging during the last four years into the Pacific War of World War II.

China proved to be a formidable foe. In Shanghai alone, Chinese forces outnumbered the Japanese ten to one, and Chiang Kai-shek had reserved his best troops for the battle. Although the Japanese managed to win Shanghai in the end, the mood of the Imperial Army turned ugly after the enormous casualties it had suffered. Their rampage after the fall of Nanjing in December 1937, is widely considered one of the worst massacres in recent history. Yasuji Kaneko's story, which follows this section, reveals the brutality of the Japanese in China.

Manchuko appeared not to be rich in oil and other natural resources as the Japanese had expected, although eventually that turned out to be wrong.[4] The Army, therefore, began to advance to Northern Indochina, with a special eye on Indonesia, a country rich in oil, iron ore, sugar and rubber – just what Japan needed. The advance to Southern Indochina brought a freeze on Japanese assets in the United States in July 1941, and a complete embargo on oil exports in August. After several months of unsuccessful negotiations with the US, including his proposal of a personal meeting between himself and President Roosevelt, Prime Minister Konoe resigned. His successor was the belligerent War Minister, General Hideki Tojo. Knowing that their oil supply would only last for one year or so Tojo and the Japanese leaders made the decision to start a war against the United States.

As justification they said the objective of the war was the creation of a Greater East Asia Co-Prosperity Sphere with their nation as the leader. Many young men willingly went to war in pursuit of this seemingly high-minded objective.

When Japan attacked Pearl Harbor on 8 December 1941, America declared war and the Allied countries soon followed suit. The die was cast.

---

4 In 1959, the Daqing oil field, the world's fourth largest, was discovered in Manchuria. The current production rate is about 1 million barrels per day.

Part One

Veterans' Testimony

CHAPTER 1

Yasuji Kaneko

Voices from the Well – Atrocities in China

He sat in a wheelchair, his hands dangling from the chair's arms and his head nodding to and fro as if his thin neck could not bear its weight. Among the dwindling population of veterans, Yasuji Kaneko was known as one of the most outspoken witnesses of the atrocities that the Japanese had committed in China. Although ninety-one and ill, he had been kind enough to accept my request for an interview.

I had come braced to hear stories of horror. But Kaneko-san welcomed me with a friendly smile. He did not look like a murderer. Despite his frail appearance, he was lucid and spoke fluently. He had grown up in a fisherman's village, and seemed proud of it. His language was rough, and he used vulgar words and expressions throughout our conversation, but I knew he could express himself in a highly literary fashion. I had read several of the novels he had written in prison and they showed that he had real talent as a writer. This is his story.

'I've done things a man should not do to an animal, let alone another human being. I am an accomplished villain. But I wasn't born a criminal. My parents didn't raise me to be a murderer. My father was a poor fisherman and I was the second son of seven kids. The extended family, eleven of us altogether, lived in a small house with only one naked electric bulb hanging from the ceiling. We lived in a small village near Tokyo Bay and had two boats – a small one for scooping seaweed near the shore and a big one for going out to sea to catch eels, shrimp and crabs.

'I was a terrible brat as a boy. But at least I worked hard to help my parents. As a child I had to get up at three in the morning to help my father dry seaweed outside. Then I went to school carrying my baby brother on my back, as other kids in my neighbourhood did. I loved having him in school with me. If I didn't feel like studying, I pinched his foot and made him cry. If he cried loudly enough, the teacher would tell me to get him out of the room, and I could play outside. When I came home, I had to work in the fields where my mother grew rice. I grew older, and joined one of the gangs in town. If I wanted to go see a movie, my mother would offer me pocket money in exchange for chores. I knew a better way. I went with my gang to a nearby temple, broke an offertory box with a rock, and took the coins in it. At the summer festival we tried to scare the lovers kissing in the bushes. We said, "Give us money, or else we'll tell everyone what you're doing." My parents were hard workers and decent people, but my brothers and I were bullies.

'I wasn't a bad student, but like the other poor kids, I quit school after six years. I never wanted to be a fisherman. Fishermen never make money. So I went to Tokyo and became an apprentice to a scrap-iron dealer. Our job was to buy scrap iron from factories and sell it to steel companies. The price of iron goes up and down, so if you knew what you were doing, as the dealer I was working for did, you could make a good profit. But he paid me just a miniscule amount. I taught myself how to cheat by adding iron sand to the scrap iron I sold, and started to make some money.

'At the age of seventeen, I decided to apply for army officer's school. For a poor boy like me, army school was a good idea since tuition was dirt cheap. Besides, the military men swaggered around the streets and got loads of respect. But I'd had too little education to get in. So I started taking a correspondence course. I was working hard, but when my uncle told my father what I was doing, my father beat me and tore up the application. "Don't ever become a soldier," he shouted. "It's the last thing any son of mine should be. In China, our soldiers are behaving like bandits."

'The Japanese had been fighting an undeclared war against China ever since my father's time. The newspapers lavished praise on the Emperor's "holy army" and never mentioned the atrocities they were committing in Nanjing and elsewhere. Every time a new city fell, the Japanese were intoxicated with joy, and went out with red lanterns and paraded in the streets. I was too busy making money to join the celebrations. When the war escalated, the price of iron soared, and my boss made an enormous profit. But since then he'd been drafted to serve in China, and so had my elder brother and my friends. I knew my turn was coming. I no longer wanted to go to war, because I'd gotten better at my job and was enjoying the sweet taste of money, and had started going to geisha houses too.

'I received my draft notice in 1940. I passed the physical exam with flying colours. Despite my father's hope, a soldier's life was my destiny. I told my mother that I would be a first class private. "I couldn't care less about rank," she said. "Just come back alive." I looked around to make sure nobody had heard. An unpatriotic comment like that would get her thrown out of the village. A brave mother was supposed to say, "Die a glorious death for the Emperor!"

'The day I left on the cargo ship, my dad and mum were there, standing among the hundreds of well-wishing parents and lifting up a big flag with my name written in *sumi* ink. The ship left the dock with all the new young soldiers lined up on deck. I didn't expect it would be sixteen years before I returned, and my parents never imagined that their son would become a blood-thirsty "Demon from the East". I was seasick for five days before the ship finally arrived at Qingdao, a city located in Shandong province in eastern China. My troop was taken to a small town where the headquarters of the Japanese Army 32nd Division had been set up. I was assigned to the 44th Battalion and put in a barracks.

'Life in military camp was a living hell. The training was aimed purely to destroy all normal human feelings and create bestial monsters instead. There never was a day I was not beaten for being arrogant, for speaking a dialect, for not learning the military code fast enough. They hit me with fists, belts or their hobnail boots. They made me crawl on the floor with a filthy shoe in my mouth. I was born at the bottom of the social ladder and here, too, I was at the bottom. No place is more rank-conscious than the army. Old soldiers were gods! When they came in after a long day outside, we had to wipe off their sweat, take off their shoes, unwind their gaiters and soak their feet in tubs of warm water. We cleaned their clothes and cooked and served them dinner.

'Once, Lance Corporal K told me to get water from a well. I drank some water at the well because I was thirsty. When I returned with a pail full of water, K asked if I had had any water. I said, "Yes, sir." Instantly he began slapping my cheeks. The beating lasted for three minutes, until fireballs sparked in my eyes. Then K grabbed my shirt collar and threw me into the air. My head hit the ground hard. What was wrong with drinking water? I was furious. Standing against the wall in front of me were dozens of bayonets. I almost grabbed one and killed him. I was always his target. Personal attacks were ostensibly forbidden, but the military's unspoken policy was that abuse would toughen the soldiers.

'We were trained to kill. In October of 1941, we were at a base in Shandong province. Armed for a drill, we marched in ranks. Ahead of us was a row of several captives bound to stakes, their hands tied behind them. We were ordered to dig a hole behind each stake. Then the commander said, "You need to learn to kill the enemy. This is a test as well as an initiation ceremony. If you don't pass the test, you won't be a soldier. Remember that the more Chinese you kill, the more you'll contribute to our country and the Emperor." My target was a young boy with large wet eyes. His face was ashen and twisted with fear. He was a peasant's son, and supposedly a communist guerrilla. I thought that his mother must be waiting for him to come home. When my turn came, the Commander yelled, "Attention, private first class Kaneko. Step forward." "Yes, sir," I said, popping up like a toy. The commander was glaring at me. My teeth chattered, my hands and limbs felt numb, and I collapsed. The commander kicked and pounded me with his boots, shouting, "You are a miserable chicken, Kaneko. Get up and charge." I jumped up and this time ran like a bull towards the young man. With my bayonet at the ready, I pierced his chest. It was an unthinkable crime, but the commander praised me.

'My thoughts were with the boy all night. I had cut an innocent young man's life short, a sin for which I would never be forgiven. But at the same time, I was glad I had passed the test.

'I got used to killing. Do you know what the word brave means? You are brave if you can kill. The more you kill, the braver you are.

The more enemies you kill, the more you contribute to your country. My comrades and I had a running competition to see who could kill the most. There were some soldiers who refused to kill and rape. We considered them weaklings, and most were court-martialed and shot.

'We had never even heard of the Geneva Convention. When we attacked a village, we raped women, killed their husbands, and stole their pigs, chickens, rice and vegetables. We cut up their furniture to make firewood. Then we burnt the village and left. The military had trained us to kill and loot, but I'll admit to you that they never told us to rape. In fact they had provided us with comfort women in order to make rape unnecessary. The comfort women were at any rural station where there were soldiers. Many were young girls from Korea, some from villages in China. Lured away by the promise of good jobs, they had been taken from their homes to faraway battlefields. The problem was that officers always got to use them first; our turn came last. Plus they were expensive. I was paid eight yen a month, and a woman cost one yen, so I couldn't afford them often. Village women were free. The screams of the women I raped still ring in my ears.

'One day my unit was supposed to attack a village. Our troops had a hard time because the village was protected by a stone wall. So we took out a secret weapon – poison gas. We used it as part of our *sanko* policy – kill, rob and run. As the smoke from the gas filled the village, the villagers staggered into the streets. We riddled them with bullets, and they fell to the ground. Then we went into the homes. I was told to kill everyone left, including women and children, because women give birth and boys would grow up to fight us in the future. We killed 130 people that time.

'Once, when we were stationed in a village, Lance Corporal Y and I prowled about with bayonets, searching for prey. After kicking down the doors of a number of houses, we found a young woman with a son of about four hiding in the back of a house. "Oi, Kaneko, take the kid and guard the outside. After I finish, it'll be your turn," Y said. Then he went inside, leaving the yelling boy to me. I heard screaming and howling. Eventually Y came out, seething with anger, his face red. "A pig-headed bitch," he mumbled, pulling the woman by her hair. "Kaneko. Come with me," he said. He dragged the woman to the village well, twenty metres away. He hauled the crying woman up to the edge of the brick wall around the well.

' "What are you going to do with her?" I asked. "I'm going to throw her in," he said. "Help me lift her up." I picked up her legs and pushed her in. The well was so deep I couldn't see the bottom. Her screams echoed, and a few seconds later we heard a big splash. Y took a tobacco plug out of his pocket and put it in his mouth. The little boy had followed us. He ran round and round the well, crying, "Ma–ma – , Ma–ma – ." After a while he ran back to the house. He came out, carrying a small stool in his arms. He placed it by the well and stepped up. Before I could stop him, he had climbed on top of the well and jumped in, calling, "Ma–ma." The voice reverberated against the wall of the well, "Mama, Mama, Mama."

' "Kaneko, aren't you a samurai?" Y said. "Show some sympathy. Throw a hand grenade into the well." So I did. In a few seconds there was an explosion at the bottom of the well, and the wailing voices stopped. But they didn't stop in my mind. Later, after I returned to Japan, got married and had my own daughter, it was this Chinese boy's voice I heard every time she cried, "Mama." It haunts me still. Indeed we were *dong yang gui*. Devils from the East.

'In the summer of 1945 we were sent to North Korea. We dug trenches to prepare for a Soviet invasion and were trained in suicide missions, which consisted of running with explosives in our arms until we hit Soviet tanks. So when we heard the news that the war had ended, I was ecstatic. It was too bad that we'd lost the war, but I had survived. Finally I could go home. The Russians rounded us up. We were overjoyed when they said, "*Japonski, Damoi*, go home." We were taken to a port and put on a Soviet freighter. The strange thing was, the ship headed north instead of south. The port we arrived at was Vladivostok. Then a train took us further north to Khabarovsk. Then we turned west, passed the River Amur, and found ourselves in the middle of Siberia. The Russians had deceived us.

'Life in Siberia was harsh. Our food was a 350 gram piece of black bread a day. We cut trees, built factories and houses, laid railways, paved roads and made bridges in the freezing cold, often twenty degrees below. I was angry with the Soviets. Eight days before the end of the war, when the Allies' victory was a fait accompli, they had broken the neutrality treaty and declared war on Japan. Then after Japan was defeated, they took 600,000 Japanese soldiers and civilians to Siberia for hard labour. I heard later that 60,000 of our comrades died of fatigue, hunger and illness in Soviet camps. I was angry with the Emperor as well. Without ever going to war himself, he had sent us to China to kill and be killed. Now we were in Siberia. Shouldn't he at least come and rescue us? I seriously believed he would come. Three years and then five years passed. He never came. I felt betrayed, disillusioned, and angry.

'We had to sit for hours in a classroom every week, chanting praise for Stalin and listening to boring Communist propaganda. Some of the other Japanese were brainwashed and began trying to convert the rest of us. With the backing of the Soviets, they abused their power, lynching former officers and anyone they didn't like. I hated them. We called them *actives*, or red radish – their red, only skin deep. They promised the authorities they would actively promote Communism when they returned to Japan. From time to time the Russians announced the names of those who were to go home on the next ship. Red Radishes were the first ones called.

'After five long years in Siberia, most detainees had been sent home, but my name had still not been called. One day the Division I formerly belonged to was rounded up. "*Damoi! Damoi!*" the Soviets shouted again. They had tricked us with this line half a dozen times already, so we didn't really believe them. But we couldn't help hoping against hope that this time it might be true. They took us to Khabarovsk, but instead of the harbour, we were taken to a train depot. Under guard by Soviet soldiers with bayonets, we were guided onto a filthy freight train that was wrapped with barbed wire. Inside, it was as hot and humid as a steam bath and the smell of animals was overwhelming. Having taken advantage of us for five years, they had the nerve to put us in old cattle cars. Three layers of bunk beds were piled up to the ceiling and the only thing you could do was to lie on a bed because, if you sat up, you'd hit your head on the bottom of the bed above. In no time we had soaked the bed through with our sweat. It was hell.

'Our last hope for *damoi* was shattered on the third day when we peeked outside through the barbed-wire window and saw a sign for the border between the USSR and China. We were ordered to get off the train, and then there was a little ceremony, with the Soviet soldiers in blue, handing us over to the Chinese in their khaki Mao uniforms. Now we were in the hands of the Chinese. We were led to a Chinese train. There, to our utter surprise, we found a clean and bright passenger train. Everyone's eyes lit up and cries of joy filled the air. I sat in a compartment that was spotlessly clean. Tears gushed from my eyes. Someone was treating us like human beings. A stir went through the place when two young nurses appeared in front of us and asked, "Is there anyone here who is sick? Can we do something for you? Do you need anything?" Tears ran down my cheeks again when a steamed bun, meat soup, roasted pork and pickles were brought out for lunch.

'The destination of our long trip from Russia was Fushun, a small city in northeast China. As we stepped off the train, we saw an ancient stone tower standing on the flat top of a bare mountain. I remembered that this was where 3,000 villagers had been massacred by our Army. We were taken to a big building with a watchtower surrounded by brick walls. The nameplate on the gate read *Fushun War Criminals' Prison, People's Republic of China*. I felt as if the world had turned black again. I was no war criminal. I had fought faithfully for the Emperor for five years and should have been thanked. Instead I had been detained in Siberia for five years and now this . . . No one knew how they chose 969 of us out of 600,000 Japanese detainees in Siberia. Among us there were Division Commanders, Manchuria Government officers and the like who really were war criminals, but why were the first and second year recruits there who had hardly been in any battles?

'But inside the building, we were welcomed with warm smiles. Beaming servants brought us tea and snacks, and then a sumptuous dinner. They were just being nice, I told myself, because tomorrow we would be hanged. Yet the next day not one of us was taken away in a blindfold or handcuffs. They kept treating us as if we were guests rather than prisoners. We weren't assigned any work. They just served us good meals and let us sleep on comfortable futons.

'Most of the prison administrators and workers had relatives or friends who had been raped or murdered by the Japanese. One worker even recognised the inmate who had killed his father. He kept gazing at the man with visible anger, his face red and his hands trembling. But he never raised a hand, or even his voice. I heard later that Premier Zhou Enlai had ordered everyone to treat the criminals humanely, that he'd said: "Even a deadly criminal is a human being. We detain criminals here not to punish them, but to help them atone." We were divided by our former military rank – officers, NCOs and *Kempeis* (military police) – and assigned to different rooms. The last Emperor of Manchuria, Pu-yi, was there, too. He was probably put in a special room with his brother. I saw them walking together in the yard.

To my shock, I was put in a solitary room separated from everyone except one inmate, S. Why? I had no idea. The others who had been thrown into single cells were the deadliest criminals. They were staff officers of the *Kwantung* Army (the Japanese Army in China) or *Kempeitai* chiefs, while I was a mere corporal. I might have killed more people than the average inmate, but the others had ordered many more deaths.

'When the prison guard came around, I asked him what I had done to deserve this treatment. He just smiled at me and didn't say a word. I almost went insane. I had no one to talk to except S. Every morning when I went out to empty the bucket that served as a chamber pot, I saw my comrades, but I wasn't allowed to talk with them. Sometimes I talked to a military doctor in a single cell next to mine. The wall had a hole in it and I stood up and talked to him through it. Conversation was prohibited, so I sang ditties like, "Oh, Doc. I fe–eel ro–tten like an eeel in mu–dd."

'The only way I could explain my solitary status was that a Russian investigator had once asked me in Siberia if I had ever worked on clandestine activities during the war. I had yelled at him. "What! Me a spy? No way," I said. "I had nothing to do with clandestine activities. All my crimes were committed in broad daylight." But he wouldn't accept my answer. He was so obstinate that in the end I screamed at him. "Go to hell, you son of a bitch. Write down whatever you like." I was stricken with fear about what would happen. Would I be taken out to the square and shot by a firing squad; would I be hanged? The Chinese were building a structure with a tall chimney in the corner of the backyard. Were they making a gas chamber? Would they throw me into a gas chamber as I heard the Germans had done to the Jews?

'When the construction was finished, we were called one by one to the building. My heart pounded and I felt faint. But as I came close, I saw the place enveloped in fragrant steam.

It was a big bathhouse! But I was still suspicious. Could they have put poison or cholera germs in the water, as some of our own troops had done? In the end, though, I couldn't resist the prospect of a warm bath, something I hadn't had since I left home almost ten years ago. Afterward I returned to my cell. A lunch tray was waiting there. I opened it and found a bowl full of steaming white rice instead of the usual brown rice. It reminded me of the cigarette I used to give the Chinese captives before cutting off their heads. It was a small charitable deed that made me feel benevolent, and less guilty about what I was about to do.

'The warm bath and the white rice had to be like my cigarette; tomorrow I would be shot . . . But the next day I wasn't executed. No one was. You see, I was in a state of constant fear and paranoia. I believed other people's minds were as evil as mine and that they would trick me as I had tricked so many. They kept giving us white rice, saying, "We know white rice is a special treat for Japanese people, so we'll serve it to you even if we only eat millet or kaoliang ourselves." It took a long time for me to understand they meant what they said.

I realised how wrong my view of the Chinese had been. Ever since we were kids, we had been taught that they were inferior people. But we had been beasts, the worst that had ever lived on earth, and these Chinese were like saints.

'We were wrong to look down on the Chinese. For two thousand years we had learned so much from China – ideographs, literature, religion, philosophy and art. How could they be inferior? I wrote a novel in prison in which I talked about a Japanese soldier, Shima, who had been wounded and taken prisoner by the Chinese. In the Chinese camp he was looked after with great care by doctors and nurses and when he was all better, they asked him whether he wanted to stay or go back to the Japanese camp. He said he'd like to go back to his camp. They drove him back there under escort. But his own company commander would not allow Shima to come in, insisting that he was a spy since Communist captors had certainly brainwashed him. He said he had already written off Shima as dead, that as a prisoner of war, he was a disgrace to the army, his family, and himself. The Imperial Army's Battlefield Law stated that a soldier should die rather than be captured: Shima had disobeyed this law. Shima turned and ran as fast as he could in the direction he had come from. But the company commander threw a hand grenade at him and killed him.

'This was a true story. You can see why Japan lost the war, can't you? The Japanese army had little respect for life, including the lives of their own soldiers. Military leaders wouldn't allow a deserter or anyone who had been a POW to come back. If any did, they would kill him or deliberately send him to the most dangerous battlefield so he could die. If he made it back home, he would be treated so badly that he would go mad or leave forever. There was a gap stretching from heaven to hell between the Chinese and the Japanese.

But Chiang Kai-shek's Army was different from the Communist one. Of the Japanese who had been captured by the former, more than 1,000 had been executed as war criminals. Later on, as you know, Mao was corrupted by his own power and ended up killing millions of his own people. But in the early days, he was different. We were very lucky to be there then, when the Communist government was still young and idealistic.

'Living alone in the cell continued to be hard. I told the guards I was going insane, and they moved me to a bigger cell with a dozen inmates. There we played mahjong and *go*. When we were tired of the games, we read books or studied Marxism as our group leader, Wu Hao Ran, encouraged us to do. To kill time, I copied the entire *Das Kapital*, but I didn't agree with Marx. So I whiled away the days writing novels about geishas and about the war. They became popular with my fellow inmates.

'In the third year of our stay, the prison leaders asked us to do something serious: confess our crimes and judge ourselves. Since our arrival in China, we'd kept our mouths shut about the war. We'd had plenty of time to reflect on our deeds and some of us felt terrible remorse, but we were afraid that if we told the truth, our punishment would be severe. But now we were being told to confess our misdeeds. Some considered this a cathartic exercise. "As in an old tale, I wanted to dig a hole, talk into it, and let everything out. I'm glad I can finally say everything out loud," one friend said. At meetings many were breaking down in sobs, while others had nervous breakdowns.

'At one of the earliest meetings, an advisor told a former lieutenant named Konishi to prepare his confession so he could read it aloud at the next session. Shortly afterward, Konishi was found dead. He had drunk toilet cleaner. His comrades said that he was a nice guy who hadn't done anything awful, but that as company commander, he'd been responsible for organising a number of campaigns. Once the sessions began, two other soldiers committed suicide.

'As for me – I belonged to the minority, a group that still didn't admit that we were war criminals. It wasn't compulsory to attend the meetings. So I was lying in bed the day my comrades from the 44th battalion gathered. My adviser, Wu Hao Ran, stopped by and asked why I wasn't at the meeting. "Because I'm not interested," I said. He talked gently with me for twenty minutes and left, saying, "Take care." He didn't change my mind. I was sure that if I confessed the whole truth, they would execute me because I had done enough to deserve death a hundred times over. But I didn't think I was responsible for what I had done. I still blamed the military leaders and the Emperor for my crimes.

'Wu Hao Ran asked me again what I thought of my wartime activities. I said, "I only did what I was told to do by my superiors – I assisted killing. I didn't willingly kill anyone." "What do you mean, you 'assisted killing'?" he asked. "It means I did it under orders." "Even if you did it under orders, aren't you the one who killed?" Normally a gentle man, he raised his voice a little and went on. "Do you think that the murdered man would forgive you because you were killing him under orders? From his point of view, you were the one committing the murder, weren't you?" I didn't answer. "Think hard about it," Adviser Wu said. Then he left.

I did think about it. I could see he was right, but even so I wasn't ready to confess the truth. I kept quiet about the rapes that no one had

Yasuji Kaneko

ordered me to do. But the extraordinarily humane attitude of the prison people moved me, and was gradually turning me around.

'In June of 1956, the inmates were divided into three groups and 320 or so of them and I were taken to the People's Supreme Prosecutor's Office. I knew this was the Day of Judgment. I was prepared for the worst. We sat in the middle of a large room, facing the prosecutors on the platform, who were wearing buttoned-up Mao uniforms. The chief prosecutor read the sentence: "During the war between Japan and China, the criminals here trampled upon international laws and fundamental rules of humanity by committing various criminal acts against the people of our country . . . They deserve punishment commensurate with their crimes. However, because of the changes in Japan over the past ten years since its surrender and the recent development of friendly relations between China and Japan, we will treat these cases with great leniency. We will nullify the indictment, acquit the defendants, and release them immediately."

'And so everyone in our group was acquitted. Some forty-five people among the other groups were sentenced to twenty years. No one was given the death penalty. I had never expected to be acquitted. I didn't even comprehend the word, "acquitted"; it didn't exist in my vocabulary. I knew I had committed unforgivable crimes for which I could not be acquitted. Can you imagine how shocked and moved I was? I had long ago given up the idea of going home. But now I was a free man and could return to Japan! I was truly impressed with my captors' dignity and generosity. I was genuinely remorseful for what I had done to the Chinese and the tough attitude I'd had toward my advisers. How could I atone for my crimes?

'When we returned to our cells, we were given new clothes instead of the prison uniforms we had been wearing for six years. Everything was new, including our underwear and socks. They even gave us pocket money, about as much as an average workman's salary for a month. In the evening they threw a farewell party for us with beer. The director, Jim Yuan, said to us, "Live a good and happy life when you go back home." That night I cried like a child – tears of remorse as well as relief flooded my pillow. The faces of all the men, women, and children I had killed went through my mind.

'We waited at the port of Tianjin. A repatriation ship, Koan-Maru, came from Japan and picked us up. Jin Yuan, Wu Hao Ran, and others were at the dock to see us off. We waved to them until they became dots on the horizon and were gone. When we saw the shadow of the Japanese island far away in the sea, I wept again. Sixteen years had passed since I had seen my homeland.

'People didn't welcome me in Japan. I was branded a war criminal and a Communist. For two years, local police officers followed me wherever I went, to check on what I was up to. I was thirty-seven, without skills because I'd only gone to school for six years. No one would hire me. One time I was given some odd jobs at a corporation. I worked hard, but when I brought my résumé in as requested, they fired me the next day. They said: "We don't hire people who have returned from the red countries." I went back to the scrap iron business. First I begged the factories to give me the scrap iron shavings from the lathes. I carried those shavings in a bicycle cart to different shops and sold them. Eventually I borrowed some money and started a small business. I bought sheets of iron, cut them into small sizes and sold them to customers who needed them to make machines and toys. I was a workaholic. Without money, I'd never find a woman to marry.

'After a while I met a good woman, Matsue. She said no at first. She had a good life, getting dressed up every day and working in an office. She was making more money than I was. I had to prove I could do better. Uninvited, I went to live with her. She saw I was a hard worker, and because she thought I was funny and smart, she finally gave in. After marrying me, she helped me at my filthy one-man factory. Cutting iron was dangerous work, and we had some terrible accidents. But I worked day and night, without days off, and we were able to make ends meet. We had two little girls, and we bought the large house that we still live in now. I had come far indeed from my poor fisherman origins.

'One of our daughters had pneumonia when she was little. I went to see her in the hospital after work. She was moaning and had a high fever, but she smiled a beautiful smile when she saw me. I prayed fervently that she would live. That night I dreamed of the boy who had jumped into the well while calling his mother. Although I'd thought of him on and off over the years, I was beginning to forget, his image buried beneath so much else that had happened. I told you I was genuinely remorseful when I was released from prison, but I was so busy after coming back that China was becoming an increasingly distant memory. Now, though, the boy's image was vivid again, his voice constantly in my ears. I hadn't completely come to terms with my war crimes, either in Siberia or in the prison in China. This was a new awakening. The reality of my crimes hit me with a vengeance.

'It was a turning point. After that I was determined to atone for my sins. I had to tell people what I and the other Japanese had done in China. The skeletons in the closet had to come out. I had been a beast, but I wouldn't be a hypocrite. There's a real risk to confessing publicly that you've committed rapes and murder. It jeopardises your integrity – well, that's a big word; I had no integrity. But people would point fingers at me, and the stability and happiness of my family would be endangered. Poor Matsue ran out of the house every time she heard me talking about the rapes and murders I'd committed.

'My old Fushun friends and I had founded a group called Chu-Ki-Ren, or *The China Veterans' Link*. We wanted to keep up with our old prison inmates. We thought we had an obligation to tell our country-men the truth about the war, and to do something to promote Japan's friendship with China. I began dedicating time to the group. I often contributed articles and short stories to the quarterly magazine, *Chu-Ki-Ren*. In the meantime horrible things were happening in China. It was the Cultural Revolution. Millions of people were dying of starvation and the Red Guards, under the Gang of Four, were treating people terribly. I felt completely disillusioned with Mao Zedong. I was worried about Jim Yuan, our prison director. I'd heard that he had been labeled a Japanese agent, stripped of employment, and sent away to a village for labour. The same could be happening to my advisor, Wu Hao Ran. We wished we could help, but there was nothing we could do.

'Eventually, Mao died and the Gang of Four was arrested. After a while we were able to communicate with Jim Yuan and Wu Hao Ran. We invited them to Japan, and they came! It was 1984, twenty-eight years after we'd left China, but they looked as great as ever. We had a tearful reunion at the airport and we took them around Tokyo. About 600 ex-prisoners welcomed them all over Japan. I suggested to Jim Yuan and Wu Hao Ran that they send their kids to school here. They did, and so did a few of the other Chinese prison workers. We hosted five boys in our house for five years. Matsue took good care of them and they went to school every day. They were good kids. They spoke Japanese fluently.

'Around this time I also began to spend more time telling my stories in classrooms and at town halls. I testified in court cases on behalf of comfort women and other victims of the war who came to Japan seeking compensation. Don't get me wrong. I didn't enjoy doing this. Who has fun saying "I raped hundreds of women and killed dozens of men, women, and kids"? I have daughters myself. I don't want them to think their dad was a murderer or a scoundrel of the blackest dye, even though that's what I really was. But even after having their parents and relatives killed, their towns burnt, their fields destroyed and their animals taken, the Chinese didn't hang us – somehow, they were even able to forgive us. At the very least I have an obligation to tell everyone in Japan that what I did should never be repeated.'

Mr Kaneko passed away a month after I met him. According to a mutual friend, 'Kaneko-san had a visit from a good friend, Shin-ichiro Kumagai, and had a lovely time. After Kumagai-san left, Kaneko-san fell over while he was in the wheelchair, and died.' I phoned Matsue-san to offer my condolences. She said, 'Toward the end of his life, when he was suffering a lot of pain, he often said that God was punishing him. At least he tried to do good in the latter part of his life. He was a good husband, a good father, and a funny man. I'll miss him very much.'

CHAPTER 2

Tadamasa Iwai

A Student's War

Tadamasa Iwai came to meet me at a train station in Western Tokyo. A trim man with erect posture, he bounded up and down the stairs with the ease of someone in his forties. I was startled to hear he was ninety-one. He explained cheerfully that longevity ran in his family. His mother, he said, had been in good health until her death at the age of 104 and his older sister died at the same age. After the delicious lunch his wife had cooked, Mr Iwai settled down to talk. Quick-minded and articulate, I could tell his longevity was not just about physical health, but very much a matter of his inner faculties.

'In the autumn of 1943 Japan was losing the war on all fronts. I was then a twenty-one-year-old philosophy student at Keio University. One day the government stopped draft exemptions for all students except those majoring in science and technology. I had known this was coming. For as long as I could remember we'd been told to go to war and die for the Emperor. We'd been feeling guilty about all the other young men dying on the front line while we read books in the library. And yet I was reluctant to go. I didn't regard the soldiers who died willingly for the Emperor as heroes. War is sordid and violent. All the officers who came to give us military training at high school were swaggering bastards, and I had heard that in military camp you get constantly beaten up for no reason.

'My idea of war was shaped by Erich Remarque's novel, *All Quiet on the Western Front*. As a teenager I found the book on a bookshelf at home. All my brothers – I have five, of whom one died in a Siberian detention camp after the war – must have read it. I read it over and over. As you know, it's the story of Paul Bäumer, a German high school boy who joins the army as a volunteer soldier. After going through training and all the meaningless hazing that goes along with it, Paul and his comrades are sent to the front, where they're all killed. My friends believed the heroic stories about war that they read in Japan's monthly magazines, but I was convinced that the truth about war could be found in Remarque's novel.

'I was also sure that Japan would lose the war. It was as clear as day that America's economic power was hundreds of times mightier than Japan's. Take oil. America had miles and miles of oil fields, while we only had rice fields. Japan had been totally dependent on America for oil until they put an embargo on it before the start of the war. America was ahead of us in science, technology and productivity. Did it require a lot of brainpower to realise that we had no hope of beating them? Our leaders argued that we would win the war with our spiritual power. But how did they know that our spiritual power was greater than that of the Americans? They said we were superior because we had an Emperor who was a god. At a climactic point, a divine wind would blow and destroy all the enemy ships, just as it did in the thirteenth century when Kublai Khan invaded Japan's shores.

'I grew up in Dalian, Manchuria. We moved there when I was four because my father, who had been an infantry brigadier general in Kyushu, believed that Manchuria was a new frontier for Japan. Even though he was retired then, he was a big shot. Officers wearing lots of medals used to come and go in our house.

'I well remember the day my father received a phone call early in the morning. "Hurrah! They've done it!" he shouted with triumph. It was 18 September 1931. Dynamite had exploded close to a railroad line, near Mukden, that was owned by Japan's South Manchuria Railway. The Japanese Army accused Chinese dissidents of attempted sabotage, and launched an invasion of Manchuria, which eventually led to its occupation. All the Japanese newspapers reported that the dynamite had been part of a Chinese plot, and that the army had been right to attack in response. Later, this came to be known as the Manchuria Incident. An odd thing was that not only my father but also some other people around us seemed to know that Japanese military personnel had set off the dynamite to give themselves a pretext for the invasion. On the street the Japanese whispered the rumour. I was only eleven and could not tell if they were critical of this act or just pretending to be and were secretly happy about it. This experience taught me that military people could be dishonest, and that war could be founded on a falsehood.

'So Manchuria became Japan's colony. We stole a big chunk of China, became the ruling class and enjoyed the benefits. When I remember the fifteen years I lived there, I get nostalgic. Life was easy thanks to the Manchurians' labour and the wealth of their land. Some Japanese treated the Chinese like slaves. I once saw a Japanese man beat a coachman with a whip, as if he were a horse.

When I was nineteen, I left my family in Dalian and moved to Tokyo. I didn't pass the entrance exam of the university I wanted to go to and had a gap year watching films and reading books. I saw good foreign films, Charlie Chaplin, Buster Keaton and gangster movies. I loved them. I was steeped in Western culture. That's one of the reasons I didn't want the Allied nations to be our enemies.

'When the war broke out, the government told us we had to defend Asia from the Western predators and we would build the Greater East Asia Co-Prosperity Sphere – a pompous catch phrase. It was true that some European nations were imperialists and had acquired lots of colonies. But hadn't Japan also done the same in Korea and China? My father's triumphant shout, "Hurrah! They've done it!" kept ringing in my ears. Now the university gates were closed to us and we were going to be shipped off to military training school. The idea of death haunted me. It seemed inevitable. I would die like Paul in Remarque's novel, and for what purpose? We'd been taught that it was the duty of a young man to die for the Emperor. There was a song, written by an ancient poet, that we all sang every day at school: "Across the sea, corpses soaked in the water; across the mountain, bodies piled on the grass. We shall die by the side of our Emperor. We shall never regret."

'I strongly resented the idea of dying for him. Who was the Emperor? What made him so great? Since when did he become God, and how? But the laws of maintenance of public peace outlawed opposition. If I spoke out against the war, tried to avoid the draft, or uttered a word against the Emperor, the military police would catch me in no time, put me in jail, torture and maybe even crush me like a vermin. There was nothing I could do but keep quiet and obey orders. So I decided I would go and do my best to defend our country. I chose to join the Navy. On a train headed for Yonezawa, the town of our family burial site, I confided my thoughts to my younger brother, Tadakuma. He was a student at the University of Kyoto then, and would also be joining the Navy soon. Our sister, who was worried about us, had said we should visit our ancestors' graves and pray for their protection. She had given us extra money so we could stop at an onsen spa nearby and enjoy what might be our last holiday.

'The train was not crowded, but I looked left then right before turning to my brother. "I have a feeling I won't come back alive from this war," I whispered. Tadakuma nodded. "Probably I won't either." I looked around again and said in a low voice, "If I have to die, it certainly won't be for Kaiser." I used the German word for emperor because it was too risky to utter the word *Tenno*. German was a foreign language we were allowed to use; English was the enemy's language, and forbidden. Tadakuma's response was immediate. "I feel the same."

'I wanted to find a cause I could die for. Sometime later, while climbing up a slope in Tokyo, I passed a middle-aged woman holding a little girl's hand. Her informal white apron suggested she was a housewife from the neighbourhood. It was an ordinary street scene with no particular meaning. But I suddenly realised that if my death would mean that this mother and her child could keep living, I wouldn't mind it so much. I felt like crouching down and kissing the earth. Since I was sure my life would end soon, everything felt dear to me in those days. That was how I reconciled going to war. Perhaps it sounds sentimental. But one thing was clear. There was nothing courageous or beautiful about the way I went to war. There must have been lots of young men like me who secretly had doubts about the war, but put on a stoic mask and went. If you can't beat them, join them. That was what I did. But I now realise that it wasn't the right thing to do. I was lucky I didn't have to kill anyone in the war, but I still contributed to a war I didn't believe in, a war that ended the lives of many millions of innocent people and hurt many more.

'I was first taken to the Naval Training Corps as a second-class seaman, the lowest rank possible. The training was fierce, but I endured it and passed all the tests. Then I was sent to an anti-submarine warfare school. This was worse than the first round of training. I didn't mind the technical courses, but the lectures about patriotism and loyalty bored me to death. And I hated the constant hazing by the upper rank seamen. One day in the fall of 1944, we were assembled in the court-yard. A top officer strode to the platform. "A new powerful weapon has been created which will change the course of the war," he said. "We will need pilots to run this machine. This is a great cause to give your life to the Emperor . . . "

'At this critical moment I must have had an attack of amnesia of some kind, because I don't have a clear memory of what happened after that. Somehow I must have applied for this suicide bomb mission and been accepted. Although I don't remember the process of applying, I can recreate my reasons. Those days my anxiety about death had grown like a monstrous tenuous balloon in the sky which was about to burst. I was terribly unhappy at camp with all the hazing and preaching, and was desperate to get out. I was going to die anyhow and it was far better to go quickly in a suicide weapon than to endure a long waiting game in which death loomed larger every day.

'Later on I was told that this suicide weapon was a human torpedo called *Kaiten*, which meant "a turning of the heavens" – the idea was that it was powerful enough to make the skies churn. It turned out that ninety-four per cent of the trainees applied for it. Isn't it astonishing that so many volunteered to die? That was because most of us had already been moulded into robots. Constant beatings paralyzed our brains and made us into tin soldiers that moved with a push of a button. Yet I was a little different. If I had to die, it was not for the Emperor as I said before. How many times did I wake up from bad dreams and trembled, hearing again and again the voice of Prime Minister Tojo, who spoke at the Meiji Jingu Shrine Farewell March for student soldiers: "You are the chosen who were born to die to help the nation in crisis. Die for the Emperor and you'll live for glorious eternity!"

'But in the end I wanted to die out of sheer desperation. Probably some believed in the weapon that would "change the course of the war" and thought it was a cause worth dying for. The truth was that this machine killed you, but seldom hit its target. I was probably selected because I was in good health and because I was the fourth among six brothers. They tried to spare the only or the eldest son of each family. It was a "generous" act on the part of those who robbed parents of their sons.

'In October, the ones chosen for *Tokko-tai*, the Special Attack units, were allowed to go to town for the last time. On the way to the station I saw rows of red peppers hanging to dry under the eaves of a farm-house. The redness shone under the brilliant autumn sun and stung my eyes. We travelled to the Yasukuni Shrine in Tokyo, where those who died fighting for the Emperor were enshrined. Those days there was a catchphrase soldiers said to each other before a death mission: "Goodbye and see you in Yasukuni." But the shrine didn't inspire me. It was built to deify the Emperor and his ancestors. The photos of the thousands of dead men which were pasted on the wall made me sad. Their lives had been taken from them under false pretenses.

'One thing I remember from this last excursion was that I caught a glimpse of my university library from the train window. It was the red brick building in which I used to read every day. Below the stained glass of the entrance hall was inscribed the motto of Keio University, CALAMUS GLADIO FORTIOR – "The pen is mightier than the sword". The university cap I used to wear – left forgotten at home – had the embroidered emblem of two pens crossed instead of two swords. What had happened to that idea?

'After the excursion we were taken to the *Tokko-tai* station. To my surprise I found my brother Tadakuma there, too. He had also applied for the *Tokko-tai*. But instead of the *Kaiten* he was assigned to the *Shin-yo*, the Ocean Shakers, small but powerful motorboats that were to be driven into enemy ships at high speed.

Our group had to move to the Hikari base where the *Kaiten* ships were docked. I'll never forget the shock I felt when I saw the gigantic, cylindrical black monster shaped like a killer whale. It was fifteen metres long and a metre in diameter. It looked demonic enough to make the heavens tremble with fear. It had no windows, and the door could only be opened from the outside. Once the hatch was shut, the pilot could not get out even if he failed to hit the target or if the machine broke down. What he would do was to die from oxygen deprivation in the little cube. This was why it was equipped with a self-detonating bomb. When I went to sea in it I felt as if I had been put in a coffin, alive and well. There was not even an ounce of warmth in it. It was bad enough to die in a dark, claustrophobic coffin; did it have to be so metallic? A comrade said, "I wish there were a soft armchair or something to sit on. For goodness sake, this is the last trip of my life."

'One day, Lieutenant Miyoshi died in a *Kaiten* during training. His machine was supposed to pass under a target ship, but because it didn't dive deep enough, the periscope had run into the side of the ship. He was hit hard on the forehead. Unlike many of the other officers, who were swaggering and cruel, Lieutenant Miyoshi was a gentle and warmhearted man. He never hit anybody. At a variety show in the camp, his sentimental song about a sweet girl at a tobacco shop was a big hit. The gods must have favoured him, taking him to heaven with them. More accidents followed Miyoshi's and fourteen of my comrades died during training missions, often having rammed their missiles aground. This showed how flawed the machine was and how little our leaders cared about our safety. Well, I guess they wouldn't have created such a machine in the first place if they had cared about young men's lives.

'Far from changing the course of the war, according to American battle reports, the *Kaiten* resulted in only two major sinkings of vessels; the oiler USS *Mississinewa* and the destroyer escort USS *Underhill*.

'In April 1945, I was given the order to transfer. The only colleague from our group who received the same order was sub-lieutenant F. After talking with each other, we came to the conclusion that we were transferred because of illness. In January, when I had come down with a cold, Dr Nakashio had diagnosed me with tuberculosis. I didn't pay too much attention because I was going to die soon in the *Kaiten* anyway. Besides, I felt better in no time. F said that he had also been diagnosed with TB by the same doctor, but since then he had been in superb health. "Dr N. is a big quack," we said to each other and laughed. But in order to defend Dr Nakashio's honour, I should add that I recently had a chest X-ray taken and was told that there was a scar on the lung from an old case of TB.

'The Navy did not seem to know what to do with me. But finally they sent me to the XX Shock Troop on a beach called Nobi. Another name for it was "a storming party". The machine we would use was called *Fukuryu*, or "Crouching Dragon". I guessed from its name that it was another *Tokko* suicide weapon. I was supposed to train young newcomers even though I was new myself. Under Captain Nitta, the underwater training began. We boarded a large sculling boat and rowed out to sea. The boat was anchored at a suitable distance from the shore and we donned our jackets. We were crouching dragons, but in our diving suits we looked more like cartoon robots – like latter-day astronauts. We loaded onto our backs, rucksack fashion, a combination of two oxygen cylinders and a square absorbent canister. For our weapon we carried a bamboo stick several metres long, to which the tip of a bomb was attached. The idea was to dive underwater and touch the bottom of the ship with the bomb. The ship would explode. Of course, there would be no chance for the crouching dragon to survive.

'First we watched Captain Nitta do a demonstration. He dived into the water all right, but didn't come up for a long time. When he finally did, he popped out of the water like a jack-in-the box and ended up on the surface of the sea, his jacket swollen like a balloon. He was flapping his hands and feet like an overturned tortoise. In the end he had to be pulled in with a lifeline from the boat. The whole scene was like watching a cheap comedy. But everyone who tried after Captain Nitta repeated the same mishap. There was only one man who had no trouble coming up from under water, and that was me. I had figured out the trick of it, and never floundered.

'This suicide bomb was a joke. Because you're carrying two bottles of oxygen on your back, you have to bend forward to balance your weight. But then your vision is limited to the floor. If you wanted to look up, you'd be knocked over on the ocean floor belly up, and no matter how much you wriggled, you couldn't get up. We laughed and said, "The inventor of this weapon must have gotten this idea from a cartoon. Has he ever worn this jacket and dived underwater himself?"

Even Captain Nitta did not object to our running this bogus toy bomb down. He would just smile grimly and turn away. He was a gentle and unpretentious man for a professional Navy officer.

'The exercise was probably comical to watch, but for us who were doing the training, it was no joke. Serious accidents often happened. One was carbon monoxide poisoning. It was treatable, but if seawater leaked into the absorbent canister, which contained caustic soda to absorb the carbon dioxide, the soda became so dense that if you breathed it in, you would burn your face, nose, respiratory tract and lungs. A later study said this was the cause of the death of more than fifty trainees.

'It almost happened to me. I heard a strange noise in my apparatus when I was underwater and asked my student to touch the canister I carried on my back. It was hot, so I immediately went back to the shore and removed the canister. Inside it looked all wet. If I hadn't noticed the noise I would have died. Another time I fainted under water. My assistant opened the air vent of my apparatus, added oxygen, and pushed it above water. A cruising rescue boat happened to see a big balloon popping out of the water, and stopped to pick me up. On shore my student removed my helmet and I came to.

'In the hospital emergency room I asked the doctors to try oxygen inhalation. I heard a doctor saying to his colleague, *Bewusstsein klar* – "Consciousness clear". Hey, they're speaking German! In my hazy state I felt happy, thinking I was back in my old life, when I was still attending university. They gave me oxygen. Later on the doctors said that they couldn't determine the true cause of the accident, but that oxygen inhalation had been the correct treatment. "To tell you the truth, we didn't think you'd make it," they said. "It's amazing you did. It's all thanks to your fighting spirit!"

'At the end of July we were transferred to an island of the Seto Inland Sea. The morning of August 6 was a beautiful day without a speck of cloud in the sky. Captain Nitta was talking to us about the day's agenda when the whole sky outside the window glittered for a second with white light. Not knowing what it was, the Captain resumed his talk. Then there was an earth-shattering roar. Later that day we heard about the bomb that decimated the city of Hiroshima. One of our students was from Hiroshima and was allowed to go home. When he returned, he didn't answer anyone's questions. His eyes didn't focus. They were the eyes of a man who had seen hell. Nine days later, Japan surrendered.'

Brother Tadakuma's story

Tadamasa Iwai's brother, Tadakuma, was a quick learner, and as a Navy sub-lieutenant, he became a trainer of younger students. Eventually he was appointed co-captain of the 39 *Shin-yo* transport ship, which carried torpedo boats, and on 22 March 1945, he left for a mission in Okinawa. The following is his own account of the experience.[5]

'At 17.10 on 22 March, when I was inside the ship, a thunderous explosion threw me onto the floor. I immediately got up and went out onto the deck. It was strewn with soldiers drenched in blood. The ship had been hit by a torpedo and lost its entire prow including the bridge. I was about to jump into the sea but before I could do so the ship buckled, and I fell into the water. The ship's tail went straight up, and in less than half a second it sank.

'The waves were enormous, but I and seven others managed to stay afloat by clutching a big board. We stayed there for three hours. When a ship finally appeared, we cried out until we were found. The sea was too choppy for a rescue boat, but after some time a big wave saved us by hoisting us on deck. We later learned that only forty-five out of the crew of 187 had survived.

'The *Shin-yo* Division of the Special Attack Unit was dissolved at the end of the war. After sending all the demobilised groups off in various ships, I stood alone in the harbour. I felt humiliated at Japan's defeat, ashamed of myself and my service to a cause I had not believed in, and disgusted by the self-righteous, incorrect historical views that my government had used as justification for the war. In high school I had thought about studying Japanese history so I could sift out the truth from the lies that the government told to justify the war, and I

5 Tadakuma section of *Tokko: Testimony of the Brothers Who Became Suicide Weapons*, by Tadamasa Iwai and Tadakuma Iwai, Shin-nippon shuppan-sha, 2002, pp. 141–2, 152–4

resolved then to follow through on that idea. I took a train to Kyoto, walked to my old university, and signed up to resume my education.'

Now eighty-nine, Tadakuma Iwai is a historian of modern Japan. The author of numerous books, he is regarded as an expert on the *Tenno* system. He served as vice president of Rikkyo University of Tokyo for many years.

His older brother, Tadamasa Iwai became a businessman in a trading company. Now he is a spokesman for the wartime generation who urge the importance of keeping Article 9 of the Constitution.

CHAPTER 3

Minoru Wada

Death in a 'Kaiten' Human Torpedo

Just as I was leaving Tadamasa Iwai's house, he gave me a book and said, "This is the diary of Minoru Wada[6] who was my classmate at the *kaiten* training school. He was a bright man with much promise, but sadly died during a training run. His diary was turned into a book after the war. Why don't you read it?"

While reading Wada's diary, I remembered the poignant poems his sister Wakana had written about her brother in a book of requiem for the war dead.[7] I read them again and wished I could share my feelings with her. I figured that she must be over seventy-five, but alive and well as Japanese women at that age often are. I wished I could visit her, but I had just returned back home to England after a round of interviews in Japan. It was not difficult to find her address and telephone number.

I dared to call Wakana-san, even though I was a stranger. A lively lady's voice answered. She readily forgave me for the impoliteness of my call and began talking about her elder brother lovingly and without knowing when to stop: 'We were a very happy family before elder brother died. Father was a doctor and ran a hospital in the family compound. My first memory of Minoru-chan[8] was of him flying a glider on the beach. He was a sweet brother and wonderful son to his parents, considerate and ready to help. He was a bookworm and played the violin beautifully. We were a close-knit family with five children.

6 Wada, Minoru, *Wadatsumi no Koe Kierukotonaku* (The Voices of the Sea Gods Won't Die), Kadokawa Shoten, Tokyo, 1972

7 Nishihara, Wakana, *Imoto-tachino Kagaribi* (The Sisters' Torch: For the Brothers Who Died in the War), ed. by Etsuko Niki, Kadokawa, Tokyo, 1980

8 Chan is added to the end of the name of a child, a close friend and family. It is a more endearing form than san, which has a respectful connotation.

We all played music. Father played the mandolin, Mother the *koto*, a Japanese harp, and I and my sisters the piano. We often played together, accompanying each other or in an ensemble. Before he went to the Navy, Minoru-chan made a record of himself playing Jules Massenet's *Requiem*. I still listen to it and think of him.'

Later Wakana-san wrote me two long letters about her brother. She also sent me a book, *Kaiten Tokko Student Force: Kaiten Was No Superb Weapon*, written by his best friend, Goro Takeda, in which Wada is often mentioned.

Minoru Wada's diary was begun in his high school days and ended when he returned to the base from his failed mission, a few months before his tragic death. Only a portion of the voluminous, original diary including countless poems and philosophical and political essays, was published. With the permission of Wakana-san, I quoted here the part of his three-year military training life. The diary in this period was often just a few lines, jotted down in a leather-bound notebook when nobody was in sight, because keeping a diary was not allowed in the military school.

Here we see an intelligent young man who grew up playing violin, writing poems, reading Tolstoy, Dostoevsky and political philosophy and concerned about rising nationalism and militarism in his country, who was suddenly shut up in a prison-like existence at the Navy school and later at the suicide bomber's training base. The doors to knowledge had been shut. All other possibilities of life had ceased to exist and he faced only death in a *Tokko* mission.

23 September 1943

What I've been fearing has happened. The government has stopped the students' draft exemption. I feel indescribably sad about having let twenty years of my life pass without finishing any of my work. At least I wanted to leave a piece of my work behind after my death no matter how immature it was.

Today the campus was quiet. All the newspapers were sold out at 8 a.m. at the news stand in front of the university where usually some are left until noon. On the ground around the stand, gingko fruits were scattered, trodden by hurried shoes.

December 9 1943

All our family sat around the table for the last time. At 4.30 am, some neighbours came over. We walked together in the dark to the station. Our German shepherd, who was later taken away by the Army, walked along with us. On the platform people talked to me and wished me luck. Somehow I was not myself. Masuda-san whispered to me, 'For these last few minutes, show a good spirit for your parents.' I pretended to be cheerful.

When the train left, I regretted I hadn't looked at my mother's face one last time. My father came along with me all the way to Nagoya. There he got off and stood on the platform as the train left the station. I saw him burst into tears before his figure grew smaller.

15 December 1943

You must have been waiting for my letter. We settled into our divisional barracks at the Otake Naval Training School and we are allowed to write letters for the first time. The seaman's uniform fits me well. Getting up at 6.20, we fold up the hanging net bed, run the parade ground, practice tough exercises and attend academic courses. I am terribly hungry all the time. Even the unpolished rice they serve tastes good. Don't worry about me.

1 February 1944

We moved to this Takeyama Marine Corps and settled into new living quarters.

To my utter surprise, I was appointed chief of the students. Being timorous, I was flustered. But I will try my best and have a new start. At a meeting it was announced that I was the first in the class of 3,354 reserve students. It gave me shudders to imagine three thousand comrades would look up at me. What a responsibility.

There are twelve Divisions which we divided into three battalions. Each of them is divided into five groups composed of eleven people each. I'm in Group 1.

4 March 1944

Group Captain Igarashi is a mean man. He reads all the incoming and outgoing letters of men in his units. He called me into his office.

'What do you think of this letter?' he said, showing me my sister Mihoko's letter. 'It is lovely. After all she is my sister,' I said. He suggested I should tell my family not to write letters which would remind me of family, home or of the peacetime world. Back at my desk, I read her letter again. I couldn't find anything wrong about it. But I had to write a cold-blooded letter telling my family to write only about business matters and words to boost my morale. I felt like crying.

14 March 1944

This time Captain Igarashi told me that he didn't like the letter I wrote home. He also said I looked neurotic. I appreciated the points he made even though his words were harsh. But I didn't agree with his heavy-handed approach. Staff Sergeant Okada said, 'He cannot touch our hearts by yelling.'

13 April 1944

In the afternoon there was a competition amongst four groups. Our group won the race in construction work, but we were beaten in volleyball by Group 2. That was due to the referee's misjudgment, but Igarashi was nasty to us about our losing. I felt sorry for our group and after he left, I tried to calm their complaints and told them to keep their chins up. Igarashi came right back and gave me three punches, shouting, 'Hey, don't assume an insubordinate attitude toward me!' Then he struck me on the head with a baton. Instead of getting angry, somehow I felt like laughing out loud. I walked past him proudly.

19 April 1944

Recently I've lost the will to speak. I just live and breathe. Every night I have dreams of home. I pine for a visiting day although I will only feel lonesome after it.

3 May 1944

The other group leaders treat us nicely when we are together and that brings tears to my eyes. Meanwhile our leader's temperamental actions and constant reproaches frighten us every day. The students of the other groups are cheerful, but we breathe in relief only when he goes away. Our conversations to each other in the hammock at night always end up on two topics: When can we get out of here? And is there a rotation of group leaders?

At the outdoor training, we saw *koi* streamers swimming in the sky celebrating Boy's Day. We heard frogs and saw red lotus flowers in the pond. They give us no solace.

9 May 1944

At noon we arrived at Kamakura Shrine. Hundreds of visitors were there. I was allowed to see my parents by the pond from 12.30 to 1.40. So happy to see my father looking plump and well, but I worry about Mother who looks thinner than before.

Officer Igarashi was watching us with binoculars. Later he said to me he was watching our every action. It's too bad we don't have an instructor we could look up to as a role model.

10 May 1944

It was a chilly morning and it rained hard during the exercise. Igarashi ordered us to run in the field while he went inside. I dragged my feet with pain and fatigue from daily abuse of my body. When finally we were allowed to go in, we were sent to dig a bomb shelter. Feeling like convicts in prison we worked in silence.

Wada's friend Takeda, who was in the same group, wrote in his book, 'I shared with Wada the famous Group One's hell life. Wada stood as a shield in front of Igarashi and took the brunt of his violent attacks. I wished I could help him, but it was not easy. Igarashi's background was at a fishery school. His knowledge was only about fish and about fisherman's boats. He was only good at shouting and beating. His face reflected his temperament which changed like the weather. His eyes were like an alcoholic's. He spoke with slurs. His bad actions were known throughout the entire twelve Divisions.[9]

9 Takeda, Goro, *Kaiten Tokko Students Force: Kaiten was not a Superb Weapon*, Kojin-sha, Tokyo, 2008, p. 46

In those days Wada's fatigue was apparent to anyone's eye. I saw him doze off and fall off the chair in a class. He had an attack of anemia and fell on the ground at a Division inspection.'[10]

21 May 1944

I had a dream again in which I returned home and played the violin. My fingers were stiff. Recent dreams are all about home, parents, and food.

22 July 1944

A week passed since we moved to the Navigation School in Yokosuka. I wonder how I survived the months in Takeyama with Igarashi without committing suicide. I was assigned to be the leader of Group 6 in the third Division.

Saipan has fallen. The Tojo cabinet has resigned. Our nation is in serious trouble.

In the morning we practiced flag signaling. Everyone drew each sign 140 to 150 times in the air. I had to do this with shoulders that were stiff from practice a few days ago. There are hundreds of things to do. We have to learn more Morse code and a table of constellations. I've been reading ten or so textbooks and am excited to think I could be steering a battleship soon.

12 September 1944

Summer is over. The rain has brought a chill to the air.

I don't want to die. Absolutely not. At the moment dying is the last thing I want. But I may never go home. In my dreams of home, I always appear dressed in a military uniform.

8 October 1944

My flaw is poor nerves. This is the most undesirable character for a soldier. I still cannot shout at anyone. I can't think of hitting my students.

The barracks behind the classrooms have been filled with new students. When they look at us, they give eager salutes. They may be

10 ibid., p. 52

older than I, but they look so sweet. I have a tendency to defy my elders and take sides with men of lower rank. The other day Ogawa in Group 2 shouted at the students, I mediated between them and calmed them down. But if you look at them closely, most of them aren't cute, but ugly. Maybe I love them just for their label, 'student'.

People say I am the most cheerful soul in the troop.

18 October 1944

At lunchtime all the students were called in to the Judo hall. Every window was shut and the air in the room was tense. Division Commander, Colonel Taguchi, in formal uniform gave a solemn speech. 'Because of the grave situation in the war, we must recruit pilots who will gladly dedicate their lives to the Navy's new powerful special attack *Tokko* weapons.'

I had heard rumours about a human torpedo *Kaiten*. They had also been creating other kinds of suicide attack weapons such as Greenpeas Ocean Shaker and *Fukuryu* Crouching Dragon.

That afternoon, my heart was pounding violently. I was totally absent-minded in the machine-gun class. Now I feel depressed.

Mother, forgive me. I think of our family's grief. This is a serious decision. Your son went to war. If you realised that his small life holds the key to destroying an enemy's big ship, would you regard me as a child of the nation rather than as yours? In my heart I will die shouting, 'Father and Mother!'

I think of Takeda. He was watching my face at dinnertime as if he knew what I had been thinking. I was moved by his deep concern for me.

I applied for *Tokko*. Colonel Taguchi asked me, 'Don't you have any regrets? Isn't it a temporary emotional excitement that made you decide this?' And he added, 'Can you come to terms with death? Can you die peacefully?'

19 October 1944

They didn't accept my application. The reason was that my family had few sons and I'm the oldest. Takeda made it since he's the fifth son. It makes me unbearably sad to see him go.

54

20 October 1944

I applied again and was accepted this time. In the evening Division Commander Taguchi gave a speech. He was sad for us and cried out loud.

I wrote a letter to my parents: 'Father and Mother. By order I will be dispatched to some place far away. I was sorry I couldn't see Toyoko one last time. Please say hello to her for me. Please tell Akira to work hard.

'Takeda is with me. So it won't be so frightening. Will you please not worry too much? I'll be gone by the time you receive this letter. This is a high security matter. Please keep this to yourself. For a while, I cannot communicate with you. Please understand. Minoru'

Takeda wrote about the day which decided Wada's fate.

'After the last inspection that evening, most of us crawled out of bed and sat around a cigarette tray. We looked at each other, but no one spoke since Colonel Taguchi had forbidden us to discuss this matter with each other. Wada was sitting in the circle. I winked at him to invite him out in the dark. We had been in the same group ever since we were in this military trap. I knew his suffering and wanted to say a word to him. 'There are better things for you to do, Wada. I'll go and you stay.' He didn't reply. In the black of night we stared at each other. After a while we started to walk back.

'Sixty years later I still wonder if my words made no impact on him. Disobeying the order, I had dared to talk to him. Why didn't I insist more strongly that he not volunteer? Given the circumstances, perhaps I didn't have enough time to think it through.

'After the war I saw the classified document on recruiting this special attack force. I was shocked to find that it said, "Do not mention the performance and the function of the weapon." Without telling us the truth about it, they asked us to apply.'[11]

Wada, Takeda and Tadakuma Iwai (Tadamasa's brother) as well as other *Tokko* members were sent from the navigation school to a temporary station in Hakata, Kyushu. Tadakuma Iwai sat in the same

11 ibid., p. 69

cubicle on the train with Wada. He wrote about the ride in his book, *Tokko*, co-authored with his older brother, Tadamasa.

'We were in the same class at the Navigation School. Wada was a very bright and thoughtful man. We were sitting together in the same compartment on a train to Hakata. Out of the window, green motorboats were skimming over the waves. Wada mumbled, "Are they the Greenpeas Ocean Shakers? By the way have you heard of the human torpedo, *Kaiten*, Iwai? Spare me from that, please." I don't remember how I responded to him. In a year or so he died in the *Kaiten* from which he wanted to be spared. I survived in the Greenpeas.

'When the train arrived at Numazu, Wada ran to a woman who was getting off the train carrying a baby on her back, "Do you know Wada Hospital in the city? Could you please tell the doctor there that his son just passed Numazu station?"

'After the war I asked his family if they received the message, and they had. Wada cared for his family tenderly. He treated other people affectionately, too.

'In 1993, when my university put up the exhibition called "50th Anniversary of the Students Draft", I asked Wada's family to put his original diaries in the show. One of his high school friends, Ide, came to the exhibit. He gazed at Wada's notebooks intently and lamented repeatedly, "I can't believe that delicate Wada died in *Tokko*." He kept coming back to the exhibit like one possessed. As a peace activist, Ide had to live abroad for a long time and hadn't heard about Wada's death. The experience of Wada's notebooks made a profound impact on him.

'Wada went to *Tokko* exactly because he had a delicate sensibility. Even though he was rejected the first time, he insisted on joining with a passionate second plea. It was his pride and his thoughtfulness. Wada knew he was a chosen one to whom everyone looked up. In front of the Navy leaders, his strong sense of responsibility as the representative of the reserve students fostered his determination. His classmates watched his every step. He wanted to show them with his actions that the students were no cowards.'[12]

After a short stay in Kyushu, the *Kaiten* group was transferred to the

12 Iwai, Tadamasa and Tadakuma, op. sit., pp. 126–8

Hikari Base in the Inland Sea. Training there was fierce. Wada quickly became a competent seaman and a capable pilot of the human torpedo.

14 January 1945

We didn't have a nice New Year's Celebration. For three breakfasts in a row, we had *zoni* soup with a few pieces of *mochi* in it. On the night of New Year's Day, a senior officer was drunk and asked me to play violin. Recently, I've had opportunities to play in the evenings. I played *Night in China*. He was so pleased that he told me to play again in a concert on the next day. I sang a song and played a serenade by Haydn.

26 March 1945

Dear Father, Lieutenant Miyoshi died. He failed to clear the bottom of a ship and crashed. Water came in from the hatch above and when he was dragged out after some two hours, he was dead – his face bloody. On the following day, we had a ceremony to bid farewell. We buried a trainee Yasaki from Miyoshi's group on the same day.

In March there was a shuffling of the *Kaiten* groups and Takeda was going to be transferred to another training base, Otsushima, which was nicknamed Devil's Island.

Takeda writes, 'I was to be separated from Wada since he was to remain at Hikari. One day we walked along the coast from Hikari to the next village. It was a beautiful beach lined with pine trees like the ones at Wada's hometown Numazu, though on a smaller scale.

'Wada's *kaiten* training was at the last stage and in a few months he would go on a mission. A capable pilot, he was chosen to go on the first mission among us. Being the top of the class and a role model turned out to be his curse. I was supposed to begin my training soon, too. So, this would be the last time to be together.

'It was too late to say anything. I only held his hands tightly and said, "Take care of yourself." What other words could I say to a man who was destined to die soon?

'We walked, talking about the past and the present. Then I stopped and asked Wada to teach me the popular song, *Bon Voyage*. Wada wrote down the lyrics on the inside of a cigarette box.

Tonight you are leaving port. I'll miss you.

A siren is hooting . . .

Write me a line when you arrive there safe and sound . . .

'We sang it loudly over and over again. In the balmy sunlight, the sound of waves accompanied our song. *Write me a line when you arrive there safe and sound.* Why were we singing this sentimental song knowing we'd never arrive anywhere safe and sound?

'It was the last time we were together alone. I was grateful to God for giving me this time with him.[13]

15 April 1945

The date for my mission was set. It will be on May 15th. I will be on I-363 Submarine with Captain Mitani and his crew. They are three NCOs and two officers, Lieutenant Shumpei Ueyama, the leader of this death mission, and myself.

Dear Father

Last night I got drunk in an unheard-of fashion. I raged about here and there, came into the NCO'S room, drank water from a vase, explained the meaning of Fichte's *Message to Germans*, and drank a mouthful of ink. The ink splashed all over the pants of a reserve candidate. Later I heard them say, 'You know, the reason why Wada is so bright is because he drinks ink from time to time'.

18 April 1945

I was frantically making a chart to measure angles for hitting moving targets. Margins of error in judging directions are getting smaller.

I love Nagao, who just turned nineteen. I also fell in love with the red cheeks of sixteen-year-old Telegrapher Kameoka. Am I homosexual? Or is it the dwindling of time – one month before the sortie – that makes me love people so dearly?

I don't feel like making big speeches like Lieutenant Nishina. Every word he utters is charged with ardent patriotism. But my cold heart shoves it down deep in quiet reflection. One might say too much

13 Takeda, op. cit., pp. 150–2

thinking is unnecessary. But for us who have learned to think, it is an unavoidable burden. Because of it, I reflect on my life and bid farewell to myself. Friends say that I look tired these days. I've been trying hard to find meaning in my death.

26 April 1945

Came back from shooting training at Otake Diving School. Now every other day we practice embarking on a sub. Excruciatingly sleepy, but no time to sleep. At Otake, I saw my old classmate, Kumada. At his lodging, I listened to Beethoven's Fifth and Sixth.

6 May 1945

The hands of a clock, which is not quite ready to give out, keep on ticking. I sometimes experience private fears.

Up until now I managed to maintain a calm front like a *Nō* mask. And now for the first time, I am truly at a loss over how to make sense of my past. I am impatiently struggling to find my true self in my remaining life of just a month. It already seems to me I no longer really exist.

I rode on a *Kaiten* which, without ever floating up, prowled over the ocean floor, and rubbed briskly against the bottom some thirty-five metres below. I operated another one that stuck in the sand of the ocean floor, at a depth of thirty metres. There was another one – when the hatch was opened, white smoke suddenly spread over the whole length of the tube because of the high internal pressure – I felt as though someone had struck me in the face.

[Wada devotes many pages of his notebook to technical aspects of *Kaiten* and points out that they should be paid attention to and improved.]

8 May 1945

Tonight the earth echoes in silence.
How I wish to have someone I could embrace and tremble with in the shadow of trees.

15 May 1945

Yesterday I was allowed to take leave and go home. Annoying rain. Took an evening train. It took me more than twenty-five hours to come up to this place on the train. At 8.30 pm I'll arrive in Numazu and I have to walk drenched to the skin. I don't have confidence. I'm afraid that as soon as I see Father and Mother's face, I might tell them everything. Then what would they think and say?

On the following day, Wakana decided not to go to school and instead walked with her brother on the beach, singing a song and clinging to him. 'I'd loved going for walks with him from the time I was really small. If I were a dog, I'd have been shaking ten imaginary tails, that's how excited I was.'[14] At the edge of the ocean, they skipped stones, trying to get them to break through the oncoming waves. When her brother saw a ship on the sea or an old lodge on the Izu Peninsula, he called out the azimuth, quickly calculating the degrees and minutes with his eye.

On the next day Wakana-san went to see her brother off at the train station. She said, 'My brother raised his white-gloved right hand in salute. The train slowly left the station. His serious face did not break into a smile. When we went back home, our house was empty and cold. I hid myself in my room and cried.'

29 May 1945 – A Postcard to his Father

Father, I appreciated your writing to me so often after my last visit with you. Don't worry, my stomach is doing well even after such a feast. The moon is beautiful tonight. I'm reminiscing about twenty-two years of my growing up under your wing. Please don't write to me any longer. I'll be away for a while. Hurriedly, Minoru

Wada carried this last note with him on his mission and brought it back to Hikari. It was found inside the *Kaiten* he died in, its ink faded yellow. It was brought home by Lieutenant Ueyama and given to his father with his remains.

14 Taya, Haruko and Cook, Theodore F., *Japan at War: An Oral History*, NewPress, NewYork, 1992, p. 330

The war situation had worsened. America had brought the Philippines under control and landed on Okinawa. Battleship *Yamato* – the pride of Japan – had been sunk.

Takeda came to Hikari one day before Wada left for the mission and attended the farewell party for him and his crew.

'I didn't realise how popular Wada was among the NCOs. He must have been loved by them since he started to play violin for them. He was invited by so many to their dorms and bid sayonara to everyone.

'Next day on May 28th Wada left for a mission. Wada, carrying a short sword given as a memento from the Emperor, walked slowly to the sea as if cherishing the last few steps on the earth. My eyes met with his. A slight smile came to his eyes. That was enough for me. 'It has been a long ordeal, but I'll keep my chin up and go,' he seemed to be saying. It was our last farewell.

'We took a small boat and chased the I-363 submarine. Wada stood on his *Kaiten* hatch with the bouquet of irises in his arms and gradually disappeared from my sight. On a boat returning to Otsushima, my head was filled with the images of that night when I said to him, 'Wada. I'll go and you stay.' He was gone and I was left.'[15]

12 June 1945

At 11.40 a.m., the order was given: '*Kaiten*, be alert!' It seemed that the target is an enemy carrier. . . . Then we missed it.

I am waiting for the enemy in the submarine here almost for a month in Ulithi [an atoll in the western Carolines], the highway for a supply route to Okinawa. I have a firm, quiet feeling in the lower abdomen. I am very happy and content . . . At night I walked up to the bridge and, off to my right, I spied the Great Dipper. The Southern Cross twinkled on the left, Corona was directly above, and the Milky Way looked like a white cloud.

Ueyama, the leader of the mission, wrote about Wada: 'Wada was a pale, thin and good-looking young man. When he listened to others talk, he often tilted his head a bit to one side and blinked his eyes shyly.

15 Takeda, op. cit., pp. 170–1

In spite of his gentle looks, one felt that there was a firm core to his character.

'For the *Kaiten* crew who rode on the I-363, two beds were prepared for Wada and me in the officers' room. But Wada always slept in a hammock with the NCOs. He played cards with the crew and sailors. On the third day when there was the first order to attack an enemy ship, we were ready to go, with the hatch shut down and engine running. We waited for a telephone call from the captain to "go". But low pressure developed and a heavy squall hampered our vision. We returned and continued the card game we had stopped before this unsuccessful sortie, as if nothing had ever happened. We laughed and yelled just as before.' [Ueyama survived the war and became a professor of history at University of Kyoto.][16]

20 June 1945

The order came to I-363 to return to base. We are still looking, but unable to find our prey. It's depressing and mortifying. How could I go back to the base and show my face in broad daylight?

Wada's last letter to his family (date unknown)

'I haven't written to you for so long. You must have been worried. The other day I returned from an unsuccessful mission in a faraway place. I understand that Numazu was bombed. Is everyone all right? American B's often visit us, too, but there hasn't been too much damage.

'Please write to me all about the family and send it to me in a fast mail. But by the time it arrives here, I may have been gone to the destination tens of thousands of miles away in the clouds.'

In order to prepare for the next death mission, Wada went for a practice run at 4.30 am on July 25th. He chose that ungodly hour since lately the American task force had been flying along the Japanese coastline as freely as if it were their own. A rescue boat was following Wada's torpedo which was usual practice. But the boat lost sight of his *Kaiten*. Then air-raid sirens blew and every rescue effort had to be stopped.

16 Ueyama, Shumpei, *Commentary on Wada's Diary*, pp. 334–5, 327

Takeda wrote in his book: '(When I received the report that Wada was missing), I was in Otsushima and was not allowed to get out. I just kept saying to myself, 'Wada, don't die! Wada, don't die!'

'I knew that even if he came back alive, he had to leave for another death mission, but I kept praying, "God, don't kill him! Please don't kill him!"

'In spite of my prayers, his hours in the small cube went over the time limit for suffocation.[17]

Imagine the depth of agony and despair he went through in the last hours of his life. What thoughts went through his mind sitting for hours and hours in the claustrophobic cube? How sad he was not to see his family at the time of death. How mortifying it was for him not to die on a mission but in a meaningless accident? Why didn't God save such a gentle and good man? He was twenty-three years old.

Wada's *Kaiten* was not found for a long time. Almost two months later on a stormy day at the end of September 1945, a *Kaiten* was washed up on the shore of a small island, Nagashima, in the Seto Inland Sea. Three of his former colleagues who were still working at Hikari went to the island. The monstrous, black cylinder was lying on the shore – an embodiment of evil, obscenely ugly and elongated. It was so unbecoming a coffin for such a sweet, gentle man. They cremated Wada on a rock ledge of the shore. Lieutenant Ueyama brought his remains to the family in Numazu. This was a terrible war crime committed by the nation against its own good citizen.'

'Did you notice that my brother stopped writing his diary after he came back alive from the unsuccessful mission? There must be a reason why he didn't write,' Wakana-san stopped and sighed over the phone. 'This is just my guess: my brother was ready to die before the unsuccessful mission, but after that he might not have been so sure about it.

'He stayed underwater in a submarine for a month waiting for the chance to attack an enemy ship. I wonder what went through his mind

17 Takeda, op. cit., pp. 196, 199–200

in the long dark nights. He read book after book in the bottom of the carrier and he must have yearned for the intellectual life he lived before. He must have missed his family and thought about the girls he used to like although he had no close relationship with any. With *Kaiten* having so many problems and little chance of success, he must have wondered whether it was worth dying for?

'According to his crewmate, Oishi-san, my brother confided to him after they returned from their failed mission, "I don't want to die." He said the same thing to another friend while they were playing music together.

'But my brother did not write so in his diary. It would have been a betrayal of himself and the cause he once believed in. Anyway, it was at the point of no return. The date for the next mission was already fixed; it would be 31 July.

'You might think that he would have died in the next mission anyway. The carrier that my brother would have been on for his next mission was hit by an enemy plane. All the *Kaitens* on it were damaged, but the crew were not on them. The war ended soon afterwards; all of my brother's mission mates survived the war'.

Wakana-san wrote about the day the Emperor announced the end of the war. 'Tears rolled down on my father's cheeks, so I cried a little. That evening, my father said, "But Minoru will be back!" Yes, Minoru-chan will be home! Mother happily started to clean the house with a broom. I played piano as if possessed.[18]

'On 26 August a telegram arrived from the War Ministry which said, "Wada Minoru, Public Death." My father crouched down, head in his hands. "Minoru. Why did you die? Why?" He howled like a wounded beast. I heard both my father and mother wail until late at night. I cried in my bed until my pillow was soaking wet.

'I was shocked that a young man who sacrificed his life for the country was dismissed with two incomprehensible words. Not a word of respect, or of thanks. Not a line of explanation about the circumstances of his death. During this war the soldiers who died in accidents

18 Taya, Haruko and Cook, Theodore F., op. cit., p. 332

or of sickness were not considered to have died an honourable death. Our family did not know the meaning of Public Death and considered it meant he had taken his own life. The words "Public Death" were later changed to "death on duty", but there was no further explanation, apology or thanks.

'The next day my father and my other brother went to Hikari. At least they found out Minoru-chan's death was not a suicide.'

Akira Wada, Minoru's younger brother by ten years, wrote a postscript to his brother's diary. 'After his death, the violin he left for me became the main tie which bound him and me. It was the instrument Father bought for him as a present for entering high school, a copy of a second period Stradivarius made in Germany. It did not necessarily have the best sound and its slight hardness bothered even my young ears. But in my mind the happy smile my brother showed when he picked up the violin, which was shining red reflecting the bright light of the room, stands out as the most vivid memory.

'The violin has a wood graining which moves as if it were alive and reflects in silence the various events that happened to my brother in his impressionable youth – a tall figure on a stage as a concert master at the high school orchestra, complicated relations with his music club friends or the centre of attention at the family concert in which he played with his aunts and sisters.

'The day the government stopped the student draft exemption was the day my brother faced death. From then on his diary shows how he tried to give an ideological meaning to his own death. He tried to write and leave everything he had learned to his siblings in thirty-eight pages of letters to us.

'Words cannot express my father's sorrow the day he received the news of his son's death. It was the deepest agony a human could ever suffer.

'Since then, every day Father has made it a practice to copy my brother's diary into a notebook, just as a monk copies Buddha's script. He wrote and reread it, sharing his son's life and death. After he finished copying the entire diary twice, we saw a peaceful expression on his face for the first time. We were allowed to pronounce the name, 'Minoru', and he began to sound it, too. It had been taboo in the entire house for so long.

'My father spent the last five years of his life quietly at home anticipating his approaching death by cancer. He passed away peacefully at a hospital in Yokohama in 1966, at the age of seventy-four.

'As I gazed at my father's face after he stopped breathing, I saw my brother's dead face overlap Father's. It suddenly occurred to me that my brother must have also died as peacefully as my father. This belief leaped over the gap of twenty years and for the first time I came to terms with my brother's death. As the hearse carrying my father drove over the hills of Hakone, the surface of the lake looked mournful. In the silent world which reminded me of Bruckner's symphony, I also saw the dark surface of the sea at the Hikari Base which I had visited with my father to pick up my brother's belongings.'[19]

Wakana-san wrote in her letter to me: 'Every year on July 25th, our family and my brother's friends gather and hold a memorial service for him. A few years ago, they had a big service to commemorate the sixtieth year of his death. His best friend, Takeda-san, came. Unfortunately he has passed away since then. Minoru-chan's crewmate, Oishi-san, came, too, and read Buddhist scriptures and prayed for my brother. He became a monk after the war. He said it was the only way he could live after the *Kaiten* experience.

'My brother was fortunate. So many people remembered him, prayed for him and wrote about him. But there were millions of soldiers who lost their lives and are not even remembered. If you write about my brother, please remind readers that he was only "one of millions." '

*   *   *

On the facing page the poems are written in Tanka form which consists of 31 syllables. There are 17 in Haiku.

19 Wada, Wataru, *About Brother Minoru*, pp. 312–20

Poems by Wakana Nishihara[20]

Delivering the Telegram to Father
Clasping the note of Brother's death
I ran through a pine forest of a defeated nation.
Cicadas sang in deafening chorus

In the *kaiten* at the bottom of the sea
Brother died
Eternal silence

---

20 *Imoto-tachino Kagaribi* (The Sisters' Torch: For the Brothers Who Died in
   the War), op. cit., pp. 203–6

CHAPTER 4

Ryutaro Hanamichi

A Heavy Bomber Suicide Mission

I took a train to visit a village on the Kii Peninsula, which juts out to the Pacific between Nagoya and Kyoto. As I traveled south along the western coastline, steep walled gorges gave way to sandy beaches. The night before, there had been a torrential rainstorm. The train stopped in a small station because our way was blocked by rocks fallen from the hill. My sister, who was travelling with me, rented a car and managed to find the little village at the southernmost tip of the peninsula. The day turned lovely. Behind a low bush along a quiet road, an old lady was hanging clothes on a bamboo pole. She heard our car approaching, looked up and her wrinkled face broke into a broad smile. She ran out and bowed to us, 'My husband has been waiting for you. Please come in.'

Hanamichi-san lived in a modest, but neat-looking wooden house which he had been toiling over for years, knocking down partitions, changing floors and the roof. We sat on a cozy couch in the living room. An *objet d'art* in the centre of the room was part of the wing of an old kamikaze plane, a piece of wreckage picked from the rice field where his comrades had crashed. The four walls of the room were covered with pictures of young soldiers, planes, bombers and the Battlefield Service Code written on yellowed rice paper. This house was a little war museum. Clearly, this gentle, youthful looking eighty-five year-old man was still immersed in the war.

'My dad was a cooper. From morning till night, he made wooden pails. Small ones to scoop water or rice, and big ones for bath tubs,' Hanamichi-san talked with the soft sing-song dialect of the region. 'The work was labour intensive because the wood pieces had to fit exactly, or water would leak through the seams.' He showed me one of the old pails his father had made. 'My parents had four sons and three daughters. We had no rice and ate sweet potato porridge. Lots of days, not even that. We had no shoes. When I started school, my father made straw sandals for me to wear. When I was ten, I made my own.

'When I finished elementary school, my teacher said to me, "You are smart. Take an exam and go to middle school." But I knew my father couldn't afford it. I asked my teacher to find a place where I could get a good job. He recommended that I go to the Training School for Aviation Engineers which was newly opened in Gifu. I passed the exam and went there with no idea what was in store. The place turned out to be a no-nonsense military school. We had to get up at the sound of a trumpet, eat with a trumpet and go to bed with a trumpet. In the morning we listened to lectures and learned about airplanes. The more I learned, the more I liked the idea of flying. When I saw powerful machines take off into the air, my heart leapt. I was allowed to ride a plane only once for ten minutes before the school was over. It took off, cruised around and landed. But since then in my dreams I saw myself being a pilot, flying in the sky.

'The next school I went to was an aviation academy in Utsunomiya. The training there was fierce. We were beaten on our cheeks with slippers, hands and fists for nothing. Our group was given training only for low-altitude flights. Later I found out why. After three years I worked at Aircraft Arsenal. My job was maintenance of airplanes, the most menial of jobs and had nothing to do with flying. I worked real hard, but I hadn't forgotten my dream of being a pilot. At the Arsenal, lights were turned off at 9 p.m. I pretended to be asleep when the night patrol came, but the minute he left, I read textbooks with a flashlight inside blankets. Thanks to my nightly cramming under the blankets I passed the exam for the recruitment of special cadets. There were four training courses – for pilots, wireless operators, engineers and navigators. They assigned me to a navigator class. This was a terrible disappointment for me, since my mind was set on being a pilot.

'But it turned out to be an important job. Radar wasn't yet used in Japan. We had to depend on conjecture when we flew over an area with no distinguishable landmarks. Usually, a strong prevailing wind like the Westerlies blows planes off course and a compass won't show a correct direction. Random wind also messes up flying speed. Velocity shown on a speedometer is likely to be incorrect. The navigator has to calculate these discrepancies every ten minutes and write down on a map the exact spot he thinks he is at.

The 62nd Air Force I was assigned to was a heavy bomber unit called *Tokko* Special Attack Force. They did not tell me what was special about it.

'Bombers, fighters and even just ordinary planes were scarce by early 1945. They had been shot down, together with most of the capable pilots. As a desperate measure, the Air Force came up with a radical idea. Heavy bombers were not meant to fly a long distance. They were to fly at low altitude to the nearest enemy destroyers and carriers. What was special about *Tokko* bombers turned out to be that the pilot and the crew had to drop themselves as well as bombs on the target. Nobody told me that I had been trained all these years to be a suicide bomber.

'I'd never heard the word *Tokko* before. After the war, I learned that young student-soldiers had been asked to volunteer to fly *Tokko* suicide bombers and many of them did under immense pressure. But we were never even asked to volunteer for it. For us it was an order. No questions had ever been asked. It was a death sentence without committing a crime. Imagine our shock and despair.

'There was something more special about our *Tokko* bombers. It was difficult for small kamikaze planes to destroy big enemy carriers. So they created heavier models. An excellent heavy bomber called *Hiryu* was remodeled by the Army into two kinds of heavy *Tokko* bombers.[21] One was called TO, short for *Tokko*. Two 800 kilogram bombs were placed in the middle of the body. While a smaller kamikaze plane was flown by one pilot, these *Tokko* planes demanded the lives of four crew – a pilot, an engineer, a navigator and a wireless operator. We were to be crammed into the plane with gigantic bombs in the middle just to navigate it to the spot. Imagine four young men dropped to be incinerated with a bomber which might not even hit the target.

21 'Development, Production and Supplies of Army's Air Arsenal,' from *The Defense Agency: Military History*, No. 87, pp. 457–60, Chouun Shimbun-sha, 1975

'The other bomber was called *Sakura*, Cherry-blossom. It was said to have developed from a drawing sent by Hitler as a present. Who knows if that was true or not? This one had to carry an even heavier bomb weighing three tons. This bomber as well as TO was not supposed to drop its bomb. We would attack an enemy ship with the whole plane with its bomb and ourselves together. It looked like a hunch-backed monster because the cone-shaped bomb was sticking out on its back like a camel's hump. In order to keep the weight to a minimum, veneer board was used for the nose, the back and the tail of the plane. After all it wouldn't matter how flimsy the plane looked, would it? It would attack the enemy and blow up after a very short flight. These bombers were so dangerous even on the ground that the residents around the base were forced to move out.

'The 62nd Air Force men would be assigned to either TO or *Sakura* and go on Okinawa missions. The targets would be the American carriers and ships which were gathering in the sea of Okinawa in preparation for an all out attack on the island. In order to carry out our mission, the 62nd Force had to move from our training base in Tsukuba to Tachiarai Airbase in Kyushu which was closer to Okinawa and whose runway was long enough for the heavy bombers to take off. The move required a flight over mainland Japan from north-east to south-west which should have been little problem for any trained pilot flying an ordinary plane, but this was done by inadequately trained pilots in the ridiculously heavy bombers and resulted in an incredible fiasco. Our Force lost more men and bombers in mishaps than in actual suicide attacks on enemy ships.

'On 12 April 1945, we were lined up at Tsukuba base, ready to fly in a formation. Our Commander Sawato was on the first plane with all the other important officers. They took off and the second plane followed. My plane was the fourth. We took off and got 150 metres up in the air when, to my horror, I saw the Commander's plane suddenly put its nose down and before my eyes dive all the way to the ground. Instantly, it exploded in a fireball. There were no survivors. To this day no one knows why it happened. Was the pilot drunk? Could heavy rice bags and canned food loaded on the plane have rolled onto one side and caused a loss of balance?

'It was an inauspicious start, but it was only the beginning of the disasters which followed. The runway of the Kyushu airfield had been the target of American air raids. When we approached, we saw the polka-dotted holes dug on the runway by the enemy's bombs. Fire was erupting from some of them probably from time bombs. We were able to avoid the holes and landed, but the next plane fell into one of them at touchdown and was badly damaged. The one which followed, probably trying to avoid the holes, ended up crashing into a nearby rice field. Another one which went missing after reporting to say that they would avoid the holes, was later discovered crashed in the sea off Shikoku.

'Our spirits sank after these losses. But in no time we were assigned to go on our mission to Okinawa using the TO bomber. I checked the engine and all the equipment to make sure that the machine was in good order. Then I stepped out of the bomber in order to get a pail of water from a farmhouse nearby. As I walked back, I could not believe my eyes. Our bomber looking perfect a minute before, had half of the body smashed. Next to the wreckage, lay another dented plane – our own fighter plane. A witness said that the fighter, which had just taken off, was buffeted by a gust of wind and slammed into our bomber.

'The TO was unusable now. So we were given a *Sakura* instead. This monster was the ultimate murder machine. If you left for a mission in this one, you'd never come back even if you didn't find the enemy's carrier to attack. Why? Because the bomb was so heavy, you were allowed to load only one way's worth of fuel. Or so they said. The tank of TO could be filled up, although those days even TOs often left with one-way fuel since we had a severe shortage of petroleum in Japan. The crew were not supposed to come back anyway. Why waste return fuel?

'The maintenance boss, Kishi, did not like the idea. He was a brave guy and whispered to his fuel man, "Fill up the tank." So those who couldn't find the enemy ships were able to return. They owed their lives to Kishi. Out of the four bombers which had taken off in the last missions, none of the *Sakuras* had returned, but the two TOs had due to bad weather.

Our *Sakura* team was ordered to make a sortie on May 25 1945. It would be the last day of my life. I would surely have been gone if we had taken off that day. However, another divine intervention prevented us from flying, although it came with the terrible sacrifice of one of our crew.

'On 22 April, we were allowed to take a day off and went to a spa in Fukuoka for the final holiday in our lives. We stayed overnight there, returned to the base and early in the morning went to look at our *Sakura*. Lo and behold, we saw a pile of ashes where the monster had been sitting. The Japanese Gestapo, *Kempeitai*, came to investigate the wreckage. The military police quickly put handcuffs on our wireless operator, Lance-Corporal Yamamoto, and dragged him away. We have never seen him again. They said that he was sentenced to death by Court Martial and was executed on August 9, just six days before the end of the war.

'I personally think Yamamoto was innocent. Yamamoto was a Japanese name, but he happened to be a Korean. Those days all Koreans had to assume Japanese names. He was a shy, gentle guy. *Kempeitai* was under pressure to quickly capture a traitor who committed this serious treachery. It was easy for them to say that this was the work of an anti-Japanese Korean who didn't want to die in a suicide mission. Don't you think it strange that the rest of his crew – Pilot Sano, Engineer Sakurai and I – were never even asked a single question? They must have been afraid that if they did, Yamamoto's alibi would have been established. Even if he was the one who had committed the crime, he was due to go on the suicide mission with us on the next trip. Isn't the death mission enough of a punishment? Besides, supposing he was the one who had burnt the plane, how could anyone blame him? We had not been treated like humans, but only like trash to be incinerated with a bomb. Being a Korean, Yamamoto had more reasons not to be reconciled to dying for the Emperor or for the nation he was not born in.

'He had gone with us on the spa holiday. He was with me on the military truck which took us back from the spa to our base. Some documents we saw later said that Yamamoto went to the billet all alone. But he went to bed when we did. He could have gone out after we were all asleep, but the air base was far away from our billet and walking there would have been extremely difficult in a total blackout. I heard that Yamamoto confessed under duress to a crime he might not have committed. Women from the nearby village saw him pass by in handcuffs, blood streaming from his face, his cheeks puffed up, and his eyes black and blue. He denied his confession at the court martial. If it were today's court, a confession would not be enough for conviction. The whole thing was an outrage. I heard that our commander begged the court to let Yamamoto join the next mission because it was his wish to die in a mission rather than from a death sentence. The court did not grant his wish.

'So our *Sakura* was gone. I was secretly happy, thanking Yamamoto or whoever for demolishing the killer monster. But they decided to send us to fly a TO instead of *Sakura*. They ordered us to fly without Yamamoto. The night before the sortie, the engineer Sakurai, came to my bed. He stood shaking there and whispered in my ear, "Hanamichi. I don't want to die. Back home I have a girl I love. I don't want to die." "I don't want to die either," I whispered back to him. I wouldn't have said this to anyone else. No one was allowed to say that. You were supposed to die happily for Emperor and country. Those who died before us went without complaining.

'We held each other and cried together in the dark, Sakurai and me. Up until then I had been resigned to my fate and felt relatively calm about it. But that night, I had a burning desire to live. I felt I was going mad with sadness and fear. Why did I have to die so young without experiencing the wonderful things life might offer. There must be a vast unknown world out there which would unfold before me. Tomorrow I would be diving from the deep blue sky into the abyss. There is no way to escape this fate. I screamed in silence, "Mom and Dad. Help me out of here, please!" I tossed and turned on the bed all night wet with tears and sweat.

'On the morning of the sortie, we were awakened early and went to the mess hall. There was a feast which belied wartime famine. But I had a lump in my throat and couldn't eat much. We went to the base and stood in a row. Commander Ono walked over to every one of us. He came to me and said, "Thank you for going." He looked at me with gentle, sad eyes. I cried.

'A wireless instructor came to ask me to do the wireless operator's job as well as that of navigator since Yamamoto was not with us. "But I don't know anything about wireless, sir," I said. Then he took me to the machine in the bomber and said, "I'll make it very easy for you. All you have to do is to push this button. At the very second you attack the enemy, you push it twice, *tu tu*. If you fail in the mission and want to blow up your own bomber, you push *tu, tu, tu, tu, tu*." "If it's that easy, why do you need a wireless operator? It would save a precious life." I was about to say, but I swallowed the words and just said, "Then I can do it, sir."

'At 6 a.m. 25 May 1945, four *Tokko* bombers of the 62nd Air Force – two *Sakuras* and two TOs – took off for Okinawa in spite of the low pressure clouds developing over the East China Sea. Our TO was told to follow Pilot Mizota's *Sakura* because we were undermanned. But we flew faster than his *Sakura* which was so heavy that it seemed to be struggling against gravity to keep aloft. It looked like a dinosaur in the sky – not meant to fly. In order to slow down, our pilot Sano went in zigzags and turned around in circles.

'In the meanwhile, the weather was changing for the worse. Heavy clouds quickly covered the entire sky and Mizota's *Sakura* was only seen in and out of them. Pilot Sano had been dutifully following the *Sakura*, but soon it disappeared completely. Sano became desperate. "Let's forget about *Sakura*. Hanamichi, Figure out the direction to Okinawa," he said. Rain, clouds and wind made it extremely difficult to plot the course, but I tried my best. At 8.57 a.m. we received a radio message from Mizota's *Sakura* 0857 – *mi-mi-mi-tu-tu-tu-mi-mi-mi* . . . meaning, "We'll make an attack now . . . " Another wireless came at 9.22 a.m. from Pilot Fukushima's *Sakura* 0922 – *te-te-ate-re-ka-u-ho* . . . "We found an enemy carrier. We are plunging into it . . . Sayonara."

'These messages put tremendous pressure on us to find a target, but we were enveloped by layers of fog and did not find a speck of a ship or an island. Three hours passed and fuel was getting low. "If we go on like this, all of us will just perish for nothing. Let's go back and refuel. We'll start all over again. Hanamichi, find a way back," Sano said, shifting the direction of his plane to the north. It was the most nerve-wracking experience of my life. Sano followed my guidance and flew on, but I was scared to death. If my guess was wrong, all of us would die.

'At long last, small islands came into sight between the clouds. I recognised the biggest one, Tokunoshima. We are close to Kyushu. We'll be all right! Everyone breathed a deep sigh of relief. But the red lamp for the fuel tank turned on. The temperature of the cylinder had risen dangerously high. The runway of Tokunoshima would be too short for a bomber with two 800 kilogram bombs on it. Sakurai and I figured out a possibility of landing somewhere else. After a frantic search, we chose Shikaya's runway and landed there safely.

'For us bad weather had been a blessing. The American planes' radar did not catch us because we flew at an extremely low altitude. After refuelling, Sano called up our headquarters and said, "We are ready to leave again." But Commander Ono told us to return to the home base. We were fearful of returning to our base. We were supposed to be dead. The morning when we left, all the troops had lined up for us, cheering and singing. But this time, they might slap us on the cheeks, box our ears and shout, "Cowards! Traitors!" and other insults. To our surprise, when we landed at the home base, Commander Ono was there waiting for us. He said, "Welcome back. I was worried about the weather. Thank you for trying." His kind words made me burst out crying.

'I had heard that *Tokko* crew who returned from a sortie alive were sometimes sent to a special cell to be tortured, but we weren't sent anywhere because our commander was a kind man. He also declined to send us on another mission. It seemed that most of the 62nd Force Commanders were sympathetic to us. After the war I read the essay written by Ono's predecessor, Commander Ishibashi. When he was told by the Commander-in-Chief in Tokyo headquarters to make the 62nd Force a *Tokko* unit, he objected saying: "The tide of war can not be turned around with *Tokko*. We cannot sacrifice men if success is not guaranteed. I don't want my men to die in vain just as I don't want to die in vain myself." He was demoted three days later.

'Toward the end of the war, the Americans had full knowledge about suicide bombers. They were vigilant around the clock for kamikaze planes. As soon as a *Tokko* was in their radar's range, they attacked it from all sides. It would perish in a hailstorm of bullets. It had little chance of reaching the target. Commander Ishibashi knew that. Neither of the two *Sakuras* with whom we went on the mission had returned, but no note of any attacks has been found in the American records.'

Mr Hanamichi breathed a heavy sigh. 'When the war ended, I felt relieved, but I felt so terribly guilty I hadn't died. Why did so many of my comrades die, but not me? Before I left the base after the war, I burned everything – my diary, military cap, ear muffs, the headband and the doll a village girl gave me – everything. I tried to shut out my past from my memory although my dead friends appeared in my dreams every night.

'Since I returned home I never talked about my *Tokko* experience to anyone – not even to my wife of thirty years. My parents died without ever knowing that I was a *Tokko* member. If I said I had been a *Tokko*, I was afraid people would call me a traitor to my country. They might say you weren't brave enough to die for the Emperor. I knew of the parents who were stoned because their son was a survivor of Kamikaze. I was also fearful of the American Occupation Force. If they found out what I was trying to do, they might come to capture me and torture me. Perhaps because I lived in such a remote part of the country, I didn't realise that people's perceptions had changed after the war.

'A frog's son is a frog. After the war I helped my father make wooden pails. During the war, wooden pails weren't in demand and my father was in debt. But after the war, a farmer asked us to make pails to keep their candied sweet potatoes in. They looked lovely in the handsome pails and sold like hot cakes. They brought us a lot of profit. We paid back all the debt and were even able to buy this house. We also bought three tans of land [a tan = 992m^2]. We bought an ox and cultivated the land. We grew rice, radishes and eggplants.

'Good things don't last. The candied potato merchants began to use tin cans instead of wooden pails. Our business was in the red again. Then I studied accounting and worked as a clerk in the village administration office. In those days the average pay was a thousand yen a month. I earned six thousand yen. We've been well off.

'In 1980, when our 62nd Force Old Boy Association asked me to write something about the war, I was reluctant. But I read the stories my friends had written and realised I had been wrong about hiding mine. If I didn't tell my stories, people would not know what we were forced to do during the war. The leaders didn't mind murdering their own soldiers, using their lives as bombs. It is my obligation to tell the stories of my colleagues who lost their precious lives in vain. So now I write for the newspapers, talk at schools and at lecture series.

'I was born under a lucky star. I have a good wife and lived long enough to see my great-grandchildren. Every morning, looking at the western sky where we flew, I pray for my dead comrades.'

Then, Hanamichi-san gave me a copy of the poem his comrade, Masatatsu Yamashita, had written to his parents before he left for a sortie on the same day as Mr Hanamichi.

> Chichi ya Haha, (Father and mother)
> You may not imagine I'm gone now
> But my spirit is back with you
> Wishing to be hugged in your arms

I happened to read a newspaper article (the *Mainichi*, July 10 2014) which quoted the same poem. It tells that in the last correspondence with her son, his mother, Matsue, wrote, 'Dear Masatatsu, dying is not the only way to serve the Emperor. Please, please, don't die. Live, live, live and live through.'

Yamashita flew a *Sakura* bomber and never returned.

CHAPTER 5

Susumu Iida

A Dream of the Greater East Asia Co-Prosperity Sphere

Susumu Iida lives in a suburb of Yokohama in a cluster of attractive, blue-roofed, white houses. A tall man, he welcomed me with a big smile and an enthusiastic handshake, something one does not often experience with Japanese men, who tend to greet their guests with polite bows. Knowing how he had suffered, I was happily surprised to find he was so exuberant. Mr Iida has been involved with many different charities, though as an eighty-eight-year-old with a heart condition, he has finally started cutting back on them. A profound thinker and prominent voice on war issues, he has written many books and numerous newspaper articles.

After leading me to a spacious room decorated with pan-Asian carved wood furniture, he sat on a reclining armchair and talked.

'I was born in Kyoto in 1923. My father was an itinerant construction worker. While in Kyoto he was promoted to a manager's position for the first time. But we still lived in a shantytown far away from the fancy streets lined with lanterns, where women walked in elegant kimonos. My father sometimes went to a geisha house to show off his small success. But he lost his job when the recession hit after World War I. Our family, which consisted of five kids – I was the oldest – moved from city to city, wherever he could find work. My parents quarreled all the time. Once I ran after my mom, who was going to kill herself after a big fight with my dad. I wrestled with her on the beach, where dark waves came surging in and almost swallowed us.

'I had to change schools every year, but I was a good student eager to learn about the world. At the end of middle school, my dad wanted me to work as a helper at a local bank, but I insisted on going to high school. I did well there, but stopped going halfway through because of a freak incident. One day on my way back from school, a student from a nearby girls' school gave me an apple and I ate it. I don't know whether the Confucian and Buddhist teachers at my school knew anything about Adam and Eve, but the Confucian ethos says that a boy over seven should not be seen with a girl, much less eating an apple given to him by her. I was called into the staff room where all the teachers shouted at me. I felt indignant. I didn't think I had done anything wrong. I couldn't bring myself to apologise, so I quit school instead. My dad, who had a hard time paying for school, didn't mind my leaving.

'I worked at a mine, loading coal, pulling a trolley or working with machines. One day my uncle came to visit from Tokyo. "Why are you wasting your life in this miserable part of the world, Susumu?" he asked. "Do you have any idea what your country is up to?" He lectured me on how Japan had created the Greater East Asia Co-Prosperity Sphere in the Pacific to liberate all Asian countries under European domination. It turned out that he was a member of a nationalist organisation. He was thirty years old and trumpeting his party's propaganda, but to me, a frustrated boy of an impressionable age, his ideas sounded good.

'My uncle invited me to Tokyo. From there he took me on a freight boat to Ponape, a Micronesian Island. He had some dubious business deal there. I became desperately bored with the sleepy, tropical life on the island and came back to Tokyo with a burning desire to go to university. I boarded with two roommates in a little flat in Tokyo. Like me, they had come from poor families in the countryside and wanted to go to university. In the daytime I had a job at an election office and at night I studied without much sleep to prepare for the entrance exams.

'World War II broke out on 8 December 1941. The three of us were nineteen and doomed – the draft was an inevitability. My dreams of attending university were shattered, but by then I had been brain-washed sufficiently by my uncle to want to help build the Greater East Asia Co-Prosperity Sphere. "When we go to war, we may not see each other again," my roommates said. So the three of us went to a photographer in Shibuya and had a souvenir picture taken. You can see the photo here on my bookshelf. My two roommates were sent to Saipan, and they both perished there. Not even their ashes made it back. After the war I went to that small island in the Pacific with a group of people who had built a monument for the soldiers who died there. Tears kept gushing down my cheeks as I hugged the granite memorial. Between its base stones, I slipped in a letter to them, and a copy of our photo.

'I didn't want to be a soldier. So I signed up for a school set up by a nongovernmental organisation. Its purpose was to educate young men to be leaders in the Pacific islands. The course consisted of history, geography and Asian languages. Martial arts were a major part of the curriculum, too. An instructor, a lieutenant general in the reserve, liked me and said, "You'd make a good intelligence officer. Why don't you become a *Kempei* (military police officer)?" In the heyday of Imperial Japan, a word from a high officer meant a lot. But I said, "Thank you, sir, for your advice, but I would rather devote myself to being a liberator of Asia. I don't need a military title." I must have sounded cocky, but I was a romantic young man.

'I finished school easily and applied for a Navy program to explore natural resources in New Guinea. I didn't expect New Guinea to be the great mecca for Asian liberation, but at least it could be a starting point. The map of the island looked like a sleepy dinosaur floating over the Pacific. The Japanese were audacious enough to enter into this heart of darkness without permission or invitation. In February 1943, our ship arrived at Manokwari, in the western part of New Guinea. It was a town that used to be the headquarters of the Dutch Colonial Government. Red-roofed buildings were scattered in the dark green jungle. It looked eerily calm, a secret island that nothing would ever disrupt.

'I was assigned to a group of geologists whose job was to study the region for oil, bauxite, gum and wood. Since I wasn't a scientist but had studied Indonesian, I served as liaison to the local people. Along with the Indonesians, Papuans were the natives, but each tribe spoke a different language. We communicated with the Papuans in Indonesian, which some of them understood. Our plan was to explore a 3000-metre high mountain range that was called the Alphak. The tribes who lived down on the coast would never go near the Alphak because the people there, who were known as the Manekiyon, were supposed to be cannibals. Our twenty-man exploration team was protected by two soldiers, but if we antagonised the Manekiyons, we might not return alive.

'While climbing high into the interior one day, we saw smoke rising halfway up the mountain. With a native guide and a comrade, I stealthily approached the smoke. Nearby was a large naked man plowing the soil. He stared at us with an unfriendly look. We smiled and flashed the necklaces and colourful cloths we had brought on the advice of the guide. But the man's face turned red; he roared like a beast and drew his bow at us. Fearing that not only that man but all his cannibal friends would run down to catch us, we rushed down the mountain, and managed to get away.

'After several unsuccessful encounters, we were finally able to befriend the Manekiyons, and traded salt and cloth for their weapons. Without their arms, they were wonderfully kind people. They didn't seem to be waiting to eat us. They guided us on our expeditions, hopping steep hills like ninjas, with our rucksacks on their backs. They said they would take us to the lakes of the Gods, Giji and Gita, hidden deep in the dark mountains. By the time we arrived there, the moon was up and the leaden surface of the lakes reflected its face. It was cold in the mountains. The natives made a bonfire and danced around in a circle, folding their arms together. We were apprehensive but happy when bare-breasted girls pulled us up to join the dance. But their body odour was unbearable. I tried to pull away, but they did not let me, their arms clasping me like vines. We had to keep dancing until midnight.

'Manekiyons didn't take baths, or even immerse themselves in water. In order to keep themselves warm during cold mountain nights, they rubbed wild boar oil all over their bodies. Animal oil mixed with human sweat produces a formidable odour. We got to know other tribes of Papuans, too, and I liked them. But it was an illusion to think we had made friends. Later on they betrayed us. They took sides with the

Dutch and Australians and became guerillas. We lost their favour because our starving soldiers looted their meagre food and damaged their crops.

'As part of the Navy's geologist team, I was safely stationed in Sorong. The Navy kept sending us to other parts of the island to investigate natural resources, even though they should have realised that it was a waste of time and money to survey a foreign land which there was little prospect of conquering. Headquarters kept us in the dark, but we knew from the pilots who flew in and out of our base that we were losing the war in New Guinea. For a while the Japanese occupied Port Moresby on the southern coast, but it was soon taken back by the Allies. Eventually the Japanese lost battles all over the eastern part of the island and our soldiers had to flee into the jungles and mountains. Tens of thousands of them were decimated by disease and starvation. We were losing the war not only in New Guinea but also all over the Pacific Islands. Guadalcanal was gone. Almost all our aircraft carriers were sunk in the Marianas. On Saipan, where my two roommates had been sent, sixty thousand Japanese had perished. Some of the local Japanese had killed themselves by jumping off cliffs.

'The war came near us when Biak Island, off Manokwari, was attacked by the American fleet in May 1944. It was a strategically important island for the Americans because B-17s, the long-distance bombers, could fly directly from there to the Philippines. As you know, General MacArthur, who had retreated to Australia, had set his heart on returning to the Philippines. The 13,000 Japanese troops on Biak Island made a desperate effort to repel the enemy, but they were no match for the Americans, who landed on the island in far greater numbers. The Japanese fled into the jungle and died of starvation and disease. Many committed suicide. After the war, eighty soldiers were found alive. Three years later, three more men were rescued.

'After Biak fell, Commander Toyoshima of the Manokwari head-quarters grew fearful that the enemy would target his base next. He decided to move his headquarters to Idore, 200 kilometres to the southeast. He flew there with a few of his staff, leaving thousands of his troops behind. Before he left, he told half his troops to come to the new headquarters on foot. He ordered the other half to go 400 kilometres west to Sorong. "Unfortunately, there is no food for you to take along," he said to his soldiers. "But there should be plenty of sago palms on your way to the new headquarters. Once a year they bloom and when they do, there'll be plenty of starch in their trunks. This is the main source of nutrition for the natives, so it should be good enough for you."

'Those who walked the coastline to Idore were attacked by the enemy. Those who went inland had to swim across rivers and trek over a 3,000 metre-high mountain range. They rarely came across starchy palms and when they did, they were not in bloom. They were lucky if they found a snake or a frog to eat. After three months of trekking through the jungle, only 700 out of 10, 000 were still alive. The soldiers who marched to Sorong had a trip as hard as the ones who went east. There were no roads. They had to negotiate mountains, rivers, marshes and jungles. Not even the natives dared to step into some of those areas. As the soldiers walked, they stumbled over the scattered bodies of their comrades who had been walking ahead of them. Only 500 out of 10,000 reached Sorong.

'I was in Sorong when a handful of these survivors arrived looking like skeletons in tattered rugs. Another group of defeated troops arrived about the same time. They were from the 35th Division of the Army, which had recently been dispatched from China to help defend Biak against the Americans. In the long voyage over the Pacific, more than half of the ships had been sunk. When the remaining ships finally made it close to Biak, the island was already occupied by the Americans. They were told to land near Sousapor, 300 kilometres west of Manokwari, and to walk 100 kilometres farther west to Sorong. But the enemy was waiting there, too. One of the few officers of the 35th Division who made it to Sorong was Naganuma. We gave him a meal of rice and pumpkin and he told us the following story.

"The Dutch and Australians had been waiting for us at Sousapor and attacked us. So we ran into the jungle. After a month-long detour in and out of the mountains, we arrived at Mega Village. We were overjoyed to see a signpost saying, 'Sorong – fifty miles west.' We were even happier when we met Colonel Morita and his twenty men, of whom we had lost track, walking along the River Mega in the same direction. We sat down together, and celebrated the happy occasion with a rare feast – in our mess tin we cooked the crabs the young soldiers had found along the shore. Then we crossed the river, thinking that soon our ordeals would finally be over. We did not realise we had to face another enemy – the Papuan guerillas – hiding in the forest.

"As we walked through a palm forest, we saw a cluster of primitive wooden houses. A few Papuans came out from behind us and said in Indonesian, 'We'll pick coconuts for you in the grove there. Come with us.' They were so friendly we followed them. Somehow the path they led us on was getting wet and sticky. We slipped and fell in the mud. It was a marsh. No palms with coconuts were in sight. Suddenly suspicious, I looked around and saw guns pointing at us through the leaves. They had tricked us. 'Run!' I cried, but we were knee-deep in mud. The sound of guns and shrieking voices echoed in the dark. In no time Colonel Morita and most of our officers and staff were dead.' "

As he talked, Officer Naganuma often choked up. His story infuriated me. I had made a great effort to make friends with the Papuans. How could they betray us? And how could experienced Japanese Imperial officers be massacred so easily by native guerillas?

'In 1943 the Americans were not bombing New Guinea any longer. Instead they headed directly to the Philippines to recapture it. Why should they care about minor posts like Manokwari or Sorong, which had no strategic value? Leave the Japs alone and they would die of starvation. That was exactly what happened. Since there was no need to fight against the Americans anymore, Commander Ikeda of the 35th Division felt he had to find something else to do. He came up with the idea of the "North Coast Campaign", which meant wiping out the local guerillas like the ones at Mega, who had murdered our soldiers. To carry out this plan he mobilised the 221st Infantry regiment. But in the end only 200 soldiers were dispatched because all the rest were sick, dead or dying.

'The trouble was that Ikeda had little knowledge of New Guinea since he had only recently arrived from China. He asked the Navy to provide him with well-informed personnel. They chose me although I was a non-combatant worker. I was given six local patrolmen. They called me "Captain." I felt as if I was one and swaggered about.

'As I told you, I was so upset by Naganuma's story about the massacre of our officers by the Papuans at Mega that I thought this was a God-given opportunity to take revenge on them. Taking Patrolman Andes along, I scouted the area around Mega. We walked in the jungle for days, making our way on trails that were barely visible. One day Andes spied a house on the ridge of a hill. It had a Dutch flag on its roof. As we came near, we saw spears, bows and arrows hanging by the door. It was dark. We crawled to the house and crouched. Suddenly I got up and pushed the door open. About a dozen men and women were sitting there. I raised my sword while Andes shone a flashlight in their eyes. One man fled, but while the light was blinding them, I tied up two men with a rope. American cigarettes, Dutch guns, and our soldiers' mess tins were scattered around the room.

'Andes pointed to the taller of the two men we had captured and whispered in my ear, "Remember him? That's Ugaro, the mayor of Mega. He murdered a woman, so I arrested him once. He was put in a prison at the Sorong base, but he escaped. Remember him, Captain? Obviously he's been hiding here." Mayor Ugaro was a known guerrilla chief. The last time I'd seen him, he had been ordered to dig a bomb shelter at the Sorong base. He'd killed a woman because, he said, she was 'Soangi'-an evil spirit that appeared in many incarnations and brought bad luck. He had mutilated her and chopped her up. And as mayor of Mega, he must have been the one who ordered Morita and the other 35th Division Japanese officers to be murdered in the marsh. This was a major catch. I felt triumphant.

'Just before I left the house, it occurred to me that I should take some of their food for starving soldiers at our base. "Can I ask you to carry food to our base?" I said to several women who were there. "I promise you I'll let you come back home as soon as the job is done. You see? I am a civilian worker and am supposed to protect you." I really meant what I said. I was a bandit who had stormed into their house, captured their men and stolen their food, but I didn't believe in killing innocent women. What had happened to the noble idea of creating the Greater East Asia Co-Prosperity Sphere? Unable to feed ourselves, we were plundering the natives' meagre food. The women were too frightened to protest. We went down to our base with four women and a child. They carried on their shoulders tapioca, sweet potatoes, pumpkins and starch from sago palms.

'Back at the camp, I was expecting to receive a hero's welcome. On the contrary, something terrible was about to happen. When I told Commander Ikeda that I had promised the women they would return home as soon as they brought the food here, he said, "No way. If I release them, they will give information about us to the men back there. They have to be killed." "No, sir. You can't do that," I said, although I knew I was not allowed to talk back to a senior officer. "Commander Ikeda, it won't make a difference whether we release a few women or not. The local Papuans already know all about us. This is their territory. They've been spying on our whereabouts every day through the branches and leaves in the jungle."

'Commander Ikeda stared at me, angry that I had defied him, and disdainful of my ignorance about battlefield practice. But I kept begging. "Major Ikeda. Most of my patrolmen are natives, too. You must worry about how they would react to killing these women in violation of my promise."

'Three deep lines were etched on the Commander's forehead. With his posture straight and his chin up, he shouted at me. "Our fellow officers and soldiers were massacred by their men. The Division Headquarters has ordered that every native in the North Coast region should be cleaned up. My mission here is to take revenge on the natives in order to honor our men. You did a good job today, Mr Iida, but you don't know what war is like." I realised how blind I was not to have remembered that Ikeda was an officer who had fought in China. His troops had raped women and pillaged and burnt down villages. According to his cold-blooded war point of view, my ideas were sentimental romanticism based on an outdated samurai spirit.

'I felt like crying. I knew I couldn't win no matter how I argued. I had ended up tricking the four women and the child. To this day I have a deep wound in my heart that is still bleeding and will never heal. I still feel like crying and often really weep when I think of these women and their large, dark eyes. They had stared at me, wanting to trust my words. I should have fought for them even if it ended up in my own death. I was a coward.

'The next day I went up a nearby mountain with a scout officer named Ishii and a young Korean who dragged the handcuffed Ugaro behind him. At a clearing in the forest, Ishii stopped and said to me, "Let's do it here." He meant to execute the mayor. Lieutenant Ishii drove a wooden stake into the ground and tied Ugaro to it. To the young recruit from Korea, he shouted, "Approach!" The Korean lad tottered forward, trembling. "Charge!" Ishii roared. The recruit drew his dagger and staggered. He reached the mayor and tried to stab him. But with his arms and legs shaking and knocking, he failed to kill the target no matter how often he stabbed. Blood gushed from Ugaro's stomach and entrails. He screamed in pain. Then the stake loosened and Ugaro leaned towards me, half dead.

'Suddenly I flung away my scabbard and swung my sword down on him. A shoulder blade dropped off and he was dead. "Splendid!" Ishii cried out. I felt nauseous as I wiped the blood off the sword and put it back in the scabbard. This was the first time I had killed a man. Did I do the right thing? The man had killed dozens of our officers, and had murdered an innocent woman. His killing was justified. Or was it? My head swirled as I tried to justify the act I'd committed. The reason I had intervened, giving the final blow, was that I couldn't bear the way the timid Korean was torturing him, killing him by thin slices. I wanted to save Ugaro from the pain. This was really the truth. Even so, I killed a man.

'The next evening we were back at Village Mega. Every house was empty, with not a soul to be seen. Ishii and I sat on a fallen tree to rest up a minute, when a shot was fired. The next second I saw Ishii fall face down on the ground. Did they aim at me, miss and kill Ishii instead?

'When I returned to the base, the women and the child were nowhere to be seen. I knew that my patrolmen were whispering behind me. I did not want to explain anything. I had no excuse for what had happened. Until that day, all the patrolmen and I had been friends. But from then on they looked at me reproachfully. I couldn't forgive myself for what had happened to the women and the child.

After this incident, I was different. Before this, I had wanted to devote my life to the liberation of Asia. It might have been a sentimental dream, but I was in earnest. But in the face of this cruel and inhuman military ethic and the ugliness of the battlefield reality, my spirit was gone. I still believed like a religion in the samurai ethos in which killing innocent people is absolutely forbidden. Even though I had heard terrible stories from the soldiers who fought in China, I trusted that the Japanese officers maintained the high principles of conduct they had exhibited in the Russo-Japanese War. But this incident shattered my romantic idealism.

'Every day the soldiers were dying. They ate weeds, lizards, snakes, hermit crabs, birds, and occasionally wild boar. They suffered from diarrhea and malaria. Medicine did not exist. They cooked the leaves of papaya and of pumpkin and called them medicine. For animal protein, they ate rats. Some tried to cook their old military boots, but even after two days of boiling they were too hard to chew and couldn't be swallowed.

'One day a Navy officer told me that the war was over. I felt as if the earth had stopped turning. Even though the American planes were dropping leaflets that said "Okinawa has fallen. The cities in Japan are in ruins." I somehow did not believe that the Emperor's country, Japan, could be defeated.

'The victors did not even bother to come. I walked to the shore, held my gun at the ready, and shot all the bullets into the sea. Staying in New Guinea was like being in a large prison. Unless we had a ship, we would be stuck there forever. We were hungry and all that we did was to look desperately for food.

Before the war, this area had been under the suzerainty of Holland. Soon the Dutch started coming back from Java, where they had been POWs of the Japanese. The first thing they did was to interrogate all the local administrators and police officers about their collaboration with the Japanese. I called the patrolmen who had worked for me and said to them, "Whatever they accuse you of doing, tell them that Iida ordered you to do it." It was the least that I could do. We had promised them liberation and prosperity, and in the end we had betrayed them.

'After the initial shock of defeat, I suffered from deep depression and wanted to kill myself. I would be captured as a war criminal and hanged anyway. I was a war criminal because I had killed Mayor Ugaro. More than that, I would be accused of the death of the four Papuan women and the child. There would be no one who could testify to my innocence. Commander Ikeda, who was responsible for killing them, had been killed along with other officers soon after the incident. They had gone to attack an Allied base and had been gunned down by artillery fire.

'One evening, I walked to a village further south carrying a short sword and a gun in a knapsack. My best friend, Sergeant Moriyama, was supposed to be there. We had once vowed to be brothers to each other. I wanted to say goodbye to him before killing myself. There was a full moon that night. My plan was to paddle a canoe into the deep sea by the light of the moon, commit hara-kiri and shoot myself in the temple. Then I would fall into the sea. Moriyama was not at his quarters, but some mobile officers I knew were drinking coconut wine nearby. "Hey Iida, nice to see you. Come here and let's drink together," they said, making room for me to sit down, one of them already offering me wine in a coconut shell. I did not have the nerve to say, "I can't stay. I have to go and kill myself." Instead I said, "I must go somewhere soon, but I'll sit with you for a short while." I ended up sitting with them for hours and drank myself into a stupor.

'Late at night I crawled into Moriyama's quarters, where I had left my knapsack. He was not there this time either. But he must have been there before because my knapsack, which I had left in his room, was empty and the gun and sword were nowhere to be seen. Suspecting my intention, Moriyama must have removed them. He often had said to me, "Calm down, Iida. You are too hot-headed." I felt desperate and burst out crying. I kept crying until I was a dried-out carcass. After that I must have fallen asleep. When I woke up, I was sober and felt like a different man. Outside, the air was calm and clean. I changed my mind about suicide. No matter how humiliating the future was, I would face it head on with dignity.

'Soon the Dutch Colonial military police came to arrest me as a war criminal suspect. I was taken to a prison in Hollandia, which was a row of shabby houses standing at the tip of a promontory. Their windows were as small as a kennel's, and their gates were twined with barbed wire. I ended up staying there for three and a half years, from age twenty-three to twenty-six. In the morning we worked at a shipyard or at a construction site. There were no pens to write with, and no newspapers or books to read. Communication of any kind was forbidden.

'The guards were Indonesians who had been labourers in the Japanese camps in Java. Having become our guards, they tortured us day and night. Inside the dark walls that isolated us from the world, nothing prevented them from getting their revenge. The look of anger burning in their dark eyes and each ferocious lashing of their whips made me realise what the monsters of the Emperor's army had done to the people of Asia. I was beaten with clubs, hoses, the bottom of a bayonet and boots. With my whole body black and blue, and my nose, eyes and ears swollen and bleeding, I was unrecognisable even to myself. I lay, sleepless night after night, tossing and turning in pain, tears of humiliation wetting the cold concrete floor.

'The food they gave us in the prison was so stale that we often had diarrhea, but there was no toilet in the cell. We had to wait until the guards came and let us use the facilities. Our old mess tins we kept from the battlefield often served as urinals. At mealtimes we had to wash them and use them as soup bowls.

But the worst anguish I endured in the prison was mental. The ideals that had sustained me through all the years of the war were false, and that realisation tossed me into the deepest abyss. When I understood that my country's stance as a lofty liberator was just a thin cover to protect us as we invaded other people's lands and plundered them, my whole belief system collapsed. I was a monster and deserved punishment. The ideas we had been taught, and that I had believed – that we were a special race, and could save the natives from the enemy's oppression – were nothing but lies.

'In July 1948, the war crime trials began. I was not allowed to speak. Most of the would-be witnesses were dead, and the ones I had asked for were not summoned. The lawyer who was sent from Japan read two pages of defense documents. I was accused not only of the murder of Ugaro, but also of involvement in efforts to subjugate the Dutch patrol force. I was also charged with another murder, one I had not committed. There was no local lawyer who could help refute the case. The military tribunal held in the name of justice and humanity ended in thirty minutes. The Dutch military court was vengeful against the Japanese. Because the Indonesians' movement for independence from Holland was gaining steam, the Dutch were eager to impress them and punish the Japanese, their common enemy. They also wanted to retaliate against the Japanese for the way the Dutch soldiers had been treated in the POW camps. In the end, the court sentenced four hundred Japanese officers and soldiers to death.

'So I was expecting the worst. I was angry with the tribunal for depriving me of a fair trial and treating me like an animal in a slaughterhouse. But I kept telling myself that by dying, I would redeem my sins as well as those of my country. I was proud that I did not try to escape punishment by blaming the dead or anyone living for what had happened. But hearing the words "death by firing squad" still came as a shock. My world blackened and I felt sad that I had had such a short life. The thought of dying in front of a firing squad frightened me. But I tried to accept my fate. At least it was a quick way to end the despair I was feeling.

'Three weeks later we were called to court again, and, for some reason, my sentence was commuted to twenty years of hard labour. Out of eight death-row prisoners, one other man and I were the only ones whose sentences were so reduced. Nobody explained why. The two of us were to be sent to a prison in Java. Before I left, I wanted to see and say good-bye to the other convicts who would remain here. After a long argument with a guard, I was allowed to see each of them through the iron lattice window of their cells. They looked pale, haggard, and unkempt. One asked me to send a will to his family. Others said, "Iida, please tell my wife not to be ashamed of me. I fought well for the Emperor." "Tell my father and mother I died in peace." "Tell Mariko I loved her." I didn't know what to say to them and tried to mumble something back through my tears. We couldn't shake hands, but I put my finger through the wire mesh and twined it with theirs. I learned later that a few months after I saw them, they died one by one in front of a firing squad.

'In the Java prison I was treated humanely. There was no torture here. The food was no prize, but there were lots of books to read. Japanese newspapers were available, and I devoured them. We were allowed to talk to other inmates, most of whom were Japanese. I learned French from a former Embassy attaché and English from a former administrative chief in Sumatra. A former government official gave a series of lectures on civil and criminal law. Every night till late, I read books on philosophy or history by the light of a dim naked bulb hanging from the ceiling. I received letters from home for the first time in six years.

'When Indonesia became an independent nation, the Dutch left Java. The war criminals kept under Dutch jurisdiction were taken to Tokyo and put in Sugamo Prison, which was run by the Americans. With 700 other POWs, I returned to Japan in January 1950, after a sojourn of seven years. What had happened to the promised glory? And to the prime of my youth? I had given all those precious years to my country, fought in an inglorious war, and come back as a loser and a war criminal.

'It was a cold, grey day. As soon as the ship landed, we were hauled into the American trucks waiting at the wharf. As dozens of trucks filled with prisoners in tattered tropical shirts drove through the streets with sirens wailing, people gazed at us with disdainful looks and quickly looked away as if they saw something they shouldn't have seen - bad dreams from the past. Tears kept falling on my cheeks as I saw their cheerless faces. The streets were dotted with grey barracks as small as matchboxes instead of the lovely houses that I remembered. Was this the homeland I had been dreaming about for seven years? Were these ruins my reward for devoting my youth to the Emperor?

'And what about the Emperor? After the war, he had confessed that he was a mere human after all. But what about all the soldiers who had died believing him to be a God? The Emperor might not have been too belligerent, but wasn't he the one who had started the war? In his name, lives were taken and discarded like trash. And yet he was not prosecuted as a war criminal. Did he feel sorry for those who had died for him? And if he did, why didn't he say so?

'We were treated well in Sugamo Prison. I had plenty of time to study and read books. Before the war, the only education I had had was about war and Imperialism. Among the 1,500 inmates, it wasn't difficult to find professors and teachers. We organised classes and they taught us science, philosophy, history and economics. They told me which books to read. I happily immersed myself in the world of books. I was also allowed to communicate with the outside world. My parents didn't seem too ashamed about their eldest son being in prison, or at least they pretended they weren't. My father was not well, and his relationship with my mother hadn't improved over the years. "Your mum is mean," he wrote. "She is so cruel, I wish I were dead." My mother wrote, "I can't stand your dad. He is a spoiled brat." But they didn't sound as fierce about each other as before. Their passionate hatred of each other had burnt itself out.

'In 1950, the Korean War started. General MacArthur wanted Japan to help in the war and ordered our government to build a Police Reserve Force. Japan's high-ranked military officers, though now stripped of their rank, were called in to advise the Force. Among these were the general staff officers whose campaigns had brought millions of soldiers to death. They had walked out free after the war without being tried at the Tokyo Tribunal. Those of us in the prison flew into a rage. "Isn't it strange that the Americans who judged the Japanese under the name of God are shamelessly taking advantage of war criminals instead of punishing them? And why do our military officers, who used to call the Americans green-eyed monsters, now wag their tails around them like dogs? While nameless soldiers and personnel like us are atoning for the sins of our nation, why are these major criminals cashing in on their former titles and rearming this country as if the no-war article of the new Constitution doesn't exist?"

'Do you know how the Tokyo Tribunal was run? Representatives from the major Allied nations were the judges. Korea and Taiwan, which were Japanese colonies, weren't invited to participate. Other Asian nations that had suffered so much from Japanese invasions such as Singapore, Malaysia, Indonesia, Burma and Indochina weren't asked to send in judges either. In the meantime 5,700 personnel were indicted as Class-B and C criminals at Allied regional courts abroad. Of these, 920 were executed and about 3,500 received prison terms.

Lots of them were brought to Japan and served sentences at Sugamo, as I did.

'The tribunals were decided by the victors. The victors' own crimes weren't brought up at the tribunals. But have you read the book *War without Mercy* by John Dower?[22] He wrote about the atrocities American soldiers had committed. He argued that their violence was often motivated by racial hatred. I was impressed that Dower, an American historian, could be so fair-minded. The book has received a national award. I respect Americans for reading such a book and praising it. There is hope there.

'We formed an anti-war group in Sugamo. We wrote letters to newspapers to protest against the new police reserve force. We cried out against war and appealed for permanent peace. Our protests attracted people's attention. Until then we had been loathed as perpetrators of evil. All of a sudden, we were victims of the war in the eyes of the people. Entertainers came to our prison and performed dances and plays. The country was recovering from defeat. People thought it was time to forget the war as history. By liberating the Sugamo prisoners, they would put an end to the bad memories of the war. After the Peace Treaty of San Francisco in 1952, the Americans left Sugamo in the hands of the Japanese government. Fearing public sentiment, the government changed the way the prison was run. In effect it became a hotel with three free meals. We were even allowed to go out and get jobs.

'I was released from prison in 1956. I married a modern dancer, Mitsuko, who used to come to entertain us in prison. I worked hard to make a living. I started a business that sold sewage facilities to housing corporations, big businesses, and hotels. I had a good head for business and did well. I also became involved with charities. A pretty, bright daughter was born and it seemed as if finally Mitsuko and I had a normal, happy life.

'But another tragedy was to befall us. To me it was even worse than my death sentence and even more personal. It was another man-made tragedy the twentieth century faced. So let me tell you.

22 Dower, John. *War without Mercy*, Pantheon Books, New York, 1986

'Our son, who was born in December 1960, was a grossly deformed child. His arms were bent and half the normal length, his wrists twisted inward and his hands had four crooked fingers and no thumbs. I was thrown into a despair that was darker than any I had experienced before. What kind of life could he have? We named him Shin-ichi. Shin means to "stretch". We wished his arms would stretch long and straight as he grew. I massaged his arms dozens of times every day. No doctors had ever seen this kind of deformity and nobody knew what had caused it. The only possibility I could think of was that Mitsuko had been exposed to radiation from the Nagasaki atomic bomb. A high school student at the time, she had been standing 1.5 kilometres away from the epicentre. I visited Hiroshima and Nagasaki and consulted many specialists. No similar cases had been found.

'In less than six months, the newspapers reported on babies in Germany with similar problems. According to Dr Lenz at Munster University, these babies were born of mothers who had taken a pill called thalidomide during pregnancy. These pills were sold under a different name by a Japanese pharmaceutical company, and Mitsuko had taken them. In spite of his deformity or perhaps because of it, Shin-ichi was the sweetest, most beautiful child to us. We would do anything if we thought it would make him happy. There were about 300 thalidomide babies in Japan, and I plunged myself into organising a group for the parents, beginning a class action against the pharmaceutical company, and negotiating with the government to establish schools and medical facilities for disabled children. For years Japan had been neglecting care for the mentally and physically disadvantaged. Our activities contributed to public awareness for the disabled, helped them to live with dignity, and promoted welfare benefits for them.

'Shin-ichi was not the kind of a boy who could overcome his handicaps and succeed in the world. That was too much to ask. He didn't like school. As he grew older, the only thing he loved to do was to go trekking with his rucksack on his back. He made many friends on those trips. Everybody who knew him loved him.

Before Shin-ichi's birth, Mitsuko had had a miscarriage, and it turned out that she had contracted Hepatitis C from the blood transfusion she had received. In the end she died of liver cancer. Thirty-four at the time, Shin-ichi was devastated. He never fully recovered from this loss. Once, Shin-ichi confided in a friend that he also had Hepatitis C. He had probably been infected from his mother at gestation – a double tragedy. But he never discussed his illness with me or even his sister, who had become a doctor. He married briefly, and when the marriage ended abruptly, he began drinking heavily. He died at the age of forty-two.

'I loved Shin-ichi so much and had tried hard to do everything I could to ensure his happiness. All my efforts had come to nothing. I was a failure as a father. I kept asking people, "Why did he die? Please tell me why, if you know. Did I do anything wrong as a father?" One of Shin-ichi's friends, a woman ten years younger than he, wrote me a long letter. "I know for sure you didn't do anything wrong, Mr Iida. He was loved by you and everybody else. It was fate that made him die young. Please forgive him."

'I asked a young architect to design a children's playground in Tibet, where Shin-ichi loved to go on his trekking trips. Using wood and tires, the local people helped build it. A big crowd of people welcomed me when I went to visit it. In a corner I placed a stainless steel plaque that I inscribed: "Shin-ichi Iida Who Was Loved by Many Sleeps Here."

'It was my wish that the spirit of my child would play among children and be happy there. Many years have passed since my son died. Gradually I came to terms with his death. Every morning when I make coffee, I place a small cup in front of the photo of him that sits on my bookshelf. Then I look at the picture next to him and talk to my young mates who died in the war. Whenever I have a problem, I ask them, "What should I do?" They are my inner gods and my conscience.

'Because I am alive instead of my son and my friends, I would like to do something meaningful for their sake. I wasted my youth in a war for a wrong cause. To my last day, I will keep telling people not to repeat my mistake.'

CHAPTER 6

Kunitami Mitsuhashi

*Artist and Writer: All my works are requiems
for those who died in the war*

A few minutes away from the busy market street of Machida, a town in western Tokyo, there is a narrow lane which leads to a strikingly beautiful wooden latticed gate. Once inside, you feel you are in old Japan at its best. This house is square with a Japanese garden in its centre. Through white *shoji* paper screens each room enjoys a different view of the garden. It gives joy to the eye and a calmness which you feel only in the depth of nature. A tall and well-built man welcomed me with a gracious smile. He is said to be ninety-two, but looks twenty years younger as he moves with ease and grace.

Mr Mitsuhashi is a celebrated artist who lives here with his wife. During the war, he was sent to Sawarati, an island off the north-west end of Western New Guinea. The island was often subjected for days on end to aerial assault by American planes. He had many different duties as his comrades died away one by one. He became a competent anti-aircraft gunner. He also took care of wounded soldiers. His survival was against the odds as almost ninety per cent of the Japanese soldiers who had been sent to New Guinea perished. He was one of two survivors in his forty-man platoon.

'For a long time after the war it was painful to face the past. All my colleagues were young men full of expectations for life. They were thrown into a cruel war and died, believing they were giving their life for a good cause. I wondered what I could do for my friends. I decided to express my feeling for them through art,' Mitsuhashi-san said, gazing at the terracotta figure of an emaciated soldier he recently created for the prestigious art exhibition, *Nitten*. 'Even now, after seventy years, all the images are vivid in my eyes. I still live in two worlds and my life in the war is just as realistic as the one in this town. All my works are requiems for those who died in the war. I'm getting old and sometimes sick, but once I start creating something, I feel alive and well.'

His art is diverse. It is made of iron, bronze, stone, clay, terra-cotta, wood and glass. He also paints, draws, and gives lectures.

'I almost died in Sawarati several times. Whenever I thought I was dying, my mother appeared before my eyes and that helped me live. The day I left for the war, my mother came running to me on the train platform among a big crowd of well-wishers. She hugged me tightly, buried her face in my chest and whispered, 'Kunitami, don't ever die! Absolutely never! You must come home alive . . . Promise . . . ' I was moved by her courage in expressing her feelings freely because in those days patriotic mothers were supposed to show no tears and send their sons away willingly for the Emperor. I realised how much she loved me and told myself I would come home alive for my mother.'

Mr Mitsuhashi has literary as well as artistic talent. He has written stories on the subject of war. *Tori no Uta* (Poems of Birds: Returning from the Death Island) is an award-winning collection of his short stories – all of them based on real events. I asked his permission to pick a story for this book.

ANTS[23]

' . . . Must be dreaming!' I muttered in my sleep.

A pale-brown, sticky, cotton-like fibre was clinging to my entire face. Strange insects were crawling around my lips and cheeks and persisted in their advance despite my repeatedly brushing them away. Some even managed to invade my nostrils.

This provoked me into picking up those insects that were crawling around my chin and pulverising them between my fingertips at one fell swoop in front of the swarm. At which point some who witnessed this

23 Mitsuhashi, Kunitami, *Tori no Uta* (Poems of Birds: Returning from the Death Island), Kadokawa Shoten, Tokyo, 2005, p. 16. 'Ants' was translated from Japanese to English by Susan Gaulter.

yelped, strenuously wagged their beards as a message to their comrades, glided to the floor and escaped into the chinks in the floorboards.

I awoke suddenly. My watch read 4:50. It was still fairly dark inside the Nipa hut. Even so, the morning sun was weakly filtering through the gaps in the roof. I expected to see the face of sleeping Lance Corporal Tsuchida, right shoulder down facing me thirty centimetres from my nose. I held my breath.

'What's happened to him?'

His face was completely filled with a brick-red colour – even his eyes and nose had disappeared. Closer inspection revealed that the brick-red colour covering his face was in fact making short, sharp peristaltic movements!

I leapt up. My gaze fixed again on Tsuchidas face. The squirming brick-red colour was clearly thrown into relief by the feeble dawn rays as a colony of countless, red-bodied, tropical ants.

The swarm of red ants moved continuously, even enveloping the nape of Tsuchidas neck as they sought to fill in every bit of exposed skin. Each and every member of the swarm scurried around busily, streaming from the orifices of the ear and nose of the already lifeless soldier and even crowding at his half-open mouth about to invade internally. One group of worker ants not allowed inside piled on top of others occupying the pinnacle of the cheekbones, each individual jostling to fulfil his duty.

I had been sleeping on my side as if to protect Tsuchida, which was perhaps why the swarm of red ants had followed their invasion of him with an attempt on me, a living being.

The body colour of the red ants emitted a certain dull glow, proclaiming their avariciousness. Some of the stragglers were still nibbling my neck. I repeated the gesture I had displayed in my dream, crushing and casting them away.

Even so, there was Tsuchida, who in the short duration of my nightmare had been reduced to a skeletal hulk. 'If only I had not neglected to look after him . . . ' I was ashamed of my personal inattention.

I folded my hands together in prayer for the soul of Lance Corporal Tsuchida and reflected on the events of the past night.

With eighty percent of our colleagues fallen, our Independent Anti-Aircraft Company was already on the brink of annihilation. Until very recently Tsuchida had not been one of our members. Due to the high incidence of losses, replacements had been made from the Field Artillery Regiment stationed on a neighbouring small island, and he had only been transferred two weeks ago.

From that day Tsuchida became my sleeping companion. In talking of his background he told me that after graduating from the Ueno Music School he had became a member of the Tokyo Symphony Orchestra as a cellist.

I knew little about music, but Tsuchida would explain to me in simple terms the attraction of an orchestra. It became a more pleasant bedtime routine to talk about this than the daily reality of hunger and fighting that threatened to harden our hearts.

At twilight one evening Tsuchida suddenly became feverish and fell asleep. Thereafter he visibly deteriorated. In addition to evident virulent malaria he appeared to have developed beriberi through quite severe malnutrition.

It was past eleven oclock the previous night. Tsuchida had been suffering continuously from a high fever of almost forty degrees for six days now. Whilst mopping his forehead with a damp cotton towel I wondered how to cheer him up.

'Tsuchida, there was a member of this section who had a harmonica. He gave it to me as a keepsake. I suppose to an expert like you it would be nothing special?'

I was surprised to see his eyes light up.

'What! You have something like that? I've never had a musical instrument since coming to the field. Please show it to me.' I produced the harmonica out of my haversack. 'I am working hard at it. I only need to master a few of the basics. Would you like to have a go?'

I was amazed at his delight. He toyed with the harmonica rapturously. ('With a fever of thirty-nine degrees, is he alright?' I wondered.) He appeared to be practising his scales eagerly.

'Right, I'll have a go. This is a tune everyone knows . . . an excerpt from *Carmen*.'

He had already started to play.

His accuracy and freshness far surpassed that of K, the former owner of the harmonica. This was a tune even I knew. His playing retained the rhythm, stirring the carpet of leaves in the dead of night and reverberating across the grassy fields of our camp. The tune even streamed into the scattered Nipa huts of the Gun Squad, lit up pale red from the kerosene lamps. The men in all the huts seemed to fall silent, as they listened intently to the sudden sound of music in the early hours of the morning.

Lance Corporal Tsuchida carried on playing, staring up at the ceiling like a man possessed. After around five repetitions of the tune, Tsuchida's flushed face suddenly looked deflated, as if something had gone wrong, and he sank back wearily. He flung the harmonica from his hands onto the pillow.

. . . The tune and his performance had ended. Shouts of 'Encore! Encore! Encore!', 'Please!', 'One more tune!' echoed from the Nipa huts from the opposite side of the grassy field.

I saw that Tsuchida was breathing hard and painfully. I replaced the damp cotton towel on his forehead and rubbed his back gently.

'Thank you so much! That was marvellous! As I might have expected – just like listening to a record! Everyone's talking about it. Thank you!'

'Oh? I suppose it's been a long time since it produced a sound.'

An encore call was heard again, from one of the Nipa huts.

'No, that's it. It hurts . . . a lot . . . '

Eyes closed, he was breathing hurriedly. Then, he suddenly opened his eyes as if he had remembered something and looked at me.

'Ah, my chest hurts badly . . . As if someone is grabbing hold of my heart. What should I do at a time like this, Mitsuhashi?'

I recalled the time when I had come down with acute pneumonia and my chest hurt.

'Tsuchida, at such a time you should try lowering your right shoulder. This will certainly make you feel better.'

'Like this?'

I helped him change position so that he faced me.

'You're right. I do feel better. But this time I feel it's no good – it's different from usual. Supposing this time . . . ?'

He stopped talking and closed his mouth.

'What's the matter? Tell me, Tsuchida!'

'If only I had some honey dissolved in water. We used to keep bees at home in Saitama and I often drank this as a child. It really bucks one up . . . That is at least what I'd like as my final drink.'

He tailed off in mid-speech, as if musing to himself, and smiled weakly. The word 'final' that Tsuchida had let slip now preyed strangely on my mind and troubled me.

I tried desperately to find some immediate way of helping him.

I went to see Tanaka, the acting medic in the adjoining medical hut. This was because I knew that he had a hoard of glucose injections, nowhere to be found now. He was the man who had become the acting medic through ingratiating himself with the senior company officials after the regular medic was killed in' action. It was rumoured that once in possession of prescribed medications, he would abuse this privilege by coolly engaging in racketeering operations for former patients.

'Tanaka, Lance Corporal Tsuchida from the Field Artillery Regiment doesn't look right. Could you come and look at him . . . ?' As I expected, his response came parrot-fashion.

'Squad Leader, our Company has no leeway to look at transferees. We are hard pressed for medical supplies now . . . '

As his senior, I was irked by the weakness of the Company personnel in requiring such an attitude to be taken.

'Really? While I do understand this, I know that since you were appointed acting medic you have been storing up a large surplus of official supplies. This is fine by me, but surely you could give Tsuchida one of the glucose injections. Won't you give me just one?'

I was bold enough to speak with menacing overtones. Even so, inwardly I was hanging my head in shame at my yakuza-like action.

'Yes, understood. I'll get one out right away . . . '

Flustered by my words he held out one ampule of glucose, but did not forget to add: 'I'm giving it to you as a special favor tonight, but don't tell anyone about it.'

I returned to the hut to find that Tsuchida's condition had changed drastically. In a period of less than forty minutes the shadow of death had starkly appeared on his face. The ashen pall around the eyes and the greasy sweat on his forehead signaled the end of life. I placed drops of the sweet glucose solution onto those lips that had played excerpts from *Carmen* and whispered into his ear: 'Tsuchida! Lance Corporal Tsuchida! Look it's honey! Do you understand? Drink some!'

He made a gurgling sound in his throat. 'Oh, that's delicious, Mitsuhashi! I never thought I could drink honey here . . . '

But the liquid was spilling out from his lips.

This was what attracted the swarm of ants after his death.

Tsuchida suddenly started to snore loudly. Perhaps the pain had eased. ('He may rally!') I once more wrung out his cotton towel.

Perhaps fatigued from the daytime work, I must have instantly fallen sound asleep with my face close to his. I had been careless.

This is how Lance Corporal Tsuchida, the cellist and musician, was reduced to a skeletal hulk.

I shifted his cold, rigid body from the floorboards so that the red ant-covered head was jutting outside. I then wound an old rag around my right wrist and knocked off the mass of ants. I continued to brush off each and every one, even those still stubbornly nibbling in the orifices of the ear, nose and mouth.

I held his face in my arms, the face of Tsuchida who had been so pleased by the 'delicious honey and water' solution I had drip-fed him. I took off his coat to purify his entire body.

In the pale morning sun a faint smile was lingering around the mouth of Lance Corporal Tsuchida.

CHAPTER 7

Lee Hanne

A Korean Guard at a POW camp

Lee Hanne, who worked as a prison guard at a POW camp in the Thai-Burma Railway for three years, was sentenced to death as a war criminal, but his sentence was later commuted. I visited Mr Hanne in his Doshin-kai office, located in a town in western Tokyo. Doshin-kai was founded by him and other Korean ex-war-criminals for the purpose of mutual help. Dressed in a chic grey suit and sitting gracefully in the President's office, he looked like an elegant businessman. He is indeed a businessman who established a successful taxi company from scratch with his fellow ex-convicts. From his gentle face one could not detect a trace of a war criminal in him. Neither does it reveal his indomitable fighting spirit with which he pursues compensation and an apology from the Japanese government almost seventy years after the war.

Here is the story told by Lee Hanne.

'I was born in 1925, the first son of a peasant farmer in South Korea. Our country had been a colony of Japan's since 1910. In elementary school, we were forced to learn to speak Japanese and to change our names to Japanese ones. My gentle name, Lee Hanne, was changed to the harsh-sounding Kakurai Hiromura. I finished school at twelve and worked at odd jobs. None of them suited me and I returned home to help my parents with their farm. Because the Japanese had confiscated their land, they were poor tenant farmers. We produced rice, but hardly ate any ourselves. I remember eating acorns and insects.

'In 1942, the Japanese Army came to Korea and Taiwan to recruit prison guards for the POWs they had captured. Earlier in the year,

105

they had occupied Singapore, Java, and the Philippines and ended up detaining more than 300,000 Allied soldiers. Unequipped to manage this many POWs, the Japanese imprisoned approximately 120,000 Caucasian soldiers and kept the Asian prisoners as labourers. The Japanese came up with the idea of recruiting Koreans and Taiwanese to guard the POWs because their own soldiers did not regard looking after them as an honourable job. The Japanese were taught that brave soldiers should not surrender in any circumstances and that POWs were dishonourable men who hadn't killed themselves.

'An older friend said to me, "They're recruiting young Korean men. There are 3,000 jobs. They'll give you a two-year contract and pay you fifty yen per month, and you'll get free meals and board. Doesn't it sound rather good?" Fifty yen per month was an enormous sum of money to me. The village mayor also advised me to apply. My father agreed, too. "It'll be a safe job," he said. "It's not like fighting in the front line."

'I went to Pusan to undergo three months of training. Instead of teaching us the Geneva Convention and other rules regarding POWs, the Japanese taught us how to use bayonets and guns. They imbued us with the idea that the POWs were dishonorable men. I respected my platoon leader, Captain Usukine. He was tough but fair and kind. But there were some mean instructors. I was slapped and beaten daily for giving unsatisfactory replies, speaking too quietly, or having poor posture. They made me lick the soles of my laced-up boots.

'After the training, 1,000 of us were put on a cargo ship that sailed south. We landed in Saigon and from there took trains to the west, and then boats on the River Kwai to the north. In February 1943, I arrived at the HQ of the POW camp in Kanchanaburi, Thailand. Hundreds of half-naked white men were sitting in a large field. It was the first time I had seen a white man. They were tall and intimidating. A Japanese captain explained the plan for the Burma–Thailand Railway. The POWs and Asian workers would work on a new railway that would extend 415 kilometres along the coastline of Burma.

'Six of us were told to accompany five hundred POWs 155 kilometres north of Kanchanaburi, where we would build a new camp. The place was called Hintok, and was in the middle of impenetrable jungle. We worked with the POWs to build cottages. We coiled ropes around gigantic, thorny bamboo, thickly twined with ivy, and pulled out roots to clear the jungle. We used the felled bamboos to build cottages, and used palm leaves for the roofs. We built nineteen shacks, small ones that accommodated fifty men and large ones that held a hundred. Motor launches would come upstream carrying food. In the summer, they brought pumpkins and squashes, but in the rainy season they stopped coming. Although dysentery and malaria were rampant, we had no medical supplies. We ordered medicine, but it never came. Life in the camp was horrific.

'Near Hintok was Hellfire Pass, one of the most difficult stretches on the railway. Five hundred POWs – later three hundred more were added – had to work from morning till night in the monsoon rain or in the burning heat, dynamiting mountains, removing rocks from rugged cliffs with pickaxes, and felling huge trees. It was life-threatening work for sick men with little to eat. I was a prison guard and my job should have been just to make sure that the POWs wouldn't escape. But our branch headquarters was understaffed and I was given a personnel job as well, probably because Captain Usukine, now the director of the Hintok Camp, trusted me.

'One of my jobs was to secure as many POWs as the construction manager needed for the following day's work. Dr Weary Dunlop represented the Hintok POWs and I liaised with him every evening, telling him how many men needed to be ready to work the next morning. Dr Dunlop was a famous man who, in the terrible conditions at the camp where the POWs were suffering and dying, cheered them up and saved many lives. Dr Dunlop seldom produced the correct number of workers, saying that many were ill or unfit to work. I said, "It's my duty to get the exact number I was asked to produce." "It's my duty to protect my soldiers' lives," he said.

As his superior, I insisted that the doctor had to get them even if it meant taking the patients out of hospital. He said no. In the end I had to go to the hospital myself to find men. Some could only crawl. I was loyal to Captain Usukine and proud of doing a good job for him. I guess I was as dutiful as an automaton. Young and healthy, I didn't sympathise with the POWs, whom I considered weak and lazy. It didn't occur to me what a terrible predicament they were in – captives in an inhospitable jungle, starving, sick and homesick.

Because of language and cultural differences, communication with the POWs was difficult. When they defied and disobeyed my orders, stole things or inserted termites' eggs into railroad ties so that they would rot, I slapped them on their cheeks or beat them up. It was what the Japanese had done to me at training camp. I only learned later that in the West, slapping a man was considered a humiliation and an unforgivable insult. To my mind, slapping was not an abuse of power. For me, it was a way of showing my authority. I did not want to be treated with contempt because I was only eighteen, small and Asian. Given that I could have brought the POWs who defied me to military court, slapping seemed a relatively mild way of punishing them.

'They nicknamed me Lizard, I suppose because I was always scurrying around the camp. My colleagues were named Bulldog and Mad Dog. Compared with those names, mine sounded cute. At least lizards don't harm others, do they?

'Long after the war, when I saw Dr Dunlop in Australia, he gave me a copy of his book, *The War Diaries of Weary Dunlop*. Lizard was mentioned often in his diary. Dr Dunlop described Lizard as "an unpleasant, stubborn, mean and a narrow-minded creature.[24] He also wrote that Lizard was "a terrible thorn in the side." He said that Lizard was enraged at the increase in hospital figures and insisted that not so many men are allowed to become ill. Dr Dunlop had also said that he hated me so much he had actually planned to kill me.

'The whole idea of the railway was a colossal blunder that took an enormous human toll. Tokyo Headquarters ordered that the work be done within a year – by October 1943 – so that they could use the railway for transporting military goods for the Imphal Campaign. Trying to get everything done by then meant pushing the men beyond their limits and 43,000 workers ended up dying. In our camp twenty-seven per cent of the POWs died. The terrible thing was that in the end the Japanese lost the Imphal campaign quickly and the railway

24 Dunlop, E. E, *The War Diaries of Weary Dunlop: Java and the Burma–Thailand Railway, 1942-1945*, Thomas Nelson, Australia, 1986, p. 232

was of no use when it was completed. What a colossal waste of human lives, labour and money.

'Toward the end of the war I was in Bangkok. I jumped with joy when I heard about Japan's defeat. It meant I could finally go home and that Korea would be an independent nation. I stayed in a temple with my comrades, waiting for the day when a ship would take us home. I heard on the radio that those who had abused POWs in the camps would be prosecuted as war criminals. It didn't frighten me at all because in my mind I had not abused the POWs; I had just done my duty. How could a non-military Korean like me be responsible in a Japanese war?

'Soon, those of us who had worked as prison guards were told to present ourselves at one of our dormitories. Seeing Allied soldiers lining up at the building armed with automatic rifles, a friend whispered to me that they had assembled us in order to identify war criminal suspects. We were told to stand in single file. Approximately fifty of the former British and Australian POWs came into the hall and walked in front of us. Four men stared at me and shouted, pointing their fingers at me. I felt as if I had been shot in the head. Fifty or so other guards were also picked. No sooner had we packed up our belongings than a military truck whisked us away to an unknown destination.

'It turned out to be a prison in Bangkok. Several dozens of my comrades at the camp were already locked up. The rumour was that British and Australian officials had decided in a meeting that as far as war crimes were concerned, Koreans would be treated the same way as the Japanese. In April 1946, we were transferred to Changi, Singapore. I was indicted and put in a single cell with special supervision. But it turned out that some of the charges against me were based on incorrect facts. I had been charged not only with abusing the POWS and forcing the ill and the injured to work, but also for the responsibility of being the director of the Hintok camp, which I had never been. As a result, I was blamed for all the shortages in food, clothes and medicine.

'The problem was I had no defense lawyer or interpreter. There was no hearing at the court, nor was I given an opportunity to tell my side of the story. After being tried in a similarly slipshod fashion, some of my comrades were sent to the gallows. The death sentence was handed out as randomly as winning a raffle prize. Day after day I sat in my dark cell, and waited for the day of my sentence, deploring my fate. One day a guard brought me a message from Captain Usukine. I knew that he was also in prison. The message said, "Hiromura, I'll take all the responsibility. Don't worry, Hiromura. I'll come and testify at your trial."

'I burst into tears and could not stop crying. Since I had been in his training troop, the Captain had always been kind to me. Unfortunately, however, this was the last communication I had with him. As he had said, he took all the blame and was executed. Half a year later I was called up to the prison office. They told me that my indictment had been withdrawn. I was overwhelmed with gratitude. The Captain must have done something after all.

'Early in 1947, I was aboard a ship sailing to Japan. It wasn't going home to Korea, but you can imagine how liberating it was for me, a jailbird who'd been cooped up in a dark hole. I stood on the deck, looked out at the vast sea and the sky and dreamed of the future. Yet my dream was disrupted abruptly. When the ship stopped in Hong Kong to refuel, an English officer appeared at my side with a summons. I felt like jumping into the sea and almost did. But I was grabbed and put into a car that was waiting at the wharf. I caught a glimpse of the beautiful Hong Kong skyline on the way to prison. It looked like an image of a heaven I would never reach.

'I was kept in Stanley Prison in Hong Kong for a month. Then I was shipped back to Singapore and thrown into a single cell at Changi again. The charge was the same as before, but the number of accusers, which now included Dr Dunlop, had increased from four to nine, and a new charge – that a man had died because I had forced him to work when he was ill – had also been added. My trial took place over two days in March 1947, at a military court under Australian jurisdiction. This time a Japanese lawyer defended me. None of the accusers, including Dr Dunlop, were present, though I understand that years later, in an interview with NHK, the Japan Broadcast Station, the doctor was supposed to have said, "If I had testified at court, I wouldn't have wanted Hiramura (sic) to be sentenced to death. He deserved some kind of punishment, but not death."

'I denied all the charges including the accusation that I had hit and abused the POWs. My cross-examination lasted forty minutes. In two hours, the trial was over. The judge told me to stand up and pronounced, his voice matter of fact, "Death by hanging". The whole world shook and blackened, and I fainted. After a while I came to with the cold touch of handcuffs around my wrists.

'I was taken to Punishment Hall, where only death-row convicts were kept. The dark cell had a bed made of concrete. The only light came through a pocketsize iron-latticed window. There were fifteen other inmates. All of us were supposed to be executed within three months. My clock began to tick the day I arrived. As time went on, sadness overwhelmed me. All the people back home must be dancing with joy because Korea had finally been liberated from the tyranny of Japan, while I was facing a lonely death. What would my family say when they heard that I had been hanged for helping the Japanese to abuse POWs? I had disgraced my family and my country. I cried every day and night.

'One day, eight months after my arrival, a guard came to my cell. My heart pounded. "This is it," I told myself. "An English officer is waiting for you," the guard said, and took me to the prison office, where a tall officer said in good Japanese, "Your sentence was commuted to twenty years." I felt dizzy, just as when I had been sentenced to death, but this time with sudden light brightening the air.

'Later I found out that Sugimatsu, my Japanese lawyer, had written a petition on my behalf, asking to overturn the judgment on the grounds that the trial had not observed the correct rules and procedures, and that the evidence given by the accusers was problematic. The accusers, he said, had exaggerated the role I had played – I should not have been blamed for the inadequacy of food, medicine and working conditions that had caused the POWs' deaths. It turned out that out of 3,000 Koreans who had served as guards at the POW camps in the Pacific islands, twenty-three were sentenced to death and a hundred and forty-eight received life or a fixed-term imprisonment.

'After being imprisoned in Autrum Prison, near Changi, for three years, I was transferred to Sugamo Prison in Japan. A thousand Japanese war criminals were incarcerated there. They fed us well. We did light work during the day, and enjoyed a variety of cultural activities in the evenings. In 1952, Japan, the US and other Allied countries signed the San Francisco Peace Treaty. As a result, I lost my Japanese citizenship and became a legitimate Korean. But in the end the treaty worked against us. Even though we had fought in a Japanese war and had been convicted of war crimes, we were excluded from receiving any benefits because we were no longer Japanese. Although a law was passed that made war criminals eligible for life-time assistance and pensions from the government, we did not receive them. The Japanese called us Japanese when they needed us and now they called us Korean and discarded us like old rugs.

'A Taiwanese and seventy Korean former war criminals submitted a petition to the Tokyo District Court, demanding compensation and our immediate release. The case was taken up by the Supreme Court, but it was rejected. We marched in the streets and in front of the Diet. My friend, Susumu Iida, was sympathetic with the Korean and Tai-wanese plight and he walked with us in the march. We've been friends since I joined the Anti-War Group in Sugamo Prison which Iida had organised. He suggested that we should go and see Mr Masanobu Tsuji, a well-known MP. Being a veteran, Tsuji might do something to help us. During the war Tsuji was a major figure at the General Staff Office of the Imperial Army. As soon as the war was over, he dis-appeared from Japan and hid himself from the Americans who were looking for him. Many years later when he had surfaced from hiding, he wrote a best-seller and was elected a MP. It was shocking that people voted for such a coward.

'Listening to our passionate plea, Tsuji fidgeted about and before we had finished talking he excused himself, saying he was busy. The cold-blooded expression on his face, like a reptile's, still gives me shivers whenever I think of him. He treated us as despicable war criminals, a description he deserved ten times more than we did.

I was thirty-one when I was released from Sugamo. Japanese society did not welcome me when I came out. I had no home to go back to, no family or friends. Where did I belong? Who was I? What was my identity? I wished I could go back to Korea and see my parents, but I had no money to travel. My mother had been praying for me ever since I left home in 1942. Every morning she prayed to her ancestors, at our family altar, asking them to protect her son. She wrote letters to me while I was in Sugamo. In the end I did not go back to Korea. I was afraid I would not be wanted there. In Korea I would be a traitor who had sold my soul to Japan and betrayed my own country.

'As ex-convicts and Koreans, my comrades and I hadn't found any jobs since being released from Sugamo. Two committed suicide, one hanged himself from a tree in a temple garden; the other threw himself under a train. After learning about this, some of the Korean inmates who were still serving their sentence in Sugamo refused to be released. In prison they were given free food, a bed and protection. We formed Doshin-kai and tried to support each other mentally and financially. We asked the Japanese government for restitution. Angered by their lack of response, we took action, sitting in the Diet or jumping over the fence of the Prime Minister's house.

'Some Japanese were sympathetic with us. There's a man I call "my father" – a medical doctor named Tomofumi Imai. Without his help many of us might still be without jobs. Dr Imai realised that the Koreans and Taiwanese had been treated unfairly. He visited Sugamo with his friends just to cheer us up. He kept saying, "As a Japanese I apologise for what we have done to you." We went to see Dr Imai every time we had problems. He was generous with financial support and always helped anyone in trouble. Every time we planned a demonstration or petition, we gathered at his home the previous night to talk about strategy. Dr Imai's wife was just as kind as her husband.

'One day I came up with the idea of starting a taxi company. In prison, as part of a programme designed to help us readjust to the outside world, they had sent us to driving school. We could put our driving skills to use and make a living. But we had no capital – no money to buy cars, a garage, or an office. At a loss, we went to see Dr Imai. He was incredibly generous again. Thanks to him, we were able to start a taxi company. A real estate agency helped us find a garage and an office in an area of Tokyo that was inexpensive and had no other taxi companies. After dozens of petitions, we obtained a license for running ten cars. All the drivers were war criminals, and so were the business managers. I was the executive director. I married a nice Korean woman and had two children. I worked day and night to support my family. I was determined not to disappoint my comrades. Within a few years we were able to give a dividend to the shareholders, all of whom were former inmates.

'In 1961 I received news that my mother had died of illness. It made me sad that I hadn't visited her before she died. Several years later, I managed to go home to see my father, who had turned sixty. We were so very happy to see each other. Everyone – my brother, sister, and relatives and neighbours – thought I was dead, and they made a big fuss to welcome me.

'Back in Japan, our hard work began to pay off and our business started to do well. We increased the number of taxis to fifty and people stopped calling it "the war-criminals' taxi company", as they had in the old days; we were finally respectable. We were able to give money back to Dr Imai. He said that he hadn't expected it, but was very happy about our success. There were other Japanese who were kind to us. Among them, Professor Aiko Utsumi,[25] a scholar who studies the post-war relationship between Japan and Korea and the other South East Asian countries. She isn't just an academic. She cares so much about us. She has pursued our problems as if they were her own.

'In 1991 I went with Professor Utsumi to Canberra, Australia, in order to attend a conference on POW camps. I was reluctant to go, because I didn't want to see the former POWs and relive my days in the camps. To tell the truth, I still held a grudge against them. After all, thanks to them, I'd gone through a hard time, and many of my comrades had been hanged because of them. But Ms Utsumi insisted that I go with her. Some of the people I used to deal with in the camp were there. Among them was Dr Weary Dunlop.

'In my long years of incarceration in Sugamo, I had done some soul searching. But in the end I blamed the Japanese for everything. I pitied myself for my bad luck, and never really reflected on what I had done to the POWs. I had only been eager to negotiate with the Japanese government about the rights of Koreans. But now I had to remind myself that I was a perpetrator in the war and that the POWs had

25 Professor Utsumi's numerous books include, *Why Was Kim Indicted?*, *Sugamo Prison*, and *Japanese Army's POW Policy*.

suffered because of me. I figured I owed the POWs an apology. So at the conference I told the POWs that I was sorry for what I had done to them. But I also asked them to listen to my side of the story. "Please understand," I said. "I was a mere civilian war worker who had been hired by the Japanese Army. I had been taught that obeying my elders was an iron rule." I also talked about the repeated tortures I had suffered at Changi prison.

'Dr Dunlop wasn't pleased. "You're asking others to take responsibility for what you did," he said. "Your actions were your problem. You can't blame others for them." He did not smile. I had been hoping to hear forgiving words from him, and this was a severe indictment. I went back to my hotel room and cogitated.

'I didn't admit to myself how I had slapped the POWs and dragged them to work even when they were ill. It was only natural that the POWs hated me; it only made sense that they had wanted me to be incarcerated and punished. Many other guards had been kinder and more sympathetic to the POWs than I was. Why had I been so insensitive to their sufferings? Being a victim myself, why didn't I try to understand how other victims felt? The POWs had been punished for no reason other than that they had collectively lost a regional war. Dr Dunlop was right: I shouldn't blame others for what I had done. But I still blamed the Japanese.[26]

'After returning from Australia, I resumed my pursuit of justice and fairness from the Japanese government. Just as I had apologised to the POWs, so should they give us restitution for all that they had done. In the past half century, we've sent a petition to every prime minister – twenty-eight of them – asking them to grant compensation to Koreans indicted as war criminals. But none has given us a meaningful answer. Some of the recent Diet members showed us some sympathy, but after Prime Minister Abe took over, we seem to have lost ground. I'm

26 Professor Aiko Utsumi has studied those who bear many crosses like Lee Hanne who was not only an aggressor in the war, but also a victim of Japan's colonial rule. 'But Lee-san was deeply wrapped up in a victim mentality and did not see he was an aggressor as well,' she said. 'When he went to Australia, he realised that his being a victim did not forgive what he had done to the POWs. It was difficult for him to learn that he was responsible for what he did.'

eighty-eight now, and Japan is my adopted home; I'll never go back to Korea again. But the war still isn't over for me. I will keep visiting the Prime Minister or the court house in my wheelchair until Japan properly apologises to us and to the twenty-three Koreans who were hanged.'

CHAPTER 8

Toshimi Kumai

War in the Philippines

I met Mr Kumai at Tokyo Sunshine Tower in Ikebukuro where Sugamo Prison used to stand. He spent eight years there after the war as a war criminal. He had been sentenced to twenty-five years, but was pardoned as were most other criminals, after the US handed jurisdiction over the prison to the Japanese government at the outbreak of the Korean War. 'Those were traumatic years that I lived here. I did my best to fight, risking my life and in the end was put in prison for it, deserted by my country. But after I was released, I found a job nearby and this area has become my territory,' he said, leading me into the super fast elevator of the tower. On the sixtieth floor the sun was flooding through the glass windows which encased the circular building.

We sat down for tea and he talked. He was articulate and had amazingly detailed memories of the war he had fought.

'On a snowy day in February 1941,' he began, 'I was at a military airport in Kyushu assigned to the Philippines when I received a telegram from home that my mother had passed away. She had been suffering from TB for some time. I was a newly minted second lieutenant but was allowed to go home briefly to be with my father. We said our goodbye, but I never imagined I wouldn't see him again for twelve years.

'Eight hours after Pearl Harbor, Japanese bombers attacked the Philippines destroying American air and naval forces. In less than a month, the Japanese had occupied Manila. General MacArthur's ground forces retreated and entrenched themselves on the Bataan Peninsula and further down on the Island of Corregidor.

'In Japan, the news reported their Army's brilliant victory, but the truth was that in six weeks 7,000 troops, two-thirds of the Japanese

65th Brigade which had chased the enemy to Bataan, had perished attacking a US stronghold, Mount Natib.

'I was recruited to be part of the reinforcements. As soon as we arrived in Manila which looked like an exotic fairyland for a country boy like me, we were transported in a beaten-up military truck towards San Fernando. On our way we saw the aftermath of the recent battles – overturned vehicles and burnt villages. The entire Bataan Peninsula seemed to be mountains covered by jungle. Our truck advanced over rough roads with lights off since the enemy could be lurking anywhere. Eventually, it stopped at our regimental HQ that before the war might have been the home of an animal.

'Next morning I woke to a faint light coming through the mouth of the cave. I crawled outside. The air was hotter than a sauna, and full of birdsong. Then there was an ear-splitting explosion nearby, sprouting a cloud of dust. I quickly ran back into the shelter. All day shells kept exploding. When we came out and shot back, the counter fire multiplied.

'In order to divert the enemy's attention, we kept in motion through the thick jungle where even tigers, lions or Tarzans would not penetrate because of thorns and prickly bamboo meshed like barbed wire. My machine gun platoon kept losing men not only from enemy bullets, but also from accidents, malaria, amoebic dysentery and exhaustion. I came down with malaria. Our machine gun weighed 55kg. We disassembled it and several of us carried the parts, as I could hardly stay upright with a 25kg gun and a 30kg tripod on my shoulder.

'Japan HQ in Tokyo and the South Army were determined to revenge the loss of the first Bataan campaign. They planned the greatest general attack ever for the Japanese Army. Artillery units, heavy bomber aviation units, infantry troops and brigades kept arriving by the thousands. On 3 April 1942, the attack began. Explosions of the two hundred cannons echoed in the mountains.

'Our men ran through a hail of bullets. We started with forty men, but were quickly down to sixteen. Bodies, Filipino and Japanese, were all about and gave off an unbearable stanch. Every day I thought would be my day to go. Delirious with fever, I caressed my sword wondering whether I should kill myself.

On the seventh night at 2 a.m., we walked down a pitch dark slope,

Toshimi Kumai

our feet faltering. As we turned a bend, we saw a bright light through the thicket. To our surprise, hundreds of enemy soldiers were sitting around bonfires in a clearing not even holding their rifles.

'We had heard a rumour about the enemy surrender. Could it be true? Commander Tanabe walked down the slope and advanced towards the bonfire. He met a tall Filipino man who was a Regimental Commander of the USAFFE (US Army Forces in the Far East). They exchanged words. The enemy had indeed surrendered. Our group broke out in cheers. I was dizzy with joy. Filipino soldiers approached us, perhaps out of curiosity. They all looked like good-natured young men of my age. I said in my broken English, 'I have the same skin colour as you. We are friends'. They smiled.

'Unfortunately, this was just the end of a regional campaign. Being so ill, I wished I could indulge myself in the luxury of peace a little longer. But in no time we received an order to leave for Balanga and work under the command of the Logistic Unit. We borrowed vehicles scattered in the area and left. When we arrived at Balanga, we were given the job of escorting a large group of POWs to Orani at the mouth of the Bataan Peninsula. The area was in utter chaos. The road was jammed with Filipino civilians as well as American POWs. In the same area the artillery of the Japanese 4th Division was preparing for the next general offensive against Corregidor.

'We were told that the POWs were to be given a bowl of gruel per head twice a day. That was obviously insufficient, but understandable since we were getting nothing but rice. The number of our soldiers who were able to perform guard duty was far too small to meet the HQ's request because half of us were as sick as dogs. There were only fifteen men in a squad, to accompany about a thousand POWs to the intersection point twenty kilometres ahead. While they were complaining about the utter chaos of the POW situation and blaming it on the lack of guards, the HQ ordered our brigade to leave Balanga in order to engage in a guerilla clean-up operation in Luzon. How would they handle those poor POWs with even fewer guards?

'We travelled in a big truck along the east shore of the Peninsula. On the way we saw thousands of POWs walking slowly, heads down from hunger, thirst and fatigue. On the opposite side of the same road,

Japanese military vehicles were advancing, kicking thick yellow sand up in the air. The POWs were covered from head to toe with the sand dust. The dead were abandoned and the military trucks ran them over, and flattened them. A large number of civilian refugees also walked along with the POWs. The procession went on for miles. Later I learned that this was called 'the Bataan Death March'. Indeed, it was. I heard that as many as 1,200 American soldiers and 16,000 Filipinos had died on the march. It's understandable that the Japanese had not prepared transportation or food for that many refugees. But it is unforgivable they had not tried to save their lives.'

Kumai-san stood up and straightened his back, saying, 'I'm tired.' We had a break and sat down again.

'On 6 May 1942, the USAFFE surrendered to the Japanese in Corregidor, but Filipino guerrilla resistance continued to be vigorous across the archipelago. Their efforts had been encouraged by General McArthur who had evacuated to Australia. Guerrillas were in effect considered as Allied Forces personnel, supplied with weapons, ammunition and equipment transported by American submarines. After a short stay in Luzon, we were assigned to fight in the anti-guerrilla campaign on the island of Panay where the resistance was the fiercest. I was one of the platoon leaders of Tozuka Unit, 170th Independent Infantry Battalion.

'In October 1942, we approached the port of Iloilo City, Panay, on a transport ship. The island looked like a tropical paradise with coconut trees along the seawall. Iloilo was the biggest city in Panay and used to be a prosperous place, famous for sugar trading. As we landed, however, we found the main part of the city a burnt ruin. Fierce fighting had been going on since the guerrillas had risen against the Japanese forces a few months before.

'The first thing we did was to watch a guerrilla suspect being interrogated by the *Kempeitai* military police. A *Kempei* poured water from a pail into the suspect's mouth. The young man choked as his stomach swelled up. Some soldiers of our unit cried, "Stop" and Commander Tozuka also called out, "Enough!" "Don't interfere with us. This is the information gathering process," Captain K. Watanabe, the Operation and Intelligence chief, shouted at us.

'Watanabe was a cold-blooded man. We did not like him, but had to obey him. Disobedience was punished by kicking, punching and even killing.'

'In the summer of 1943, a special squad of eight hundred soldiers was established to sweep-up the guerrillas. General Staff, Colonel Hideumi Watanabe (no relation of Captain Watanabe) was the architect of the campaign. He ordered Captain Watanabe to be a leader of the operation rather than the weaker Tozuka, so the operation was bound to be cruel.

'The sweep began on July 7 and covered a wide area. When it was difficult to tell guerrillas from locals, which was often the case, we were told to kill them all. So, some of the victims were killed, as if they had been pigs or chickens. Stealing cattle, food and killing were all done in the name of the Emperor and, therefore, justified. The guerrillas retaliated in kind. Panay had turned into a blood bath. What had happened to the ideal of the liberation of Asia and greater Asia's co-prosperity?

'In December 1943, our force headed south to attack a guerrilla stronghold. Along the tributary of the Aklan River we met an American who was bare-footed and limping. "My name is King," he said, under interrogation by Captain Watanabe. "I used to be a guerrilla officer, but with the Japanese campaigns, my unit scattered. Neither the guerrillas nor the villagers took me in since I look American. That's why I'm here wandering along the river by myself." Threatened by Captain Watanabe, King told him that more Americans were hiding near the town of Tapaz, thirteen kilometres north of Calinog. Watanabe and his troops immediately took the path to the town. The Americans had no chance to escape. Some were found in their dugouts and others were caught while trying to escape. By the evening, all of them had been captured and rounded up. The Captain came back to the base with a dozen Americans including young children.'

The Edge of Terror by Scott Walker[27] tells us the story of these brave and ill-fated Americans. They were extraordinary people – mostly

27 Walker, Scott, *The Edge of Terror*, Thomas Dunne Books, St Martin's Press, New York, 2009.

missionaries who had come from America before the war and had dedicated their lives to helping people in the Philippines. Among them, Dr Frederic Meyer and his wife, Ruth, came in 1919 on a missionary appointment, settled down in the small coastal city in Panay and set up a much needed medical clinic in the area. It had grown to be a big hospital to which people came from all over the islands. He was a skilled surgeon and a mentor for young doctors. The nursing school he built educated hundreds of local nurses. On Sundays he was an inspiring preacher at a Baptist church. Ruth was a concert soloist and sang at churches throughout the island. They were parents of three boys. When World War II broke out, however, the busy, but peaceful world of the Meyers abruptly ended. Under Japanese control, all Americans became hunted prey.

After Christmas in 1941, less than two weeks after the Japanese invaded the Philippines, the USAFFE ordered Dr Meyer to abandon his hospital and to evacuate to the interior of the province. They moved to Dumalag where the military hospital was. In April 1942, 4000 Japanese troops landed on Panay. The Meyers, the head nurse and the nursing students sped south in two trucks. They were pursued by a Japanese fighter plane, but narrowly escaped to the town of Calinog near Katipunan. A Baptist pastor, Reverend Delfin Dianala offered them a place to stay.

But it was soon clear that the area would not be safe. Japanese planes frequently flew overhead, often at low altitude. Reverend Dianala guided the refugees further into the foothills to a bushy area in a forested canyon. The missionaries decided to build their hideaway there and named it Hopevale. They lived in canvas tents under the dense tree cover. Reverend Dianala and his confidant, Mr Rio, provided food and security for Hopevale.

Life was a struggle with roaches, snakes, rats, iguanas and monkeys. Eventually, the Americans arranged for the local people to build them traditional nipa and grass houses. Eleven such houses were built, tucked away along the hillside and covered by jungle foliage.

In July 1942, Japanese planes crisscrossed Panay, dropping leaflets announcing that the Americans must surrender to Japanese forces within four months. They would be executed if found after that. The missionaries at Hopevale were determined not to surrender despite this ultimatum. For some this decision was based upon their advanced age and poor health. For others, it might have been wishful thinking that the enemy would spare the lives of those who served God.

There was a group of American mining engineers' families who had also fled to Hopevale. They came to the Philippines to dig gold during the Depression. Unlike the missionaries, the miners were determined to escape from Hopevale.

One of them, Claude Fertig, was working under Panay's guerrilla chief, Lieutenant Colonel Peralta. Claude asked his engineer friend, Spence, to assist him in developing a submarine rendezvous point that MacArthur had requested and to construct a radio station capable of communicating with him in Australia and with Peralta's mobile headquarters. Claude and Spence walked over difficult mountainous terrain to the northwest corner of Panay where the project was to be developed.

Soon Calinog was occupied by the Japanese, who transformed it into an infantry outpost. Now Japanese troops were based within a day's march of Hopevale. The missionaries still insisted on staying there. But Claude and Spence came to pick up their wives, Laverne and Louise, and they walked through the jungle again to reach the area free of Japanese troops. It took two months before they finally settled down in a safe place when Laverne found out she was pregnant.

Laverne insisted on seeing Dr Meyer because he was the only doctor she trusted. Hopevale was a long trek back and it was not a safe place, but she was determined. In the end they trekked all the long way back to Hopevale. They were exhausted, but warmly welcomed by the missionaries.

Spence called another meeting in Hopevale and suggested that they should not remain bunched up within the confines of the camp. After deliberation, the missionaries decided again that they should not leave Hopevale but rather stay close together as a mission family.

Claude and Laverne settled in a new nipa house twenty minutes away from Dr Meyer's hut in Hopevale. Spence and Louise were forty minutes away.

On 17 December a reconnaissance plane flew over Hopevale barely above the tree tops. On the next morning Claude was at work at his command post. Spence was dressed when Pilo, his Filipino aide rushed in. 'Sir, the Japs are on this side of the Panay River running in this direction.' Spence bolted from the hut, binoculars in hand, and sprinted up a hill beside the house. They had only minutes to flee.

Spence, Louise and Laverne left and waded through a mountain stream so as not to leave footprints. They crawled up a long sloping hill. Looking back at the valley below, they gasped. Dr Meyer's nipa house was a flaming torch. Other huts were also burning. But they had to go on. Scrambling across the ridge, they plodded up the stream bed. Finally they made it to Claude's command post, but safety had not been reached. Together with Claude, they kept going.

Back to Mr Kumai's account: 'Among the captured Americans there was one gentleman who spoke perfect Japanese. He came up to me and said that he was Reverend Covell and used to teach at a university in Yokohama.'

According to Scott Walker's book, Reverend James Covell and his wife Charma had been missionaries in Japan in the 1920s. He taught the Bible and English at Kanto Gakuin University in Yokohama. As the Reverend began to protest against the church's acquiescience in the rising militarism in Japan, the Covells were reassigned to the Philippines. He had been teaching at the central Philippine University in the city of Iloilo before they fled to Hopevale.

Mr Kumai said, 'Reverend Covell had a gracious and dignified manner and spoke persuasively. I introduced him to Captain Watanabe, thinking that even the Captain's cold heart would be softened by this quiet and courageous man and that he would treat the Americans in a kind manner. The Reverend spoke with Watanabe and pleaded with him to spare his colleagues' lives. Watanabe seemed to have been moved by him.

'I had to leave then since, based on Mr King's information, my platoon had been ordered to hunt for an American miner who had become a guerrilla officer, his wife and friends. I left hoping that the talk between Reverend Covell and Captain Watanabe would bring a good result and that all the Americans would be sent to the internment camp in Manila.

'Our platoon walked in the dark, often crawling as we made our way with a local villager as a guide. We reached the place and kicked and banged on the doors of each little hut, but nobody was found. The Americans must have already fled. After going on for miles, we finally gave up. We returned to the field headquarters at midnight.

'Next morning, I looked for the Americans – Mr King, Reverend Covell and the other missionaries, women and children. None of them were in sight. I asked a soldier about them. He said that all of them had been executed. "What!" I was outraged and saddened, as were my subordinates. "How could he kill those innocent children and families? They were obviously good people." Neither Watanabe nor Commander Tozuka said anything.

'Sometime later, I was promoted to Adjutant and was now allowed access to the wireless record at the Panay headquarters. I found out how the fateful decision had been made. The record showed that Captain Watanabe's report of the "glorious war results" – meaning the capture of the American missionaries – had been sent to General Staff H. Watanabe at the Punitive Operation Headquarters in Cebu-city. The report was forwarded to Manila. The Manila office responded to the field headquarters with severe criticism instead of the praise which Captain Watanabe had expected. They ordered the Captain to "dispose of the captives immediately without letting any nearby locals know." I believe that in Manila, the top HQ did not want to get involved in the capture of missionaries.'

According to Scott Walker, the Americans were allowed to meet alone for a time of prayer before the execution. At 3 p.m. on 20 December 1943 they walked back to the place of execution, singing a hymn of faith together. Mr Kumai surmised that Swordsman Otsuka and his disciple Kuwano in Watanabe's company had been ordered by the Captain to do the killing. They had the sword skills necessary to instantly and silently behead a person. A hut had been chosen, the victims were called one by one into a room and beheaded. Then the bodies were burned, hut and all.

'Even after seventy years I think of the deep, sad eyes of Reverend

Covell,' Mr Kumai says. 'When I parted from him, he looked at me as if he trusted me. I betrayed him. It is my mission to tell people in Japan what a terrible injustice was done to such good people.'

I wrote to Scott Walker about this story. He replied: 'Watanabe was obviously an individual who did not mind committing atrocities. However, when Jimmy Covell talked with him, he made an impression on Watanabe. Perhaps the words of Jimmy Covell somehow touched him. He hesitated to draw his sword . . . However, when Watanabe contacted his superiors by radio, they contacted their superiors in Manila. With each step the decision became less and less connected to real people. Small children were not seen. The power of Jimmy Covell's words was not heard. By the time the request reached Japanese Headquarters in Manila, the seventeen (*sic*) American missionaries and three children had become statistics. And it is much easier to exterminate statistics than it is to murder individuals . . . This is the danger of war. In war, people become faceless statistics.'[28]

As for the miners who escaped Kumai platoon's chase, they kept trekking through Christmas and New Year so that they could get as far away from the Japanese as possible. Laverne's baby was due any time. Claude and Spence found an isolated spot and made an arrangement with a tribesman to build a one-room hut. It was camouflaged by dense growth, and close to a clear stream. The hut was completed just in time.

Dr Teruel, a civilian doctor who was helping the guerrillas, came to deliver the baby and Louise found herself serving as a midwife. The delivery was blessedly short and Susan Beatrice Fertig was born. Her loud cry brought smiles to everyone's face and lit up the dark room.

Shortly after Dr Teruel left, Claude grew feverish and delirious. Another Filipino doctor was brought in. He examined Claude and gave him sulphur tablets. Just before he left, the doctor checked Louise who had not been feeling well. After a quick examination, the doctor said to Spence, "Sir, the señora is pregnant!" Now it was the Spencers' turn to go through what the Fertigs had endured for the last nine months.

28 Walker, Scott, in a letter to Hiroko Sherwin, 5 June 2014

In February, they moved to a camp in a safer place Spence had built. The day they arrived at their new house, Claude received great news from Peralta. General MacArthur, enraged by the news of the Hopevale massacre, had decided to rescue all the American civilians on Panay in a submarine pickup. These communications were possible thanks to the radio work Claude and Spence had established.

They were beside themselves with joy. An exhausted mother with a newborn baby, a pregnant woman and two men started off again. They crossed a high range of mountains and made it to the rendezvous point in time to board the submarine *Angler* on 20 March 1944. As they left the island, their thoughts were with the missionaries and the other friends who were not there with them.

They arrived in Darwin, Australia. Shortly after, Louise Spencer gave birth to a baby boy in an army hospital. The Spencers returned to the US. *Guerrilla Wife*, the book Louise wrote about her wartime experience was published in 1945. Claude Fertig worked for the US Army until the end of the war and became a lieutenant general. The two families went their separate ways after the war, but their friendship never waned from time or distance.

'In the meantime, the Americans were gaining momentum in the Pacific,' Mr Kumai resumed his side of the story. 'The turn of the tide was palpable in Panay. After Hopevale, the relentless mop-up campaign that had lasted for six months was ended. Our garrison returned to Iloilo city. As for Captain Watanabe, he was sent to Negros Island to fight a battle with US forces. He was hit by a mortar shell and killed in May 1945.

'Panay was considered strategically useless by the Japanese after the US forces advanced to Leyte Island in October 1944. Abandoned by Tokyo headquarters, we were besieged by 23,000 well-equipped guerrillas and they attacked us relentlessly with bombs, mortars and dynamite.

'In the morning of 18 March 1945, heavy explosions awakened me. That was the day 7000 US troops landed on Panay. The Filipinos were cheering, eagerly waving little American flags as hundreds of tanks and trucks of the US forces drove down the road.'

'Our garrison set out on a silent march to the mountain region in the west-central part of Panay called Bocari which we had chosen as a final hiding place in case of defeat. Local Japanese women, children and old folks came along with us. Enemy fire followed as we marched. The shells and bullets passed right over our heads. We hid in the jungle by day and marched at night guided by the compass and the Southern Cross. But the front line commander was wounded. Another company commander was killed. The number of soldiers kept dropping. Some were injured and could no longer move on. Others took their own lives.

'The Saito force was made up of elderly men and women, children and patients of the Army Hospital. In the beginning they carried large bags of their belongings on their backs. Exhausted, they dropped their bags one by one. Some soldiers carried children or bags. Some said, "Don't let babies cry. The enemy will hear them and chase us. What are the parents doing?" Others even shouted, "Kill the child."

'Five days later about seven hundred of us made it to Bocari. A river flowed in the valley and on both sides was a small village, a terraced rice field and a garden where a variety of vegetables grew. But before we had time to relax, sad news about the Saito force reached us. As the Saito force was so slow, the guerrilla siege was able to close in. The US artillery started a vigorous bombardment. The repeated explosions cost the local Japanese whatever spirit and energy they had left. The principal of the Iloilo City Japanese School stopped at a coconut grove. "We cannot go on like this any longer," he said to the group. "We'll be burdens to the soldiers. Let us end our lives here."

'Far away from mainland Japan, a local Japanese school principal was imbued with the idea of suicide in case of defeat. For him, it was imperative to obey the Field Service Code: "Rather than live and bear the shame of imprisonment by the enemy, die and avoid leaving a dishonorable name." It was not clear whether everyone agreed with him or not, but, eventually they bowed in the direction of the Imperial Palace in Tokyo and began shooting themselves in the ears or on the temple. Mothers asked soldiers to help kill them and their children. They used bayonets and hand grenades. Approximately, forty men, women and children perished.

Left: Yasuji Kaneko

Below: Tadamasa Iwai.
The young Tadamasa Iwai
and his brother Tadakuma
(standing on the left) are on
the jacket of the book.

Above left: Minoru Wada (sitting) with his friend Goro Takeda

Above right: Susumu Iida in recent years

Below left: Ryutaro Hanamichi

Below right: Susumu Iida (right)

徴兵検査を翌年に控えて、同居人の二人と撮った記念写真

(著者右央)

Left: Kunitami Mitsuhashi

Below: 'Starving Soldier' by Kunitami Mitsuhashi

Above: Lee Hanne

Below: Osamu Komai and Eric Lomax at Eric's house in Berwick-upon-Tweed, England

Above: Toshimi Kumai

Below: Tokuro Inokuma

Above: Michiyo Arakawa, editor of *Chu-ki-ren*

Below: Taeko Sasamoto, founder of the POW Research Network Japan

Above: Keiko Holmes, founder of the Pilgrimage of Healing and Reconcilliation

Below: Eriko Ikeda, director of the WAM Museum

Left: Ayako Kurahashi
Below left: Professor Aiko Utsumi
Below right: Yoshiko Tamura

'I remember the day we heard the Emperor's surrender broadcast. The soldiers were overjoyed. At last we were relieved of the daily combat we had endured for more than three years. But for a war criminal suspect like me it was the beginning of another dark war. We officers were separated from the rest, placed in a black van and driven through the streets with US soldiers guarding the front and back of the van. Along the way local residents came rushing towards us, shouting curses in Japanese. Some raised their fists and others mimicked beheading us with their hands. We were taken from one prison to another until we finally settled in a camp at Nicholas Field in the suburbs of Manila. Day after day we had three meals of a cup of thin corn soup and water. I was so feeble and dizzy that within two weeks I could not stand up straight.

'At the preliminary hearings, the cases were focussed on incidents during the six months punitive campaign in 1943. Two thousand Filipinos had died during that period. I realised there was no chance for me to come out free. I was in total despair. Every day I looked blankly upon the mountains east of the camp. I was getting increasingly angry, too. Now I was a criminal, abandoned by my country to which I had dedicated my life. I decided that I would fight for my life if nobody helped me.

'I came up with the idea of escape. It was the only way I could avoid my fate. But a few nights before I planned to escape, there was a big commotion in the camp. Three of our fellow prisoners had run away. Several days later, outside our camp, I saw them in a wire mesh cage. They were so starved that they had surrendered. One of the three escaped again and surrendered again. He was sentenced to death.

'Even then the idea of escape did not leave me. Several colleagues wanted to join me. We did meticulous research on the landscape of the region, the place where our Army's weapons were stored, the area where our ships could be found, the current and the trade wind between Luzon and the Sea of Taiwan. We collected sea salt, malaria pills, a magnet, a map, a knife, mess tins, water bottles and an American tent.

'Unfortunately, before I had a chance to try to escape, I was taken to the War Crime Tribunal in Manila with my fellow suspects. We were all put in cells, unbearably hot and dark. The sound of waves from Manila Bay made me sad. The dream of going home on a stolen ship had vanished. What infuriated me was that the US Military Commission decided not to prosecute Staff Officer Watanabe. He was the mastermind of the Panay mop-up operation. He had teamed up with Captain K. Watanabe and forced everyone to follow their brutal policy. Why did the Americans decide not to indict this arch-criminal?

'Colonel Tozuka was sentenced to death. Otsuka, the master swords-man, indicted for killing the Americans on Watanabe's order, stood calmly in court, prepared for his destiny and seemed to concentrate only on saving the life of his subordinate, Sergeant Kuwano. Every time the local resident witnesses mentioned Kuwano, Otsuka said, 'I am to blame for that.' He also tried to save a spy for the Japanese Army named Jesus Astrologo. He was Otsuka's disciple and was facing trial himself because collaboration with the Japanese was treason. Otsuka did not contradict any of Jesus' testimony and chose to give answers only to be helpful to him. The sentence for Otsuka was death by hanging. Kuwano received life.

'My trial was held on 4 July 1946, the day the Philippines celebrated its independence. Even from my prison cell, I could hear a brass band parading and saluting salvos from US warships stationed in Manila Bay. I was accused on three charges. One was the incident in which they said I tortured a fifty-year-old local man and ordered my assistant to kill him. Two and a half years had passed since that incident and I did not have a clear memory of it. I made up a well-crafted scenario about the event and drummed it repeatedly into my head so that I would not contradict myself.

'In the second case, a villager accused me of treating a blind old woman brutally, binding her to a tree and leaving her to die. I testified to this charge by saying, 'I don't recall.' My defense attorney Simon interrogated the villager about discrepancies in the facts, but the witness explained everything with confidence. For the third charge, a farmer testified that he had seen me behead three local men one after another. Strangely, the witness suddenly stopped talking half-way through the testimony and refused to say anything except "I don't know."

'I wondered where justice lay in this kind of trial. The prosecution accused me on inaccurate evidence. I testified to my side of the story with a well-crafted scenario. The prosecutor and the defense lawyer Simon argued about false testimony. At the end of the trial, the prosecutor summed up the case against me, "I demand for Kumai the sentence of death by hanging," he declared.

'I had to wait two days for the verdict. The words "death by hanging" kept ringing in my ears and I felt the rope tightening around my neck in my sleep. On the day of the judgment, I went to the court accompanied by military police. Judge Ottoman made me and Simon stand in front of him. I was shaking and trying hard not to collapse when I heard the voice: 'Twenty-five years hard labour.' I felt a sudden lightness in my head. Anything was better than death. Two MPs came up and took me out of the court holding me up by the arms. Simon ran out with me. His smile felt like a beam of sunlight.

'In January 1947, I was sent back to Japan and was put in Sugamo Prison. In February 1954, I was pardoned and released from the prison. Three years of war, and eight years and four months as a war criminal, had thoroughly exhausted me.,' Mr Kumai said.

The Mr Kumai I saw sixty-eight years after the war was a man who cared deeply about what had happened in the part of the war in which he was involved. He visited the Philippines six times after he was released from prison, talked with the villagers and apologised for the Japanese atrocities. The former guerrillas treated Mr Kumai as an old friend every time he visited them.

On one of the trips, he went to the area where the mass suicide had taken place. Thanks to help from the local people, particularly from the former guerrilla officers, the spot was located. Mr Kumai organised a memorial service and had a monument built for the dead. It turned out that, at the scene of the suicide, guerrilla soldiers and local citizens had rescued five Japanese children, four of whom grew up in Iloilo. Mr Kumai went to thank the people who had raised the children. He made inquiries in Japan and from the information he received, helped establish the identity of their parents.

Recently, he began corresponding with Susan Fertig-Dykes through the introduction of Yukako Ibuki, his translator and good friend. She says, 'Kumai-san never dreamed that a baby could have been born in the jungle after her parents had escaped from Kumai platoon's chase. He was very happy he had failed in the hunt for her parents. Susan is a symbol of the triumph of the defiant spirit of her parents and their friends who helped each other to survive. She grew up to be a peace worker. She lived for six years in Croatia and in Bosnia during the conflict and afterwards. She also visited Japan for a conference on Comfort Women.'

Yukako gave a message written by Mr Kumai to Susan at a conference in Pittsburgh. Susan felt uneasy about accepting a letter from the man who had tried to kill her parents. But later she wrote, 'I could even consider friendship with him more than six decades later. It wasn't really a question of forgiveness; it is not for me to forgive. Not only was I not harmed and my parents not killed, but it was not even for me to judge what happened. That belongs to God – to my God who chose to spare me, for some unfathomable reason.'

Susan wrote back to Mr Kumai. So they are corresponding through Yukako. 'Whenever I talk about Susan, Kumai-san's eyes shine with tears,' she says.

CHAPTER 9

Tokuro Inokuma

A Boy Soldier taken to Siberia

Inokuma-san volunteered to go to war at the age of fifteen. He was sent to China and ended up in a Siberian detention camp after the war. Because of his early age at the start of the war, he was only eighty-two, the youngest among all the veterans I would meet. A week before my visit, his wife had passed away after a long illness. I was hesitant to visit him, but he insisted on my coming. 'You'd better come now. Then I won't feel lonesome.'

From his address I figured that he lived along the Pacific coast, not too far from Kamakura, an old temple city. I took a train going to the southwest of Tokyo, imagining his place was likely to be in one of the beach towns which dotted the coastline. I got off the train at Nobi, and following the instruction, rode a bus. Somehow, it took me to a quiet, remote village. From there I climbed a sharp slope, tracing stepping stones hidden among weeds. According to the map, his house was on top of the hill. The strange thing was, that walking all the way, I did not come across anyone, not even an animal. No house or structure was in sight. The sea could not be seen in any direction. I was rather happy to find such quiet and uninhabited space so close to Tokyo. But I began to wonder how an old man could live here all alone in this deserted area, climbing up and down the sharp hill.

On top of the hill was an old house made of wood. As I stood at the entrance, I could hear cats meowing from inside. I remembered some-one had said Inokuma-san was a cat lover. Suddenly the door slid open. Standing there was a well-built, youthful-looking man. My worry was unnecessary. He could easily hop up those steps much better than I could. It was a traditional Japanese house and we sat on the floor around a low table. Cats were running around everywhere. They all looked identical to me and I could not tell how many there were. 'There are four of them. Aren't they lovely?' he said.

He turned out to be an articulate and intelligent speaker. He was obviously in superb shape for his age, not only physically, but also mentally. Inokuma-san was born in 1928 in Tokyo and was a pharmacist's son. He was the youngest of four brothers and a sister. His mother was hospitalised before he started school and died six years later.

'I don't know how my father managed to raise five kids by himself, but I was a good boy and did well at school. We were taught that Japan was a special country and it was our duty to build a Greater East Asia in order to ward off the threat from the West. After its initial success, Japan did not do well in the war. One day in 1944, my teacher told us that we could volunteer to be boy soldiers by applying for the army cadet school newly set up for boys aged fourteen to eighteen. Enormous numbers of soldiers were dying in the sea, in the air and in the fields. The country was so desperate that they began recruiting boys. "They need your help. You'll be trained quickly and will be sent to the battlefield. Apply if you want to make a contribution to your country."

'I was fifteen. I instantly made up my mind and told my father I was going to the war. My father's face turned pale. "No, you won't." His voice was stern. His three older sons had been taken to the war. He wanted at least his youngest to stay home. We argued day and night. I refused to eat for four days and never changed my mind. On the fifth day my father said in a husky voice, "You can go, Tokuro." To this day I haven't forgotten how all of a sudden he looked old and haggard, his cheeks hollow and his shoulders sunken. "You have only one life to live, Tokuro," my father said. "Cherish it. Don't die." He couldn't say anything else because if he had, he would have burst into tears. He turned his head around so that I wouldn't see his face. The day I left home was the last time I saw him. He passed away before I returned from Siberia in 1947.

'I understand that 420,000 boys volunteered for this programme. Some boys from families with many sons were forced to volunteer because the teachers told them to go in order to meet the quota the Army had assigned to each school. The numbers of the boy soldiers were four times the 100,000 university students who were drafted. We were given the choice of becoming sailors or aviation crew. I loved the idea of flying and joined the latter group. The sailors turned out to have worse luck than we. In 1944, a transport ship which left Moji Harbour with 2,500 boy sailors on board was sunk by an American submarine. The suicide boats the brave boys steered in the sea of Okinawa and the Philippines all perished like cheap toys.

'After a year and a half of training, I was assigned to Mito Airfield. One morning there was a massive American air-raid. My classmates were in a detached barrack, learning Morse code. I happened to be in another class. Right after the bombing, I went to the barracks with friends and found our classmates lying dead all over, their bodies chopped to pieces, heads with a receiver on, legs with boots on and hands clutching a pencil or a telegraph paper. We collected the body parts from the far corners of the room and matched the limbs with bodies and the arms with hands. We put eleven bodies together. They were all my good friends. Over breakfast a few hours before, we had been talking about our hometowns, talking about local food, a renowned sumo wrestler or a singer. We were homesick and talked about our families. The air-raid destroyed four hundred planes and killed a hundred and eighty personnel that morning.

'That was the day I realised the reality of the war for the first time. The romantic image of a brave soldier on a velvety horse I had kept all through my childhood was shattered. The war was not a cool thing. It was about killing each other and there was nothing beautiful about seeing guts exposed and heads cut off. I realised that boy soldiers like us had been collected as throw-away slippers.

'In April 1945, I was sent to Chanchun, Manchuria, and joined the 22nd Anti-aircraft Wireless Corps in the 2nd Army. I was assigned to work at a wireless station in the airport. Luckily, no active battles were being fought in the region. I went to China, naively believing that we would help and protect that backward nation so that we'd achieve the ideal of the Greater Asia. When we won the war, we'd cooperate with each other and make the whole region prosperous. What I saw there shocked me. I rode a bus with several soldiers in our troop. None of them bought a ticket, saying their troop would pay for it later. At a market, one started a conversation with a merchant, while others snatched his groceries away. I saw a soldier yelling and kicking a Manchurian Chinese who looked like a beggar.

'A soldier's life was sordid. Probably because there was no fighting to let out their pent-up energy, many spent their time hazing, bullying and lynching boy soldiers like us. On Sunday there was a queue in front of the comfort station. Almost all the upper rank soldiers seemed to be there waiting for their turn. I was sixteen and I did not feel right about it. "Why do I have to buy a woman?" I said to my leader. Immediately, he slapped me and shouted, "If you can't even buy a woman, how can you kill an enemy?" Then he laughed and gave me a condom. Those who didn't buy a woman were ostracised as weaklings. It required more courage not to buy. In the end I went. I felt terrible for the women who had been put up in a house worse than a jail.

'I was transferred to a few other cities. I was always assigned to wireless stations in airports and was getting better at it. No fighting was going on, but we were preparing for possible Soviet attacks. In 1941, the Soviet Union and Japan had signed a five-year Neutrality Treaty, but in April 1945, before the term was over, the Soviets declared that they would not observe the extension of the treaty. Therefore, an attack from them was a real threat. Urgent efforts had been made to build up defenses. Every available young man in Manchuria was drafted. Two hundred and fifty thousand of them became instant soldiers.

'But there were few arms or ammunition and I had to share a rifle with two other comrades. No aluminum canteens were available. We carried water in bamboo tubes. We had to wear straw sandals instead of leather shoes. The pilots were trained to fly toy-like gliders at the airport and were told to attack the Soviet bombers and fighter-planes with them. I wondered how it was possible to win the war.

'I understand that Stalin had secretly agreed with Roosevelt and Churchill to enter the war with Japan at the Yalta meeting a half year earlier. Stalin knew the war was about to finish. Jumping on the winning bandwagon and sharing trophies was not a bad idea. The Allies welcomed Stalin because the Soviet push would be the final blow to the Japanese.

'On 8 August the Soviets declared war against Japan.

'On 9 August people close to the border heard an ominous chorus of drones and looked up the sky. They saw something like black snakes swarming toward them. They were gigantic fighter planes and dropped thousands of bombs like hailstones all over Manchuria. On the same day in Chanchun, where I was stationed mammoth tanks were advancing in the main thoroughfare carrying Soviet flags with the picture of a hammer and sickle. At the same time the Communist Chinese troops were marching toward us. We tried futile retaliation by throwing grenades, but the whole city quickly turned into a scene of carnage.

'I learned later that the Soviets attacked us with 5,000 bombers and 5,000 tanks while we had 200 planes and 200 tanks. The number of Soviet troops was four times more than ours.

'On 17 August we were told that we had lost the war. Our headquarters were busy burning important documents and we were left alone to defend ourselves. We went to get food from our army warehouse where vengeful Manchurian mobs threw rocks at us. We were quickly rounded up by the Soviets. We had been taught that to be a prisoner of war was a deadly shame. A few soldiers had already killed themselves by taking potassium cyanide or pouring gasoline on themselves and setting it alight. The rest of us discussed what we should do. Some insisted on running away while they could. Others said they would resign themselves to the mercy of fate. In the end, five comrades walked away with meagre food and arms on their shoulders. Nobody saw them again. Soon the Russians soldiers called us: "Tokio Damoi, Skola Damoi." (Go home to Tokyo. Go home quickly.)

'We believed their words and jumped with joy. The war was over and finally we could go home! In my eyes I saw my father who had been anxiously waiting for me. Pretty soon I could really see him. I'd be a good son this time and help him out. The Russians took us to the railway station. But they betrayed us. The train went north instead of east. It stopped in Khabarovsk and turned west. It went over the river Amur and we were dropped off. Later I found out we were half way between Khabarovsk and Irkutsk, the city along Lake Baikal.

'It was 17 September 1945, and it happened to be my seventeenth birthday. It was already snowing. I did not know what kind of fate was waiting for me. I stood in front of the vast silver river and thought about my father again. I came to war in spite of his desperate objections. He was right. I should have listened to him. Now I told myself that no matter what I had to go through, I would survive and go home to see him. We were put in a Lagel, a prison. We were packed on three story bunk-beds like sardines in a tin. It was freezing with only a thin blanket to keep us warm. Some of those who slept in the lowest bed froze to death.

'Three hundred grams of black bread and four hundred grams of salt water called "soup" were the whole day's ration. Every day we were taken out to work unless it was below -38°C. On the days of snow storms diamond ice dust covered us. It was like walking in a vacuum. The man walking next to me was invisible and sound was muffled. We went to the forest and cut trees. When you touched a metal saw with bare hands, they froze and your skin peeled off. Some days we were assigned to building roads or railways or worked to reinforce the bank of the river. We worked all day without anything to eat because in the morning we couldn't resist eating the meagre bread, half of which was meant for lunch.

'We worked until dusk fell on the snow. Usually on the way back to the camp, acute fatigue and hunger would suddenly attack me. My whole body would feel frozen and wouldn't move. Then despair would grip me. Eventually I dragged along my heavy feet, crying and longing for my father. My limbs and ears were frostbitten. My left toe developed gangrene. With my friends' help, I had to cut part of it off with a knife.

'In the forest we put thin wire into the holes of pine trees, scooped bugs and caterpillars and ate them. They were sweet. We nibbled at leather off our shoes. I cut my belt in half and ate it. We cut a few inches off the sleeves and hems of our overcoat and exchanged them for bread at the market. For poor Russian farmers, a few square centimetres of wool were precious. We were happy when our comrades were sick because it meant that the rest of us could share their food. When someone died, we stripped his clothes and shoes off and put them on ourselves, saying that they were his keepsakes.

'My good friend became delirious with fever. He suddenly sat up and said, "I see a boat coming. I can go home and see my mother. I can drink miso soup." Then he fell back on the bed and died. Because we were working at a wood factory, the Russian supervisors allowed us to make a small coffin for him. We had to cut his limbs off with an axe in order to fit him in the small casket.

'Pretty soon there were too many to bury. We just carried the bodies on a carriage, a sled or a hastily built stretcher. Oh, how light the bodies were! Everyday, there was a funeral procession. We just walked silently and tears instantly froze on our cheeks. We first burnt branches to melt the frozen earth, but the earth was frozen solid two metres underground. It took a whole day for several of us to dig a hole. In the end the naked body had to be buried in a shallow bed. We left them after we put our hands together and prayed. In spring when the snow had melted, we went back there, but found nothing left. Even the ones inside the casket were gone. Wolves or wild dogs had feasted on their remains.

'The war was over, but in this camp the military ranks still held sway. The Soviet authorities kept them to control order in the camp. Food was served first to the officers who took the biggest portion. NCOs like us had to eat the left-overs even though we were the ones who worked the hardest. The officers ordered us around to do chores like washing and cleaning. They made us observe the ridiculous military rituals such as getting up in the morning and bowing toward the east in the direction of the Emperor's palace. We decided to tell the officers to take off their insignia of rank. We had a meeting and suggested this gently to them, 'This place shouldn't be run by the military system any longer. If everyone takes off their badges of rank, this will be a democratic place.'

'A few officers agreed and removed the symbols of rank from their collars. The others were silent. "The Soviet authorities wanted to keep things as they were," a captain said, with his chin stuck up. One of the angry young soldiers who had a grudge against the captain walked up to him and ripped the badge off his collar. The others did the same to other officers and a mob scene developed. I tore off the insignia of a lieutenant who was haughty and a swaggerer.

'The Soviet guards saw this and reported it to the authorities. To our disappointment they cracked down on our efforts. The officers got golden badges back on their collars and triumphant looks on their faces.

'After a third riot, the badges were permanently removed from the officers' uniforms. This improved the situation a little. But then the Soviets decided to take advantage of the rebellious energy of the young men like us. They tried to brainwash us for political purposes. They organised classes and taught us Communism. Some young men became passionate Communists. The Soviets wanted these "Actives" to proselytise Communism in Japan when we returned home.

'A newspaper *Nihon Shimbun* was published three times a week at the suggestion of the Soviets. Having been thirsty for any news and even for just seeing printed words, we read it voraciously. The editor was a Russian, but there were fifty Japanese staff working on it. The paper reported international news from the Soviet point of view. There were a lot of articles criticising the Emperor and militarism, denigrating capitalism and glorifying communism.

'At first, I thought some of the articles were enlightening. The idea of Communism was refreshing to me as I had grown up learning only about militarism. But some of the propaganda turned me off. The final blow came when they told us to send a letter to Stalin which was nothing but shameless flattery and adulation. It said something like: "Thank you, Mr Stalin, for liberating us Japanese from the misery of the war and from the evil of burglar warmongers! We are forever grateful to you, Mr Stalin, for teaching us the joy of work! You are our ultimate hero."

'I said that I would be the last person to sign the letter. Stalin killed 50,000 Japanese during six days of war and declared victory. He imprisoned 600,000 of us in 2,000 camps all over Siberia for his country's post-war industrial effort and made us work in terrible conditions with little food. Do we have to sign a letter to thank Stalin for all this?

'Luckily, I was one of the earliest who were allowed to return home. It was November 1947. I'm sure it was a random choice, or because of my young age. Some people had to stay for five or seven more years. The last ones came back eleven years later. Sixty-thousand of our colleagues never came back. They were buried under the snow of Siberia. If I had not gone home then, I would have been punished by the Aktives as a traitor. They captured those who were defiant 'reactionaries' and hauled them before a kangaroo court. Lots of the former officers were also severely tortured. Some were even beaten to death.

'On the returning ship I couldn't wait to see my father. How happy I would be to spend time with him. I would leave the memories of the terrible war behind once and for all and work hard to be somebody to make my father proud. I was still only nineteen and a bright future should be ahead of me. But when I finally reached my town in Tokyo, there was no sight of my house. It had been burned down in an American air-raid. And my father was nowhere to be seen. My sister told me that he had survived the war, but had died in a car accident just a year before I returned.

'My world turned black, I almost passed out. I squatted down on the ground where my house used to stand and cried like a child. As if that were not enough, I was told that my third brother had been killed near Okinawa, attacked by an American submarine, on the way to his mission in a human torpedo, *Kaiten*. He was eighteen.

'My country which had sent me to war as a boy soldier did not welcome me. I visited the junior high school from which I had not been graduated and asked what I could do to continue my education. They said that they would give a graduation certificate although I had missed the last academic year. But there was nothing else they could do. I had no money and could not afford tuition for high school or university. They would not accept me anyway unless I caught up to their academic level. My sister and brothers were kind, but they had little money to help me.

'I had to look for a job to survive. When I said I had been in Siberia, no one hired me. There was an invisible discrimination against the Siberia returnees which haunted all of us for more than ten years. Not only the Japanese police, but also the American Occupational Government kept an eye on me and came to my neighbourhood to ask people what political thoughts I had. When I went out at night, I often found a man following me. If I ever sang a Russian folk song or whistled its tune during work, I was fired instantly as a Communist. Only in 2009, did the government finally pass a law to pay a small token to the former Siberia detainees and publicly apologised for their past ill treatment.

'For many years I had only menial jobs such as delivering newspapers, an electric technician's helper or water sanitation work. Finally, after getting an accounting degree through correspondence courses and mastering the use of the computer, I became the head manager of a medical organisation and later head of the accounting department of a construction company.

'None of my siblings had an easy time, but somehow they managed to establish their careers after the war. My eldest brother, who had been sent to the Pacific islands during the war, became a businessman. My second brother, drafted in the student mobilisation, was assigned to the special attack plane *Tokko*, but he survived because he was a member of the ground crew. After the war, supporting himself as a doorman at a hotel, he studied medicine and became a doctor. My sister became a surgeon and later a professor at a medical school.

'The war robbed most men of my generation of something precious. Lots of us lost our dreams, if not our lives. In my case, I suffered so much from lack of education. I still read a lot and educate myself even if it's for nothing else but sheer joy. Our generation is dying out. Our era is ending. And yet I still haven't come to terms with it. I am angry at myself as well as at my country. Why did I make the wrong decision in spite of my father's objection? Wasn't it because of the education which painted war as something glorious and romantic? A fascist nation enticed young boys to the war and killed half of them. It did not help those who had returned. It punished them again by giving them no chance of education.

'Hopefully, nobody will ever be stupid enough to repeat these mistakes.

'It wasn't only men. Women also suffered. My wife had a big share of the hard times with me, but she was always courageous and positive. She raised two good sons. I pray she will rest in peace.'

Part Two

From War to Post-War

Did the Japanese Mourn?

My interviews with veterans brought to light the common experiences they had, no matter where they had been sent to fight. 'You can see why Japan lost the war, can't you?' Yasuji Kaneko said to me. 'The Japanese army had little respect for life.'

Indeed, that 'little respect for life' was the common thread woven through all the stories told by the veterans. That may not have been the only reason Japan lost the war, but the lack of respect for human life answered my question why the Japanese had waged so savage a war. Had they respected life more, the Geneva Convention would not have been ignored, peasants would not have been used for bayonet practice in China, and the lives of thousands of civilians in Nanjing would have been saved. American soldiers and Filipino civilians would not have been subjected to the Bataan Death March. Allied captives would not have been kept in inhuman conditions in POW camps.

The disrespect for human life also applied to Japan's own soldiers. The leaders told young men to go on suicide *Tokko* missions. They let student soldiers like Minoru Wada die in the *Kaiten* torpedo, a defective machine with a very low success rate. They lured boys, aged fourteen to eighteen, to war and used their lives as sacrificial pawns. They imposed a fanatical moral code on soldiers and even civilians: 'Kill yourself rather than surrender.'

Japan was over-ambitious and stretched the war to the far corners of the Pacific – the Aleutians in the north and the Solomon Islands and New Guinea in the south, as well as to India. Millions were sent without assured supplies of food and medicine. In the last year of the war, sixty per cent of the Japanese soldiers who perished did so due to starvation and disease rather than enemy action. Mismanagement – poor analysis of the situation and the failure to learn from earlier mistakes – led to the deaths of millions which could have been avoided if the men's lives had been a priority.

Japanese military training was meant to expunge soldiers' humanity and produce warriors who could kill without mercy. In training camps, recruits were hazed, bullied and tortured until they became killing machines. Soldiers were taught that the more enemies they killed, the greater contribution they would make for the Emperor.

Life's transience had been a theme of Japanese literature for a thousand years, repeated in images such as life being 'fleeting as a petal of a cherry blossom,' or 'a bubble in a stream.' The leaders used these phrases to encourage students to die gladly for the Emperor.

Prime Minister and General Hideki Tojo made a speech to thousands of students gathered at the Meiji Shrine before they left for war: 'Your blazing spirit, your youthful body and fresh blood are treasures of our nation. Dedicate all you have to our Emperor. Die for a great moral cause and you'll live to glorious eternity!'[29]

Why did the Japanese leaders glorify this sacrifice? It could be argued that notions of human rights had not been fully developed in Japan, as they were in Western countries at the time of World War II. Japan had been a feudal society until the middle of the nineteenth century, when Commodore Perry forced the nation to open its gates to the world. The Japanese made Herculean efforts to catch up with the West and within a short time it looked as if they had been successful. They set up a modern government, patterned on Western democracy, but their fundamental ideas of human rights required time to grow. When the Japanese leaders sought to achieve their grandiose dream of conquering Asia, they found it easy to trample on these budding concepts.

The Japanese soldiers in Part One of this book had the bad fortune to come of age during the war years. They had no choice but to accept their fate and go to war. Some of them beat the odds and survived, but the soldiers of the lost war were not welcomed back home. The country was eager to close the book on that ignominious

29 Tojo's speech given at the Meiji Shrine to the student soldiers, *The Evening Asahi*, 21 October 1943, and in Hanto, Kazutoshi, *History of Showa, 1926–1945*, Heibon-sha, 2004, p. 419

chapter in its history. The veterans kept their mouths shut about what they had done and seen. Some leaders and top generals were convicted of war crimes and executed. The Emperor was spared criminal prosecution. There were public debates about his responsibility for the war and the possibility of abdication was discussed even among his entourage and the nationalists, but Hirohito never indicated his willingness to consider his role.

In the meantime, thousands of foot soldiers had been convicted as war criminals in tribunals abroad. The public was sympathetic to those such as Susumu Iida, who had been convicted abroad and brought to Sugamo Prison. The Parole for War Criminals Movement, made the government pardon Sugamo detainees by the end of 1958. The problem was that people barely questioned what crimes these convicts had committed, nor did they think about the suffering and death that they and other soldiers had brought to many millions abroad.

In the 1950s, the novel *Human Conditions*, by Jumpei Gomikawa,[30] was a best-seller. Later on, it was made into an epic film trilogy. It was the first serious attempt to confess and reflect on the atrocities committed by the Japanese in Manchuria. Despite this, most soldiers were still reluctant to talk about their own part in the war and most civilians were not aware of atrocities that had been committed abroad. Trying to forget the past, people worked tirelessly to rebuild their country and became successful economic animals.

Psychologist Masaaki Noda argued in *War and Guilt*[31] that after the war the Japanese lost the ability to grieve. In his words: 'We as a nation have forsaken responsibility for our actions during the war.'

He recalled a spring night in 1985, when he emerged from the Ginza subway station in Tokyo and found himself among thousands of people walking with lanterns and flags on the street: 'Seeing this parade, I could not figure out when and where I was. Were they celebrating a national gymnastic event, or was I watching a military parade in a pre-

30 Gomikawa, Jumpei, *Ningen no Joken* (Human Condition), Iwanami Shoten, Tokyo, 1956
31 Noda, Masaaki, *Senso to Zaiseki* (War and Guilt), Iwanami Shoten, Tokyo, 1998

war film with a pompous announcer shouting in a dark theatre? The red circles of flags and the lights of lanterns flickered in front of me like will-o'-the-wisps.'[32] It was a parade celebrating the sixtieth year of Showa, Emperor Hirohito's reign, and people looked euphoric. One said, "There was a war and hard times, but as a whole, Showa has been a good era." The reality of the war seemed to have been forgotten. People seemed to be intoxicated by a shallow happiness brought on by material success . . . '[33]

A German friend once said to me: 'After the war we did soul-searching and went into mourning. The whole nation apologised to the Jewish people in the world for what we had done. It was a voluntary act, but also a political one. Our national border touches eight other European nations. We had no choice but to apologise in order to be accepted by the neighbours.' Living in an island nation, the Japanese had no daily contact with the people they had hurt.

I visited Japan with my American husband around that time. Japan's prosperity was at its height. 'People in Japan seem to be always smiling and laughing,' he said to me. It was true. People looked oblivious of the fact that they had fought a war not long before. I felt as if materialism and an easygoing attitude had replaced the spiritualism that had been the backbone of wartime discipline in Japan.

But the real explanation of the Japanese attitude is probably more multi-faceted. The public was relatively happy, not just because they were suddenly richer, but also because democracy, freedom of thought, the growth of the middle class and social equality had transformed post-war Japan.

However, the economic bubble which had been created from 1980 onwards, when real estate and stock prices were greatly inflated, began to deflate in 1990. The subsequent decline lasted for more than a decade. Many businesses failed and the number of suicides increased. People began soul-searching and reflection. It was probably not a coincidence that the issues of the war they had tucked away for a long time came up again at such a time.

32 Noda, ibid., pp. 3–4
33 Noda, ibid., pp. 6–7

One event that forced the Japanese to reflect on the war was the court case of a prominent historian, Saburo Ienaga.[34] The trials, which would eventually number ten, would last for thirty-two years.

During the war, Ienaga had been a high school teacher. He taught war propaganda and the imperial divinity myth to students who would be sent to the front. Though opposed to the war, he knew he would be incarcerated or killed if he did not do as the government had instructed. After the war, he wrote a history textbook that discussed the 1937 Nanjing Massacre and the experiments carried on by Unit 731. Ienaga was told by the Japanese Ministry of Education to make 200 revisions to his text. He refused, and in 1965 launched his first lawsuit against the Ministry, contending that it should not have the right to screen all textbooks.

The lawsuits Ienaga brought against the Ministry were a crusade motivated by wartime guilt, but also by his desire that the public realise the truth about the war. Although he could not get his books adopted by schools for many years, he drew attention to their contents through his lawsuits; his stubborn campaign for the right of free speech won him national and international acclaim. In 1982, the Ministry's right to screen textbooks became a diplomatic issue when the media in Japan and neighbouring nations gave extensive coverage to the changes that Ienaga had been ordered to make. In 1990, pressure on the Education Ministry prompted a reform of the textbook screening process, and it is now more transparent, though no less controversial.

Another case, brought by a Korean woman, Kim Hak-Soon, in 1990, also attracted public attention and helped raise awareness about hidden and unresolved war issues. Introducing herself in public as a 'comfort woman' for Japanese soldiers during the war, she brought lawsuits against the Japanese Government and asked for an apology and compensation for all Korean victims like her. Yasuji Kaneko testified on behalf of the women and apologised to them.

34 Ienaga, Saburo, *The Pacific War: 1931–45*, Pantheon Asia Library, 1979
  Ienaga, Saburo, *Senso Sekinin* (War Responsibilty), Iwanami Shoten, Tokyo, 1985, and
  Ienaga, Saburo, *Japan's Past, Japan's Future: One Historian's Odyssey*, New York, Rowman and Littlefield, 2001

Also coming forward to claim compensation were Taiwanese and Korean men, including Lee Hanne. The government's stock response – 'The case has already been dealt with in the San Francisco Treaty' – and the rejection of the plaintiffs' claims upset many Japanese. Such cases gradually made some Japanese realise that their country had been the perpetrator of the war rather than its victim.

The dispute over the Emperor's war responsibility has never died down. Although he tried to avoid war, once it started, the documents show that he was not a puppet of military leaders, nor the passive, reluctant monarch that he and his protectors claimed, but a strong supreme commander of the Imperial Army and Navy who actively participated in daily discussions about the war, played a decisive role in operations, and in whose name every important order was given.[35] For instance, on 5 November 1941, the Commanding General had showed him the plans for Pearl Harbour. Without his approval, the attack would not have been carried out.[36]

In Japan, Emperor worship was so deeply ingrained in people's psyche that many were afraid of criticising him, but there were some who said that he had a moral obligation to the soldiers who had died for him, and the millions of people to whom he had brought tragedy. A number of the ex-soldiers who appeared in Part One expressed doubt, anger and disappointment about the Emperor.

Herbert P. Bix, in his groundbreaking biography, *Hirohito*, wrote that a major concern of his book was 'Hirohito's failure to publicly acknowledge his moral, political and legal accountability for the long war fought in his name and under his active direction.'[37] He also says that 'Hirohito became the prime symbol of his people's repression of their wartime past. For, as long as they did not pursue his central role in the war, they did not have to question their own.'[38]

35 e.g. *The Diary of Kido Koichi*, University of Tokyo Press, 1966
36 Yoshida, Yutaka, *Japanese View of the War: Change in the Post-war History*, Gendai Bunko, Tokyo, 2005, pp. 200–201
37 Bix, Herbert P., *Hirohito and the Making of Modern Japan*, HarperCollins, 2000, p. 16
38 ibid., p. 17

Japan has come under worldwide criticism for not expressing apologies for the war. In fact, Japanese prime ministers repeatedly expressed their remorse and offered apologies to individual countries such as Burma, Australia, Korea and China since the 1950s, but much too tentatively and inadequately in view of the enormity of the tragedies that the war had brought to the people of those countries.

Although Prime Minister Yasuhiro Nakasone visited Yasukumi Shrine, he later changed his view of the War and made a statement in 1986 saying that it 'was a war of aggression.'

At the annual war memorial service in August 1993, the newly elected Prime Minister, Morihiro Hosokawa said that World War II was a 'war of aggression' and 'a mistaken war'. He expressed responsibility and condolences to the war victims and survivors in Japan, its Asian neighbours, and the rest of the world.

Prime Minister Tomiichi Murayama issued the following statement two years later, on the occasion of the fiftieth anniversary of the war's end: ' . . . During a certain period in the not too distant past, Japan, following a mistaken national policy, advanced along the road to war, only to snare the Japanese people in a fateful crisis, and, through its colonial rule and aggression, cause tremendous damage and suffering to the people of many countries, particularly to those of Asian nations. In the hope that no such mistake be made in the future, I regret, in a spirit of humanity, those irrefutable facts of history, and express here once again my feelings of deep remorse and state my heartfelt apology. Allow me also to express my feelings of profound mourning for all the victims, both at home and abroad, of that history . . . '[39]

In the 1980s and the early 1990s, a time of unprecedented economic prosperity for Japan, the government might have felt that a show of remorse was politically necessary in order to appease the ill-feelings that people of the former enemy countries still carried against Japan. At the same time, the statements made by Prime Ministers Hosokawa

39 Ministry of Foreign Affairs of Japan: Statement by Prime Minister Tomiichi Murayama on the occasion of the fiftieth anniversary of the war's end, 15 August 1995, http://www.mofa.go.jp/

and Murayama also coincided with a growing awareness among the Japanese about the war and its consequences.

While writers, historians, artists, journalists and educators expressed their reflections on what the country had done during the war, some became openly defensive, proclaiming that Japan fought a war out of economic necessity and for self-defense against Western threats, although it wasn't clear how the invasion of China could be explained as self-defense.

In 1996, a group of nationalists, counting conservative politicians and scholars among its members, got together and wrote a revisionist history textbook. They argued that history taught to the children of the post-war generation had been too critical of their nation. They said that the children should be proud of their heritage. Currently, all Yokohama schools are using revisionist textbooks due to the decision of the Yokohama Education Board. Four per cent of schools in Japan use these texts.

And yet, until recently, testimony of old soldiers, research by historians, and work by artists have done much to dispel the revisionists' efforts. The media has also helped people's awareness. NHK, the national broadcasting company, ran a television series of interviews with veterans for several years and there has been extensive coverage of the war's legacy in newspapers.

An *Asahi Newspaper* editor, Yoichi Jomaru, ran a series of articles in 2010, called 'Passing on the Recollections of the Battlefield,' in which he wrote about dozens of people, young and old, whose lives had been disrupted or destroyed by the war. He wrote a postscript after he finished the series:

After the war, many Japanese wrote about it, but the majority of them talked about their experiences as if they had been the victims of natural disasters. The soldiers who were detained in Siberia described the misery and the hardship they had suffered, but they did not write what they had done in Manchuria during the war.

. . . Often the Japanese were only sorry for their countrymen's deaths. How much imagination and sympathy did we expend on the peasants who were killed for murder training?

Probably this is not only a Japanese problem, but a universal one. I wonder how many Americans really lamented the Japanese who had been killed by the atomic bombs. But that does not excuse us from caring for the victims of Japanese atrocities.[40]

However, the Japanese political climate has moved sharply to the right since the current Prime Minister Shinzo Abe, who maintains a nationalistic view of the war, took office in 2012. The emboldened nationalists rally round him and support his aggressive agenda. The revisionists' strident voices are destroying the healing process Japan has gradually brought about with Korea and China after the war.

In the first several decades after the war, most Japanese rejected the nationalists who tried to whitewash history. But they gradually gathered force as the soldiers died away and the pains of war receded in memory. The new generations who had no experience of war and had not been taught much about it are now taking centre stage. The revisionists' theories that the Japanese fought the war for self-defense and that their grandfathers did not commit atrocities sound sweet to their ears. The society which had not done enough soul-searching after the war and did not educate its children to the true facts is now paying the price.

The theme of Part Two of this book is 'Did the Japanese Mourn?' I interviewed people from the post-war generations to find out how they have coped with the legacy of the war. Some young Japanese seem to consider the war just as a chapter in a history book. When I brought up the topic of war, conversation stopped. After a long silence, someone might say: 'I heard it was a difficult time. My grandparents' house was burned. I have a distant relative who died in Hiroshima.' They mentioned the sufferings of their own family, but seldom talked about the tragedies our country had caused to other people.

But I found many people, especially those whose fathers had fought in the war, grieved indeed. Sons and daughters suffered for their father's sins as well as their death or the nation's defeat. Some of them even travelled overseas to apologise to the victims' families and friends.

40 *Quarterly Chu-ki-ren*, #49, Postscript to 'Passing on the Recollections of the Battlefield', January, 2012

The earliest reconciliation efforts were made by the soldiers themselves. 'China Returnees' Association, (*Chu-Ki-Ren*)' was organised by the former inmates of Fushun War-Criminals' Camp, such as Yasuji Kaneko. They have devoted themselves to telling the truth of the war in public. Some groups were organised by the post-war generations in an attempt to help heal the wounds of the war and reconcile with former enemies. Organisations such as 'POW Research Group' (Chapter 12) have helped the former Allied POWs and their families, 'Women's Active Museum on War and Peace' (Chapter 13) has been dealing with 'comfort women'. 'Bridge for Peace' has been working for reconciliation between the Philippines and Japan. These groups were mostly founded in the 1990s or later.

It should be noted that many of these organisations were created, and are being run, by women. Women seem to be the conscience of Japanese society when it comes to war issues. Part of the reason perhaps is that women do not mind working for non-profit organisations. Men who engage in this kind of reconciliation activities are likely to be part-time volunteers or retired people. It was heart-warming to find out that although Japan as a nation has been unrepentant about the war, at a grass-roots level, so many are making positive efforts of reconciliation.

CHAPTER 10

Chu-ki-ren
(China Returnees' Association)
War Criminals Mourn Their Actions

In 1957, *Chu-ki-ren* was set up by the former soldiers who had returned to Japan from the Chinese war criminals' camp. Right after the war, they had been taken to Siberia and detained there for five years. They had rejoiced when the Soviets cried out, 'Damoi', and put them on trains. But the train station where they got off was Fushun, China, and they were taken straight to a war criminals' prison. They were to stay there for another six years. It was not clear why these 969 prisoners had been chosen to be taken to China out of the 600,000 Japanese who had been kept in Russia. While some of them such as the high officials in Manchuria and the Army commanders, could be deemed war criminals, there were others who were only first year recruits and had hardly fought on the battlefield.

In surprising contrast to the Russian camps, however, they were given no work to do and were well fed as if they had been special guests (as Yasuji Kaneko described in Chapter 1). The prison guards, whose parents or relatives had been abused or killed by the *dong-yang-qui*, Devils from the East, held back their anger and acted like saints. Seeing this, the *dong-yang-qui* reflected on their own activities and regained their humanity. They were remorseful by the time they were released and allowed to go back to Japan in 1956, eleven years after the war.

They formed *Chu-ki-ren*, originally to ask the government for financial help. But they decided that the purpose of their association was to pursue reflection on their conduct and to tell the public about their experiences in order to contribute to peace and friendship between China and Japan. In post-war Japan they played an important role in testifying to the truth of the war and informing the people who had not known what kind of war had been fought abroad. The following are examples of the testimony of the *Chu-ki-ren* members. Unlike most veterans, who kept their mouths shut about the war, the *Chu-ki-ren* members had the enormous courage to tell the truth in public, jeopardising their integrity and reputation. Since these veterans are deceased, I owe their stories to the books and articles written about them, which are listed at the end of this book.

Ken Yuasa, a doctor who conducted vivisections:

Ken Yuasa was born in Tokyo in 1916. Following in his father's footsteps, he became a doctor. He hoped to have a rural practice traveling to remote villages to treat patients. But it was 1942. He was drafted and deployed to Changzhi (then Luan) in Shanxi Province, China. Within six weeks, he was conducting vivisections of prisoners.

Two Chinese farmers were brought in, one stoically calm, the other, screaming and trembling. They were handcuffed to operating tables. The room was hushed as gas anesthetised the prisoners. With nurses assisting, twenty doctors took turns practicing incisions on various parts of the bodies. After three hours, the mutilated bodies were dumped in a hole near the hospital.

Yuasa was nervous during the course of the first vivisection, but by the third, he was a willing participant. Under a secret order of the Japanese North China Army, doctors were trained in vivisection practice twice a year in each Division. During his three years' service, Yuasa participated in the killing of fourteen men in such sessions. He also provided dysentery and typhoid bacillus strains for use by Unit 731 of the Japanese Forces.

Although the war ended on 15 August 1945, Chang Kai-shek kept fighting against the Communist Army and hired several thousand Japanese soldiers and technicians in Taiyuan, Shanxi, where Yuasa was stationed. He decided to stay on and helped treat soldiers in a hospital. Eventually, he married a local girl and had two children. In April 1949, when Taiyuan finally fell to the Communists, most Japanese returned to Japan. But Yuasa stayed on at the same hospital, treating Chinese patients and giving lectures to their doctors.

One day in 1951, without any warning, Yuasa and his family were put on a truck and taken to a local prison. Yuasa did not comprehend what he had done to deserve this, as he had no sense of guilt. 'I thought that Dr Shiro Ishii of Unit 731, who had masterminded biological warfare and vivisections was bad, but we ordinary doctors faithfully obeyed the orders from above which were absolute.'

At the end of 1952, Dr Yuasa and 142 other Japanese were moved to the Taiyuan War Criminals' Prison. The prisoners were treated in the same humane way as those in the Fushun Prison. Dr Yuasa was even paid for treating patients in prison. Advisors suggested the prisoners should confess to the crimes they had committed during the war. Yuasa wrote about the vivisections he had conducted although he still insisted that he was only fulfilling his military duties. His advisor rejected Yuasa's confession as being based on insufficient reflection.

Six months later Dr Yuasa fell ill with TB. The Chinese doctors took good care of him with the newly discovered antibiotic they had acquired from the Soviet Union. As Yuasa was recovering from TB, he received a letter from the mother of a vivisection victim:

'I am the mother of a son who was murdered by you. One day my son was taken by a *Kempei*. I went to the *Kempeitai* office and stood in front of the gate all day. The next day the gate was suddenly opened and I saw my son tied up with rope, being hoisted on a truck and driven away. I ran as fast as I could, but with my bound feet I quickly lost sight of the truck. I looked all over, but he was nowhere to be found. The following day an acquaintance told me: "Your son was taken to the Army Hospital and a Japanese doctor murdered him."

'I was so sad and angry I almost died. I didn't feel like eating. I couldn't till my field as I used to any more. I heard you had been incarcerated. I just asked the government to give you the harshest punishment possible.'

Yuasa couldn't hold back his tears when he read the letter. He had been trained to see a patient as a body on an operating table. He didn't even remember this man's face because he made it a practice not to see the face so as not to feel sympathy. But as he read this letter, it came home to him that he had deprived a precious human being of life. It also dawned on him that he was to blame for killing the man whether it was an order from the Army or not. He was the murderer. He was ready and willing to receive the harshest punishment. But in June 1956, the Communist Government suspended an indictment for Dr Yuasa and most of his fellow prisoners. Yuasa came back to Japan after fourteen years.

After being treated in Tokyo for the TB which had not yet been cured, Yuasa worked at a clinic there for the rest of his life. He joined Chu-ki-ren, and talked about his vivisections and biological warfare in classrooms and public halls all over the country. He said, 'Wars turn men into devils, not just madmen, but anyone. People must realise it. I have to tell everyone in Japan never to start a war.'

Up until then none of his former colleagues had spoken out in public about the vivisections. One of them sent a letter to Yuasa saying that he felt threatened since. He now had a guilty conscience, which before had been successfully suppressed. An anonymous letter criticised Yuasa for exposing skeletons in closets. But his brother, a year older and practicing medicine in Hokkaido after the war, praised Ken for his courage in telling the truth. The brother had been feeling sad about his own experience in the war. He understood what Ken had gone through. 'I went back to China three times this year,' he wrote. 'Something takes me back there again and again. It is my ardent wish to see China recover from the devastation we caused. I bought a camera and took pictures of beautiful natural scenery there. I did so with a feeling of atonement . . . I've ordered more of your books today. I'd like my daughter, her husband and their son to read your book as a Bible.'

Yuasa stopped practicing medicine at the age of eighty-four, but kept telling his story until the end of his life. 'I should have been sentenced to death sixty years ago. I was allowed to live, but it didn't mean my sin was forgiven. I have to tell the younger generation not to make the mistakes our generation made.' He died in 2010 at the age of ninety-four.

Yoshio Tsuchiya

Former *Kempei* Yoshio Tsuchiya tortured and killed 328 Chinese. A son of a peasant, he was a gentle boy who saved worms when he tilled the soil. In 1931 he joined the Army and went to China. In 1936, when

Lance-Corporal Tsuchiya was stationed in Qiqihar, he captured the family of Zhang Huimin who was making radio contact with the Soviets. Tsuchiya tried to work with Zhang's family, but Zhang would never confess his spying activities. Eight members of the family were shot by Qiqihar *Kempeitai*.

Humane treatment in Fushun prison made Tsuchiya a new person. After returning to Japan, he actively worked for *Chu-ki-ren*, but he was still so troubled that he had to do something more to atone. In 1990, he went back to China and visited the Zhang family's grave. He kneeled down in front of Zhang Huimin's grave stone and said: 'I am Yoshio Tsuchiya, the man who murdered you and your brother as well as six of your family fifty-four years ago. I am truly sorry.'

Tsuchiya insisted on seeing the remaining members of Huimin's family. Zhang's fourth daughter, Quiyue, agreed to meet him. She said to Tsuchiya, 'Life was difficult after my father was murdered. A few years later, my mother died of overwork and starvation. I started to work in a factory when I was eight . . . ' Tsuchiya bowed on his hands and knees, and apologised, crying. When Tsuchiya was about to leave the room, Quiyue took his hand. That was more than Tsuchiya expected her to do for him.

Yutaka Mio

In another case, the victim's son forgave his father's murderer, Yutaka Mio, and the enemies became best friends. Yutaka Mio was a *Kempei* in Dalian in 1943 when a radio message sent from the city of Dalian to the Soviets was intercepted. The Dalian *Kempeitai* captured the sender of the message, a Korean anti-Japanese activist, Shen De Long. A wealthy entrepreneur, Wang Yao Xuan had provided the funds for the operation. Sergeant Mio was ordered to find Wang who was hiding. He captured Wang in Tien-jin and took him and his group to Dalian *Kempeitai* station.

The captives were first tortured by waterboarding. Then they were classified as 'special categories,' which meant they would be sent to the 731 Unit. Mio had no idea what that unit had done to make it so notorious, except that those who had been sent to it never came out alive. Only after the war, Mio was told that political criminals and notable POWs were sent to this unit and used for medical experiments. Mio took the group – Shen De Long, Wang Yao Xuan and two others – to Harbin and handed them over to the 731 Unit. Until Mio was put in Fushun prison and asked to reflect on his conduct during the war, he did not think he was responsible for the fate of the four men. True, Mio was the one who put handcuffs on Wang, but he was just performing his duty. He did not kill them. But in the process of reflection, he began to realise that he had played a major role in their murder.

In the summer of 1995, Mio attended the International Symposium on Unit 731 held in Harbin. Wang Yao Xuan's son, Wang Bing, was also there. One evening during the conference, Mio went to see Wang and apologised to him for his father's death. They talked for almost two hours. Shaking with rage, Wang accused Mio: 'You are the murderer. If you hadn't captured him and taken him to the Unit, my father wouldn't have died . . . ' Mio was eighty-one and had just had a cancer operation. Fragile and in pain, he stood in front of Wang during the entire time. Tears flooding his eyes, Mio apologised to Wang many times.

In 1997, Mio testified as a plaintiff's witness in the lawsuits of ten Chinese war victims and their families, including Wang Bing, that had been brought against the Japanese government asking for compensation of 100 million yen. Mr Mio testified that he took the plaintiff's family to 731 Unit and said, 'By invading China, Japan brought unfathomable tragedies to its people. The Japanese government should apologise and compensate the victims.' He was the first Japanese soldier who testified in court in this series of lawsuits.

Mio was unhappy about the revisionists' denial of the Nanjing Massacre and the rewriting of textbooks. When *Chu-ki-ren* members decided to start a quarterly in 1997, *Chu-ki-ren*, Mio gave all his assets to the magazine. His busy life, testifying in court and launching a magazine was too much for an old man ravaged by cancer. Mio passed away in 1999 at the age of eighty-five. He said to Setsuko Kobayashi, who visited him in hospital twelve days before he died, 'In the other world, I will look for the people I sent to death and will apologise. I was happy I was able to meet some of the victims' families in this world.'

Soon after Mio's death a letter from Mr Wang arrived at *Chu-ki-ren*'s office. 'Please send my sincere condolence to Mr Mio's family . . . Over the years I and Mio Xian Sheng [a way to address someone one respects] from deadly enemies became closest friends. He reminds me of an old Chinese story about a man who discarded a deadly sword and became a Buddha. Mio Xian Sheng! Please rest in peace.'

Shin-ichiro Kumagai

Shin-ichiro Kumagai was born in 1976. He grew up in economically booming Japan where the war had become a forgotten chapter in history. One day a friend of his showed him the quarterly, *Chu-ki-ren*. 'I was very much moved by what had happened in Fushun Prison. The story of the rebirth of the war criminals made me regain my belief in humanity which I had almost lost through reading about the Nanjing Massacre and biological warfare by Unit 731. I called up the *Chu-ki-ren* office right away and Yasuji Kaneko answered the phone. It was the beginning of my lifetime commitment to this group and the magazine.'

Kumagai thinks that one cannot underestimate the impact the magazine had on the public. It had only about a thousand subscribing members, but the quarterly had broadening ripples of influence like a little stone dropped in a pond. It brought up all the issues of the war hitherto hidden or reluctant to be discussed – the Nanjing Massacre, comfort women, inside stories of the military system, and the anti-war activities by the Japanese POWs captured by the Chinese Communists.

In 2002, *Chu-ki-ren* wound up after forty-five years since so many of its members were passing away. But Mr Kumagai announced that the younger generation would found the *Uketsugu-Kai* – 'a group to pass down'. Although a busy man, with his job as an editor of a major publisher, he said he would continue its quarterly. 'We are determined to keep the legacy of *Chu-ki-ren* and pass it down to posterity,' Mr Kumagai said. 'The self-examination and sincere reflection for war crimes voiced by the Fushun and the Taiyuan returnees was what the whole nation should have been doing after the war.'

Michiyo Arakawa

Michiyo Arakawa, another editor of the renewed *Chu-ki-ren*, is just as dedicated to the group as Mr Kumagai. She is so youthful and gentle-looking that one wonders why she is interested in old war issues. 'Once I read a book called *Travel to China*, written by Katsuichi Honda. This was a collection of interviews with Chinese victims of war. They were ordinary citizens and what they had gone through was so horrific that I often closed the book and couldn't go on. The book opened my eyes to the shocking reality of war. Then I read *Chu-ki-ren* and found myself emotionally involved in it. The editor-in-chief, Mr Kumagai, invited me to do interviews with old soldiers. I started to work for the quarterly.'

Ms. Arakawa has a keen sense of justice. She is the kind of person who cannot just be sitting on a couch when she sees something wrong. She goes out of her way to make friends with the mistreated in the world. Before she joined *Chu-ki-ren*, she worked as a staff member of a group to protect children from violence. This is also clear from the story she told me about how she became a good friend of an eighty-one-year-old Chinese woman, Xia Shuqin.

Xia's mother and sisters were raped and killed by Japanese soldiers in Nanjing in 1937. A professor in Tokyo wrote in his book that Xia was a false witness of the incident. Xia filed a suit against him. Ms Arakawa, although busy with helping in another law case and other work she did with her husband to make a living, went twice to Nanjing to get to know Xia. Finding her frail, distraught and full of sadness, Ms Arakawa was determined to help her.

When Xia came to Japan for her court hearings, Ms Arakawa accompanied her everywhere, hand in hand. She was able to protect Xia when a right-wing group shouted at her outside the courthouse. 'We became fast friends, calling each other sister,' Michiyo-san says. 'I jumped with joy and hugged Xia each time she won a stage of her case. She won it all the way through the Supreme Court.'

Michiyo-san talks about the future of the quarterly. 'Since the war-time generation is passing away, it is facing a question how to pursue its course toward the future. We'll pass on the legacy of the brave veterans to the younger generation, but we will also discuss today's issues such as wars which are happening all over the world and discuss the new relationship with China. We hope that this magazine will always reflect the conscience of this country.'

CHAPTER 11

Osamu Komai

The Son of a War Criminal Visits England to Apologise

Osamu Komai's father, Mitsuo Komai, was hanged after the war at Changi Jail in Singapore. Osamu grew up bearing a cross as 'the son of a war criminal'. After retracing the steps that led his father to a death sentence, he visited Eric Lomax, the author of *The Railway Man*, in England and apologised for his father's sins. Osamu's father was a vice warden at a branch of the Thai-Burma railway POW camp. When a radio was discovered in Lomax's hut, Mitsuo Komai and his men beat two of Lomax's colleagues to death and left him with severe wounds. After the war Lomax reported to the British Authority that Mitsuo Komai was the culprit and advised them to put him on trial.

Readers of *The Railway Man* may remember that the interpreter Takashi Nagase, rather than Komai, was Lomax's archenemy. 'Verbal abuse was even harder for me to bear than physical. I spent longer hours with Nagase face to face,' Eric said to me when I went to interview him at his home in Berwick-upon-Tweed for my book about POWs, *Even So I Survived*. The story of Eric's hatred for Nagase and their ultimate reconciliation was the main theme of the latter half of *The Railway Man*, but it took a long time – more than fifty years – before Eric ever thought of forgiving Nagase.

Nagase realised the extent of the cruelty of the Japanese when he joined the Allies' search group for abandoned graves along the railway after the war. He became a Buddhist and devoted his life to atoning for the sins of his countrymen. He visited Thailand several times a year (135 times in all), funded the education of Asian children, gave scholarships to young people who entered medical and nursing schools, constructed Buddhist temples and made friends with local people.[41]

Nagase eventually convinced Eric to meet him on the bridge over the River Kwai. He also invited Eric to Japan. Eric wrote at the end of his book: 'Meeting Nagase has turned him from a hated enemy, with whom friendship would have been unthinkable, into a blood-brother.' At the end of the book, he says, 'Sometime the hating has to stop.'

Osamu Komai read the translation of *The Railway Man*,[42] in which his father was mentioned. He also read the books written by Nagase. He wrote a letter to Lomax and asked Nagase to send it so that Komai could visit and apologise to Lomax in England. It took six years before he finally went to England to meet him. In the summer of 2007, I read in an English newspaper an article about Osamu Komai's visit with Eric Lomax. Osamu was seventy by then and Lomax, eighty-nine.

I met Mr Komai in Tokyo. He is an amiable man with a ready smile, but one could tell by the way he stands straight (the Japanese expression is, 'like a young bamboo cut fresh and sharp'), that he is a man of principle and speaks in a forthright way. 'I'm sorry for what my father has done,' he said in front of an audience who came to hear him talk. 'The Japanese military, unfortunately including my father, ignored the Geneva Convention and treated the POWs inhumanely. Under the name of War, they lost their conscience and did something shameful. It's still not too late. Let's apologise to the whole world for whatever we did wrong.'

But Mr Komai talked lovingly about his father. During the war Mitsuo wrote letters to his five-year-old son every week from the camp in Thailand. When Osamu was told that his father had been hanged as a war criminal, he thought that it must have been some kind of mistake. Osamu traced the life of his father to find out what had made him into a war criminal who had been given the death penalty.

'My father was born in 1904 to a shoemaking family in Morioka. He was a romantic youth who went to university to read literature.

41 Mitsuda, Yasuhiro, *Rainbow over the River Kwai: Takashi Nagase's Post-war Years*, Nashi-no-ki-sha, Tokyo, 2011
42 Lomax, Eric, *The Railway Man*, Vintage, Great Britain, 1996

My shoemaker grandfather said to him, "How can you make a living writing poetry?" and stopped sending tuition money. So he went to another university to study economics. He dated my mother Yaeko, the daughter of a lunch shop owner, in the ruins of an old castle where they read poems together. Eventually they married. Theirs was a modern style of marriage for those days. They had four children, but two died young.

'My father worked for a big corporation, but had a year's sojourn at the Army cadet school. When he was drafted in 1939, he was sent to Korea as a second lieutenant. He was a reluctant soldier. According to my mother, before he left for the war the last time, he cried in front of her, saying, "I don't want to go to war." She asked him why. He said, "I have a premonition I'll die."

'The Noguchi Unit to which my father belonged recruited POW guards in Korea. My father trained these Korean civilian workers and took them to POW camps in Taiwan, French Indonesia, Singapore and Jakarta. In 1943, my father was sent to Thailand to help build the Thai-Burma railway. At a camp in Kanchanaburi he supervised 7,200 POWs with the help of 130 Korean guards and several Japanese soldiers. The 415 kilometre railway was completed within fourteen months in the harshest conditions imaginable. In Kanchanaburi, POWs were kept in several hundred bamboo huts. In one of them lived a group of eight British Royal Signal Officers who worked at a shop to repair machines and trains. One of them was Eric Lomax.

'In August 1943, a radio was discovered in their hut. The possession of a radio was considered a spy activity and strictly prohibited in the camp sites. Thew, an expert radio man, and other mechanically adept colleagues had collected scraps of material and managed to make a radio. Every evening after work, the men gathered around Thew's bed and listened to the news about the war. The news was relayed from hut to hut and spread to the whole community of POWs. It was the only source of information those prisoners received from the outside world. There was nothing which cheered up their morale more than hearing the news of the Allies gaining ground in the war.

After discovering the radio the Japanese were determined to give the harshest punishment to the men in the Signalmen's group. Each was kept in a cage as small as a kennel. The *Kempeitai* tortured them and my father, with the help of Korean guards, and beat them hundreds of times with pickaxe shafts.

' "Then I went down with a blow that shook every bone," Eric wrote in his book, "which released a sensation of scorching liquid pain which seared through my entire body." Sudden blows struck him all over and he felt himself plunging downwards into an abyss. When Eric came to, both his wrists were broken and the skin peeled from his back. The Dutch doctor who treated Eric and his group said that evening he counted 900 pickaxe strokes by the time the beating of Eric and his colleagues ended just before dawn.

'The next afternoon, another group of POWs were sent to the same place where Eric had been the previous night. They stood under the scorching sun all day. At about ten o'clock at night a squad of thugs went into action. Eric heard from his hospital bed "the dull sounds of wood on flesh, the roars and screams of anguish, and the shouts of the drunken NCOs." The next morning the doctor was allowed to go and see how the victims were doing. He found two of them dead. They were Captain Howley and Lieutenant Armitage, Eric's good friends. "My father was responsible for their deaths," Osamu Komai said. Right after the war, he was captured by British MPs. He was the first war criminal to be executed in Changi on 14 March 1946.

'During the war, our family moved from Osaka to my grandmother's home in Morioka to avoid the nightly air-raids. It was a small city in the North, but in no time American B29 bombers began visiting even this peaceful place. One night three incendiary bombs were dropped on our small house. It was burnt to the ground.

'On a hot day in August 1945, we gathered in the square where a radio was placed. Men listened to the Emperor speak with their heads hung low, but I heard women whisper, "Great! It's over!" My mother spoke into my ear with a smile, "Now Daddy will be back!" I was so excited that I jumped up in the air three times.

'I still keep my father's weekly letters from Thailand. There are eighty of them. In one letter, after congratulating me for getting into kindergarten, he wrote, "O-chan, last night I had a dream about you and it made me very happy. Please don't forget to give flowers and water to your brother." The last sentence referred to my brother, who had died of an illness at eleven. My father wanted me to keep his tombstone clean and to put flowers on it. Another letter says, "O-chan, I read your letter over and over again. Please write me again." My mother kept telling me to sit at a desk and write a letter to my father, but as a child, I hated to write. I wish I had sent him more letters. I hardly remembered his face, but I knew from those letters that he loved me dearly. I waited and waited for him to return.

'My friends' fathers came back from the war. I kept asking Mother, "When will Daddy be back?" She said, "Daddy is in a foreign land far away south. It'll take time for him to come back." Father never came home. A notice arrived on March 1946, a week after he was hanged. Soon after that my uncle came and said to me and my sister, "I'm going to announce something important to you today. Sit down there."

'Just as we sat down and were ready to listen to my uncle, my mother ran into the room, tears rolling down her cheeks, put her hand over her brother's mouth and screamed, "Stop. Brother, stop." "I got it," my uncle said calmly, and nothing more. I felt confused, but I kept quiet, thinking that something terrible must have happened to my father and he died because my mother had been crying every day.

'When I was alone with Mother, I asked her, "Did Daddy die an honourable death?" Even a seven-year-old kid like me knew those words, because the families who had lost their loved ones in the war proudly talked about their honorable death. Those words must have been the only consolation for them. When I asked the question, her face turned red and ferocious, and my mother shouted at me, "Stupid!" After that, my sister and I promised each other never to ask her about my father. I asked my relatives about him, but they quickly changed the subject. I tried not to think about him.

'Somehow or other, I eventually got the idea that my father was a war criminal and had been executed by the British. Since the Tokyo Tribunal had begun in 1946, it had become taboo to speak the words "war criminals". People only uttered those words in whispers behind your back. The term referred to the sinners who had not only committed atrocities but had also brought shame to the nation. My mother kept saying to me, "Osamu, be a good boy. Don't do anything to make people point fingers at you behind your back." She told me that those were the words my father wrote for me in prison just before his execution.

'Even though I tried to be a good boy and did not do anything shameful, people talked about me behind my back. Most of my mother's friends had abandoned her after finding out about her late husband. We had to move three times in the city because of icy treatment from the neighbours. Even when I learned at school about the meaning of war criminals, I didn't believe my father could have committed any war crimes. How could the man who had written such sweet letters to me do anything terrible? It must have been a mistake.

'In 1953, seven years after my father was executed, my mother passed away of an illness. I was in my first year in an engineering high school. When I was sorting out the stuff she had left in her drawer, I found a copy of a Japanese newspaper published in Singapore which reported the execution of my father in Changi.

My sister and I were orphans with no financial means. I worked my way through high school, but it was not possible to go to university. When I applied for a job, my teacher said to me, "If you are asked about your parents, don't tell them that your father was a war criminal. Tell them he died an honorable death in the war."

'It was none of his business, I thought. In my first job interview, when asked about my father, I said, "He was a war criminal." The teacher was right. I was not called back again. For the second interview, however, I gave the same answer. But this time they said, "I'm sorry to hear that. You must have had a hard time growing up." They gave me the job. I worked hard at the company. The president of the company liked me and introduced me to a nice woman, Yukiko. We married and had a daughter. For the first time, my life was shining with blessings. The cursed words which had been binding me with thorns – son of a war criminal – were a thing of the past.

'It did not mean that I had forgotten about my father. I've seen war films like *The Bridge on the River Kwai* and *Merry Christmas, Mr Lawrence*. I kept wondering what my father had done to deserve a death sentence. I attended the reunion of the Burma-Thai Railway

Unit. They welcomed me. Some shook hands with me and said, "You look exactly like your father." Others talked to me with tears in their eyes. I travelled with them to Singapore and visited my father's grave. I asked them, "Can you tell me what you know about my father's case?" They looked at each other, but no one was willing to tell me anything.

'Through the help of a parliament minister, I got hold of a copy of the Singapore Tribunals. I was staggered to read that my father had beaten two POWs to death and that he had abused and severely injured several others. I acquired the original British document of the BC class (officers and soldiers who had been tried in a local court) war criminals' trial records and it said that in the trial my father had admitted his crimes. It was a moment of truth, fifty-five years after the war. It was not a mistake. My father did commit war crimes. I cried, tracing his name with my finger on the death sentence written in English. What was he thinking at the moment of death? How sad he must have felt to die far away from home, leaving my mother, my sister, and me.

'But then the images of the British victims' families appeared in front of my blurred eyes. They must have waited for their sons' and husbands' return just as I had for my father. How did they feel when they were told that their loved ones had been beaten to death? I relived the victims' suffering and their families' mourning. My secret hatred against the British for my father's death was replaced by sorrow and guilt. I wished I could apologise to the families of the victims. I visited the cemetery for the soldiers of the British Commonwealth in Yokohama and prayed for those who might have died in similar circumstances in the Japanese camps.

'I visited Takashi Nagase, the man whom Lomax had passionately hated – possibly more than my father for some reason. He was the man Lomax had often thought of killing even fifty years after the war. But Nagase was Lomax's "blood brother" now after having gone through the long process of reconciliation. I talked to Nagase about my wish to visit Lomax and apologise to him for what my father had done to him and his friends. Nagase understood what I had gone through and agreed to send his friend a letter I'd written. I felt rejected by Eric's reply through Nagase. It said, "I'm wavering on the question.

I'm not ready to meet him yet. It took a long time before I finally agreed to see you, Nagase. It's a similar situation. You are saying that Osamu Komai looks exactly like his father. I am not sure whether I could welcome him with a smile when he appeared in front of me. I fear that the anger I have suppressed for sixty years might suddenly explode like a dormant volcano." In the end it took six years before I went to see Lomax in England, although the delay was also caused by a number of other reasons.

'Just before I left for England, Eric asked Nagase if I knew that it was Eric who had advised the British Authority that Mitsuo Komai should be hanged. "Even so, does Osamu Komai want to see me?" "I already knew that," was my answer. On a warm day in July, 2007, I travelled with Yukiko to Berwick-upon-Tweed in the north-east of England.

'When we exchanged greetings, Eric gazed at me with his pale, blue eyes and said, "You are a mirror image of your father." We drank tea in the living-room where Japanese wood-cut paintings hung on the wall. We went out in the garden full of flowers. There was a small pond with carp. Back in the room I was ill at ease communicating with Eric through an interpreter. I hesitated to bring up the subject for which I came all the way from the other side of the world. After a long suffocating silence, or so I felt, I gathered my courage and bowed my head down to my knees. "I sincerely apologise to you, Mr Lomax," I said, "on behalf of my father for what he did to you and to your friends."

'Eric looked pale, and stayed silent without responding to me for a period that felt like an eternity. Then he stood up, his face haggard and anguished, and said in a heavy voice which almost congealed my blood: "For me it is unthinkable for you to apologise to me. It is painful for me to accept your apology. I am the one who pointed a finger at your father and told the authorities to give him the death sentence. I told them to hang him as quickly as possible. I can't comprehend how a son wants to apologise to the man who has sent his father to death."

'He sat down, his face gentler now and his voice calmer. "I know you lost not only your father, but also your mother while you were young. Your mother must have suffered a lot," Eric said. "You had a hard time growing up as a child of a war criminal. I'm the one who brought grief to your whole family. It is extraordinary that you didn't hate or resent me. Instead you came all the way across the ocean to apologise. I really appreciate your coming here. But it is not necessary for a son to take responsibility for what his father has done."

'I did not come to England to ask Eric to forgive my father's sin, but I thought he might at least accept my apology. At least Eric was taking me seriously. He had been suffering a lot, too, though in a different way. Probably I had provoked his anguish by coming to him. But I told myself to think positively. Coming to see him had been necessary for me if not for him. At least he understood how I felt. Gradually, we were more relaxed and talked about things both of us were interested in such as trains, stamps, sumo and cycling. Eric and Patti suggested that Yukiko and I stay for one more night, but we had to catch a flight the next day. Before I left, Eric gave me a piece of paper on which the following words were written: "No matter how often you look back in the past, it won't change. Let us not cry for the past and live our present fully for the better future. That's what we should do now."

'I don't believe that my father was born an evil man,' Osamu Komai said. 'After reading numerous books about Japanese soldiers, I tend to believe that so many of them, particularly weak minded ones, turned into monsters because of a shamefully inhuman military system. Their terrible philosophy of disrespect for those who surrendered led them to the most horrible abuses of POWs. But that does not absolve my father from what he did. He did something which a man should not do to his fellow men. I'll go on telling my story to our countrymen, particularly young people. Wars inevitably bring out the worst in otherwise normal men and hurt innocent people.'

I wrote a letter to Eric Lomax after I read in an English newspaper about Osamu Komai's visit with him. I had read his book, *The Railway Man*, a few years before and was planning to ask him whether I could interview him for the book I had been writing. 'You wrote in your book that for many years after the war you hated Japan and avoided meeting any Japanese. Eventually, you reconciled with Takashi Nagase and recently with Osamu Komai. Do you still hate Japanese? Could I ask you what you think of them now?'

Soon, a letter arrived from Mr Lomax. It was written with a shaky hand, but in the same meticulous fashion he had drawn the Burma-Siam railway map for his book. 'I cannot answer your question easily in a letter. Can you come and visit me here in Berwick-upon-Tweed?' he wrote and went on, 'It will probably be easier to take trains rather than to fly. The train takes only five to six hours from Bristol to Berwick.' A rather worn-out time table between Bath-Bristol and Edinburgh was enclosed. He circled the possible trains I could take in red ink, and carefully wrote the names of the stations at which I should change trains. At the age of eighty-nine, he was still a railway man.

I wrote him back right away saying I would love to visit him at his earliest convenience. I figured that if he still hated the Japanese, he would not have invited me – Japanese and a total stranger – to his house with instructions about the train trip.

The train stopped at a town in an inlet where old stone houses stood facing the sea, like a fortress. The sky was a deep transparent blue. Outside the quiet station a tall lady was standing waving at me. She must be Patti. I told Eric I would come by taxi to his house, but she was there with a warm smile. 'Can you take a scenic route, please,' she said to the taxi man. He took me to the promontory where white waves splashed at the foot of a lighthouse and then drove along the ancient red brick fortress which stood at the border of Scotland.

The taxi stopped in front of a white iron fence in a quiet street where I saw a gentle-looking old man standing with a stick in front of the door. When he saw me, his face broke into a sweet smile and he asked me, 'Did the train arrive on time?' He guided me into a hallway where a large painting was hung. Yes, it was the very painting Eric wrote about on the first page of *The Railway Man*. I even remembered a part of the description: 'It is a large work set in St Enoch Station in Glasgow on a dusty summer evening in the 1880s. A woman in late middle age, dressed in dark and modest clothes and carrying a parasol, is standing tense and distraught . . . ' I felt as if I had already seen this painting before because its image was so vividly articulated in the book.

For a long time I could not take my eyes off the work. It was more beautiful than I had expected.

'I bought this at an auction in Glasgow,' Eric said, 'because the woman reminded me of my mother.' The woman looks tense and distraught because the train is leaving, taking her son off for a long journey. She reminded Eric of his mother of whom he had had the last glimpse amongst the crowd at the train station from which he left for war.

He kept thinking of his mother during the war. 'Eric screamed, "Mother! Mother!" when the jailers had tortured him with water,' I remembered reading in one of Nagase's books. When Eric went home after the war with the happy expectation of finally seeing his mother, he learned that she had died a month after she saw Eric's name in the missing soldiers' list.

Eric offered me a chair in the living room. Saying, 'I'm suffering from a type of muscular dystrophy,' he said as he sat himself with great effort in an arm-chair. 'All these books are written by POWs – about three hundred of them,' he said, pointing at the bookcases on both sides of the fireplace. Among them, there were a few books co-authored by the blood brothers, Eric and Nagase. More books in cardboard boxes are piled up in the next room, making it look like a book store's warehouse. 'Eric is a collector, Hiroko,' Patti said with a smile. 'More boxes are upstairs – some filled with train tickets and stamps.'

After a while I asked Eric what he thinks of the current Japanese. After a silence, he said, 'Now Japan is a peace-loving country and it seems that they are mostly decent people – except for the extreme nationalists. One thing which bothers me is that I hear many young Japanese don't know the history of the war. I want them to learn about their past.'

He talked about Nagase. 'We still write to each other, but both of us are old and ill. Probably I won't see him again. He is a great man. After the war he did so much to make up for the past, while I was consumed with anger and spent many sleepless nights scheming up detailed plans to kill him. I could have written a book on my various scenarios for murder.'

On the second day of my visit Eric did not feel well, suffering from chest pains as well as the muscular dystrophy. Trying not to disturb him, I went for a walk. Following Patti's instruction, I walked on a narrow path between the tall stone walls. At the end of the path the sea opened up in front of me, thousands of white ripples twinkling over the surface of the water. I walked a long stretch of the promontory to the lighthouse. The tower looked deserted. White paint was peeling off here and there. Weeds covered patches of sand, shriveling in the wind.

I leaned on the railing and looked at the deep blue sea. Far away over the horizon lay the continent of Europe. South East Asia and Japan were even farther away. I thought of the tens of thousands of young men like Eric who went over the sea seventy years before to fight the war. Some never returned. A seagull came and perched on the railing.

Eric Lomax passed away on 8 October 2012. A film, based on his book, came out in 2014.

CHAPTER 12

Taeko Sasamoto, Yoshiko Tamura
and Keiko Holmes

The Allied POWs' Tombstones

Taeko Sasamoto

Taeko Sasamoto lives near the Commonwealth War Cemetery in Yokohama. When I visited her, she met me at the train station and drove me to the graveyard, which has an entrance almost hidden in the bushes. Inside, a vast green field spreads out with hundreds of bronze plaques laid in perfect order, each adorned with summer flowers in full bloom. Secluded from the noise of the city, the place looked like a part of heaven. 'The first time I was here I wandered among the tombs,' Taeko said. 'I was surprised to find that all the names inscribed on the plaques were foreign men and that the dates of their deaths were all from 1942 till 1945. It meant that these men died during World War II. I was born three years after the war ended, and to my knowledge, no war had been fought on our soil. So why were so many young foreign men buried here? Having no confidence in my English, I didn't have the nerve to ask any questions of the Western man sitting in the office.

'It was the summer of 1997. The mystery was solved when I read a local newspaper article about the memorial service which had just been observed at the cemetery. The service was held for the British Commonwealth soldiers who had died in the labour camps in Japan and had been buried here. I went to see Professor Amemiya, one of the organisers of the service. He talked for five hours about the POWs buried here, as well as about those who had been imprisoned in other parts of Asia. He also showed me the film called *One Man's*

Redemption – the tale of Takashi Nagase, the interpreter at the Thai–Burma Railway camp.

'In the film I saw thousands of bones of workers being dug up along the railway. The icy cold eyes with which the former POWs gazed at Mr Nagase gave me goose bumps. What was it that had brought them such hatred for the Japanese? We had never been taught at school that any kind of POW camps had existed either in Japan or anywhere else. I had casually assumed that the British and the Japanese had been good friends since the end of the war. Intrigued by the story of the POWs, I found myself often walking in the cemetery wondering about the men who had been left here far away from their home. Did their families know what happened to their loved ones? Did they know where and how they died? But isn't it our duty to find out about these soldiers? Without letting their families know what had happened to their missing husband or son, could we be reconciled; could they and their countrymen forgive us?

'Those days, I was a freelance writer for television programmes. I thought of making a programme about this cemetery. My plan did not materialise, but it was the beginning of my long and active involvement with POW issues. I was no historian and had no idea where to start, but I first wanted to find out who was buried here, what kind of life they had lived in the camps and how they had died. I went to the library to find books or materials about the POWs. There were none. I was told that right after the war, the Army had burnt all the records so that no proof would be left for the occupying force's investigation. By groping in the dark for a long time and pulling thin threads, I located the former camp sites (ninety-one of one hundred and thirty camps in Japan remained at the end of the war) on the map.

'During the war, Japan suffered a labour shortage in the absence of its own men. The military shipped some of the POWs to Japan and made them work in factories, shipyards or coal and mineral mines. They often worked in terrible conditions with meagre food. Out of more than 35,000 POWs taken to Japan, 3,480 had died. The number must be higher if you count those who died on the sea on the way to Japan either of disease, or from American bombs and torpedoes.

'After the war the bodies of the Americans and the Dutchmen were sent back to their own motherlands, but approximately 1,840 British, Australian, Canadian, New Zealander and Indian soldiers were buried here, observing the rules which had been decided at the Commonwealth Military Convention after World War I.

'One day I met Yoshiko Tamura, who had also been visiting the cemetery, impelled by a curiosity like mine. Yoshiko's father was one of the rare soldiers who had made it back from New Guinea. Naturally, she had a keen interest in war issues. Both of us were busy mothers, but we started to visit the camp sites one by one scattered all over Japan. Few sites had kept their original shape and most of the records had been destroyed. We gained some knowledge about the camps by visiting local ward offices and archives, but it was a long way to find the information about individual POWs.

'Along the way, many people cooperated with us. We met like-minded people and pioneers in the field. Together with them, we founded the POW Research Network Japan in 2002. There was one lucky break. A member of the group, Tetsu Hukubayashi, found a crucial clue when he discovered the "Roster of Deceased Allied POWs in Japan Proper" in the National Diet Library. It was the U.S. GHQ (Gubernatorial Headquarters) documents, which contained the names of more than 3,000 POWs who had died in Japan. From this list we were able to identify the men who were buried at the cemetery, where and how they died. Two years later we launched a website with the database which lists the detailed information gathered. The media both in Japan and abroad wrote this up and we were inundated with letters like "Thank you very much for what you have done. For the first time I found out where and how my father had died."

'The members of the POW Research Network Japan are all volunteers – housewives, journalists, school teachers, university students, retirees, veterans, some over ninety years old, and foreigners living in Japan and Japanese living abroad. We completed the database for those who had died in Japan, but we are still working on those who died overseas. At the request of the Dutch National Archives, we just translated from Japanese into Dutch all the detailed individual information of the Dutch soldiers. This database is now on view in the Archives' website.'

There is no question that Taeko is the driving force and the leader of the group. It has done so much and its efforts have been so widely recognised overseas, that the Japanese government started to cooperate with the group. Every year they invite former POWs from Britain, Holland, America and Australia to Japan. Every time they come, Taeko organises occasions to invite Japanese citizens to meet them and to listen to their stories. Taeko and her friends take the former POWs to the old camp site where they worked during the war.

'Some of them come with old wounds still oozing after seventy years. The children and the grandchildren of the POWs visit, too, carrying the traumas and the burdens of their fathers and grandfathers. But when they go home, almost everyone says that they were happy they had come and that their wounds are finally healed.'

Taeko wrote a book called *The Allied POWs' Epitaphs* .[43] It is clear from the book that she has the talents of a successful researcher – a passion for the pursuit of truth, the methodical and scientific approach of a detective, and the thorough and conscientious attitude of a historian. 'Our POW group was originally a research centre, but we are making efforts to promote friendship between the countries. The war generation is dying, but for their children and for the future generation's sake we will continue our efforts.

'We have a lot to do. I'm determined to devote the rest of my life to this project. I have good daughters who understand my cause and are busy working out their own careers. My husband is retired now and spends half of his time reading and cultivating a garden in the mountain cottage he built. I'm fortunate the whole family is supportive of my work.'

Yoshiko Tamura

'My involvement with the POWs, like Taeko's, began with a visit to the Commonwealth Cemetery in Yokohama. In 1974 when I was

43 Sasamoto, Taeko with assistance of Yoshiko Tamura in information gathering. *The Allied POWs' Epitaphs*, Kusa no Ne Shuppan-kai, Tokyo, 2004

newly married and a newcomer to Yokohama, my husband said, "I'll take you to a beautiful, sacred place not many people know about."

'It was only ten minutes' walk from our house, and the most beautiful cemetery in which I had ever stepped. I walked amongst tombs of hundreds of young men with foreign names. Why did they have to die so young and lie here far away from their homelands? I had the same questions as Taeko when she was here for the first time. Even after going home, the images of the inscriptions did not leave me. They had left loved ones home and never seen them again, never married or if married, perhaps never seen their own child. How homesick must they have been? I found myself walking around the cemetery again the next day. When I asked an Englishman at the office – who happened to be the cemetery director – about its history, he brought down a bundle of thick yellowed documents from a shelf. "The answers to all your questions are written in this book. Why don't you read it?"

'I skimmed through it. It was the history of the war. I remember reading the same line in a history class at school: "On 15 February 1942, Singapore fell." It did not mean much to me then. I had never imagined, following this simple line, what tragic dramas had ensued. The fall of Singapore and of the Pacific islands had produced 140,000 Allied POWs, and some of them sadly ended up lying here.

'Because I spoke some English, the cemetery director asked me to come there to welcome visitors from abroad. Many former POWs wept before their friends' graves. One said to me, "You might think that we won the war, but we have no pleasant memories of it at all. We've lost our precious youth. Our friends lost their lives." The POWs and their families' stories were sad and I was able to understand their sorrow because my family also had its shares of war's woes.

'My paternal grandmother used to say that she was blessed. She sent four sons to the war, but all of them came back safe and sound." She was really fortunate compared with my husband's grandmother, who lost her husband and her two sons in the war.

'People often told me I'm lucky because my father returned alive from New Guinea. He did not say much about it, but my mother told me about the first night she was married to him. That day she had placed flowers in a vase in their bedroom. At midnight my father suddenly got out of bed and yelled, "Wake up! Look. Those flowers are edible. Let's eat them." My mother thought she was married to a madman.

'One day my father placed two thick books in front of me and told me to read them. One was a collection of war stories written by soldiers of various ranks in his Division. The other was the Division's war record written by an officer. I started to read them. Each one was such a terrible story of starvation and death that I couldn't keep reading. I closed the books and put them up in the highest corner of the bookshelf. I should have read them through and talked with my father about his experiences. At least I should have been sympathetic. But the next time I opened the books was after he had passed away.

'My father had been in Manchuria having a relatively easy time, but his Division was ordered to go to New Guinea to help, since the Japanese were not doing well there. He got rid of his winter coat, said a teary goodbye to his horse and sailed down the Pacific in a convoy of sixteen transport ships. The soldiers were shoved like sacks of rice into the bottom of the ship which had no beds or toilets. I know well that the POWs who were transferred to Japan during the war had a terrible time on the so-called "hell ships," but the Japanese who went down the Pacific Lane did not have an easy time either. On the way, ships were hit one by one by American torpedoes as my father's was. He clutched on to a bamboo raft which had floated his way and was eventually saved by a rescue boat.

'After a little rest on an island, a new ship took the survivors to Sorong, a base in northwestern New Guinea, and then in small boats to Manokwari, 300 kilometres to the east. Those who had been waiting for the newcomers' arrival were disappointed since they found arms instead of food in the ship. They had not been fighting but starving. My father came down with malaria and almost died. His comrades brought him frogs, lizards and snakes and told him to eat.

'The Division Commander in Manokwari had meetings with the officers and decided to carry out a strategy of decreasing the number of mouths to feed. Troops were told to walk back to Sorong from which they had just come. Thousands of soldiers perished before they reached the destination, falling off cliffs, swallowed by torrents or just collapsing and dying. Only one out of ten arrived in Sorong in three months. The survivors looked like ghosts. There was not much fighting in Sorong and if there had been, no one had the strength to carry a gun.

'Luckily, my father was considered too ill to walk this death march. He was assigned to a food-supply team. They travelled on a small ship in the pitch of darkness and dropped food at specified spots along the coast. My father recovered his health thanks to the rest he had in the daytime, hiding in the shade.

'After the war, my father was taken to Hollandia and worked in a labour camp under Dutch supervision. The guards often threatened the workers at gunpoint. My father wrote in his memoir that, if only he had known a few words of Dutch, they could have communicated with each other better. That must have been the reason my father encouraged me to learn English ever since I was a child. He was more than delighted when I got a job after college at a Dutch bank, even if he had had hard times with Dutch soldiers at the camp.

'He was also very happy about my involvement with the former POWs. He came to the cemetery with me. He did extensive research for a former POW from England to find the old mine in a remote region of western Japan where he had worked, and arranged to go back there.

'At my work place the branch manager and most people were very kind to me, but a few were not. Although they seemed to try to smile, their eyes were icy cold. I asked my Japanese boss why they were that way. "There are a few people here whose families had a hard time during the war. Particularly, Mr A. He was living in Indonesia when he was a child. The war broke out and his two brothers were killed in front of him by Japanese soldiers. His mother was taken by them and never returned."

'I was shocked and saddened to hear the story, but I did not realise the depth and the scope of the tragedies of the war until I visited the Cemetery for the British Commonwealth Soldiers in Yokohama. For the first time then, it dawned on me that I should do something to atone for the sorrows the Japanese had brought to other people during the war.

'A woman from England came to visit her husband's tombstone for the first time and burst into tears. Another woman cried in front of her father's inscription. "He left for war on my fourteenth birthday," she said. "Every day my mother and I prayed for his safe return. Then we received a letter from the War Office which said that he had died in Japan in 1943 as a POW. We have had a hard life since then. How I hated Japan . . . " Even so, she later wrote to me, "My dream is to build a bridge between England and Japan by placing one small stone at a time." The letter moved me so much that I replied saying that I would do the same.

'I've made good friends with the visitors to the cemetery. They are from all over the world – Australia, Canada, Holland, America and England. I've been trying to build a bridge with their countries one small stone at a time. I was fortunate to be able to work with Taeko and others at the POW Research Network Japan and do something – no matter how little – to mitigate their and their families' pain.'

(Both Taeko and Yoshiko were given an MBE in The Queen's Honours for their service to the Commonwealth POWs.)

Keiko Holmes

Keiko is a recipient of an OBE for her services to former British POWs. She is well-known among them, but lives alone quietly in a modest house in Croydon, in the outskirts of London. 'My husband passed away and my sons are grown up and live far away. Many of the ex-POW friends who treated me as if I were part of their family have passed away now. I miss them,' Keiko says, gazing at hundreds of photos of POW friends pasted all over the wall of her living room. 'But I still continue with the AGAPE organisation I founded for the purpose of healing their old wounds. Its members are now only me and another Japanese woman, but I still take former POWs and their families to Japan every year. Japanese airlines, corporations and wealthy people donate enough money to pay the travel fares. Those who still hated the Japanese after half a century – all of them come home loving Japan. Some of them go back there three or four times.'

Keiko Holmes was born several years after the war in a village called Kiwa-cho in the southwest of mainland, Japan. When she was a student in Tokyo, she met a Londoner called Paul Holmes. They married and moved from Tokyo to London in 1979 with their two sons. Paul was a devout Christian and she became one, too. Sadly Paul was killed in a plane crash in 1981 while on a business trip. It was her faith that helped Keiko through the dark years of her life.

'When I visited home in 1988 to see my parents, I noticed that the old graveyard in Iruka (now part of Kiwa-cho), with a simple wooden cross I used to see when I was a child, had been turned into a beautiful memorial garden,' she said. The copper cross stood in the centre of the new cemetery surrounded by deep forest. On its right hand was a stone on which sixteen soldiers' names were engraved under the inscription, "Roll of Honour."

'On the left side of the cross stood another marble monument on which the following words were inscribed:

A HISTORIC SITE:

CEMETERY FOR FOREIGNERS

CULTURAL HERITAGE PROPERTY DESIGNATED

BY KIWA TOWNSHIP

On 8 June 1944, the three hundred British Far East POWs who had been working in the Malaya Area were sent to work at the copper mine in Iruka under the supervision of the Japanese Military. Most of them worked in the mine, some in ore dressing and others in cultivating farmland. They were efficient workers, proud and cultured British gentlemen. However, loneliness, the anxiety of captivity and various illnesses caused the death of sixteen soldiers before the end of the war in August 1945.

After the war, 284 men returned home. They left the following inscription for their dead colleagues on the original tombstone:

REMEMBERING THE BRITISH SOLDIERS WHO,

UNDER THE GREAT GLORY OF GOD,

PASSED AWAY HERE DURING

THE WAR YEARS OF 1941 TO 1945

Keiko said, 'It was almost a mystical experience for me to see this place with the inscriptions on the tombstone and the shining cross adorned with fresh flowers – like finding a precious gem hidden in a dark forest.

'I knew how poor the town had been since the mine was closed down. What a big project it must have been for a small village to rebuild the cemetery! It may have been the undertaking of Ishihara Industry which owned the mine, but even so it must have required some persuading to build a Christian cemetery in a village of mostly Buddhists and Shintoists. Out of respect for the dead soldiers, however, the townspeople built the new cemetery and have kept it beautifully.

'Reading the names of the dead soldiers out loud, I thought of the anguish of their families. As a mother of two sons, I imagined how they felt about having their loved ones buried in a faraway land. I wished to let their families know how beautifully the graves had been looked after by the villagers. I also wanted to find the former Far East POWs who had lived in Iruka, and to share my excitement with them.

'Back in London, my search for the Iruka Boys began. After much difficulty, I attended the annual FEPOW conference held in Barbican Hall, London in 1991. The minute I entered the hall, a roar of boos and jeers erupted. I was shocked to realise how much hatred these old veterans had toward the Japanese. I knew then that I was being urged by God to work to help the healing process for war wounds and reconciliation. Wherever I went, angry words or flat rejections were waiting for me. But the small book I wrote called *Pilgrimage of Healing and of Reconciliation* started to be read among the former POWs. They slowly began to talk to me.

'Through word of mouth the Iruka Boys got in touch with me one by one. My proposal, "Let's go to Japan and visit Iruka," at first met a half-hearted response. But my persistence and enthusiasm won out and I finally began to grip their hearts. Fundraising for their travel fare was even more difficult. In the end, many Japanese corporations, airplane companies and individuals donated enough to fund the trip. Finally in 1992 I led the first Pilgrimage of Healing and Reconciliation to Japan. This was mainly for Iruka OBs and they were met with an almost explosive heros' welcome, not only from the villagers but also from all over Japan. As a result of the trip, many FEPOWs told me that their hatred of Japan had disappeared.

'Since then I have taken more than five hundred former soldiers and bereaved families to Japan. For several years, there were so many who wanted to go, I travelled there twice a year.

In 1998, a letter with golden seals arrived in my mailbox. It came from the most unlikely and unexpected address – Buckingham Palace. I opened it with much trepidation. It said that I would receive an OBE from Queen Elizabeth. I did not even know the meaning of OBE. But all my POW friends were terribly happy for me.

'My sons, Chris and Daniel, and the former FEPOWs who had just been to Japan with me met the Queen and Prince Philip. They talked kindly to them as well as to me. I was also invited by the Emperor and the Empress who visited London that year. They encouraged me to continue my efforts.

'The Emperor's visit rekindled the anger of the former FEPOWs against Japan. They stood on both sides of the street with their backs to the Emperor on his way to the Palace. One of them, Jack Caplan, burnt a Japanese Flag in protest. A few weeks after the incident, Jack phoned me and asked me to visit him. He wanted me to know why he had burnt the flag. He said that he still could not forget the horrible treatment and abuse he and other POWs had received at the camp and is still burning with hatred for Japan. I apologised to him and we talked all day. At the end of the day, he offered to come to Japan on my next trip. Doctors told him not to go because, confined to a wheel chair, he was in no condition to travel. Government officials in both countries advised him not to. But we did not give up the idea. Four years later in 2002, Jack was on the plane to Japan with me. After the trip he was a different man. He became a great fan of Japan and we became fast friends.'

Keiko's pilgrimage of reconciliation did not stop in Britain. She travelled to America, Australia and Singapore, met former POWs and tried to mitigate their pain. Keiko brought a bright smile wherever she went. Her enthusiasm and positive attitude backed by her faith melted old men's hearts.

CHAPTER 13

The Comfort Women and Human Dignity

The Women's Active Museum on War and Peace is tucked away on the second floor of a quiet building complex in Tokyo, with only a discreet sign, 'wam', to announce its presence. The wall of the entry-way is covered with one hundred and fifty-five enlarged faces of the so-called 'comfort women'. The wrinkles etched on the women's faces speak not only to their age, but also to their pain, sorrow, fear and shame. Some seemed to stare at me with anger and hatred, while others gazed out with desperately sad eyes. The museum is a big room divided by panels, every surface of which is covered with stories of the women whose lives had been torn apart by the experiences they had during the war. They are also on every page of the periodicals published by the museum.

Here are a few of their stories:

Lu Man-Mei

'I was taken from Taiwan to Hainan Island in the South China Sea at the age of seventeen, lured by the promise of a nurse's job. When soldiers first came into my room, I didn't know anything about sex. I fought back, panic-stricken. Soldiers came in one after another around the clock. In 1944, when I was eight months pregnant, they didn't want to keep me anymore and let me go home. The baby died a month after birth. I did anything I could to support myself, picking tea leaves, carrying building blocks, or selling insurance. I got married at thirty-eight, but my husband heard a rumour about me and ran away with another woman. Since then I've been working as a laundry woman.'

Tomasa Salinog

'I was born in Panay Island in the Philippines. My mother died after giving birth to me. My father, a carpenter, loved me and we lived a peaceful life until 1942, when Japanese soldiers broke into our house. One killed my father, cutting off his head, because he tried to protect me. Then they took me to a big house nearby, and the man who had killed my father, Captain H, raped me. I was thirteen. From then on I was locked up in the house and raped by dozens of soldiers every day. One day I found a key they had left and ran away. An old couple protected me, but on the third day, when I was getting water from a well, I was captured by Colonel O. He and his men treated me like a slave and raped me over and over. They said they'd kill me if I tried to escape again.

After the war, I refused every proposal of marriage. 'I couldn't deal with the prospect of sex – shivers ran down my spine whenever I thought about it. I made a living sewing dresses with a machine my mother had left behind. In 1991, after making some money selling blankets, I went to Tokyo to sue the Japanese government. But the court dismissed the case. I felt like killing myself. I didn't think I could go home after such humiliation. It was only after the Women's International War Crimes Tribunal in 2000 that I finally felt I had regained my dignity as a human being.

'Money won't compensate me for my loss of dignity or for my grief at losing my father. So I refused to accept the Fund for Asian Women that people had set up. But after my landlord kicked me out of my old house, I was happy to live in the house Japanese supporters had built for me.'

Li Xiumei

'I was born in Jinguishe, a mountain village in the north-west of Meng Xian, Shanxi Province, which was a stronghold of anti-Japanese Communists. Therefore, it was a strategically important area for the Japanese and they had a big base in the area. In 1942, when I was fifteen, four Japanese soldiers broke into our house. They struck my mother and knocked her onto the floor. Then they dragged me to their camp and locked me up in a dark room inside a stone house. There was no heat in the room and I wasn't even given a futon. A handful of mixed cereal once or twice a day was all I was given to eat.

'They raped me every day and night. The red-faced troop leader was particularly violent and I was determined to resist him. He beat my face with a belt buckle, and as a result I permanently lost sight in my right eye. He also kicked me with his boots on my back, arms, and thighs. He hit me on my head, and it bled badly. I later learned that my mother had worked hard to save six hundred silver yuan to buy me back, and that she had been in despair when they told her it wasn't enough. Eventually my brother came up with enough money, but when we arrived home, we found my mother had hanged herself.'

Kim Hak-Soon

She was the first woman to come to Tokyo and identify herself as a 'comfort woman'. She asked the Japanese Government to apologise and compensate her and other Korean comfort women.

'I grew up in Pyongyang, Korea. My father died when I was a baby. I went to a free school, organised by the city church, for four years. When I was fourteen, my mother remarried and I did not get along with my step-father. He sold me to a family who made it a profession to train girls to be *kiisens* (geisha-like court-singers).

'In 1941, I was seventeen and too young to work at a licensed house. My stepfather decided to make me work in China and took me on a train. But as soon as I arrived in Beijing, a Japanese soldier stopped us. He asked my stepfather, "You are a Korean. Are you a spy?" and without waiting for an answer, the soldier took him away. He put me in an army truck and took me to an empty house. There I was stripped, my clothes ripped open, and I lost my virginity.

'From there I was moved to another house. Three more Korean women were there. Twenty to thirty soldiers came every day and we were forced to serve them. If we rejected them even a little, we were beaten or our hair was pulled. We were dragged naked around the hall. We were never paid. During the day, we delivered ammunition, did laundry, cooked and worked as nurses. I was thinking of nothing but running away. Luckily, a Korean man helped me to escape. We lived together, moving from one place to another. I believe that he was an opium broker. Eventually, we went to Shanghai and settled down in a French settlement. We had a daughter and a son.

'My family went back to Korea when the war was over, but even then misfortunes kept coming in battalions. My daughter died of cholera. My husband died in a traffic accident. He used to get drunk and abused me in front of our son. He called me "a filthy bitch" and "a prostitute for Japs." So I had mixed feelings about him, but when my son died of heart failure at nine, I was devastated. I wanted to kill myself and took pills several times, but did not succeed.

'From then on I drifted around, drinking and smoking. Finally, in my mid-fifties, I cleaned my feet of an aimless life and became a housekeeper. Now I live on welfare from the government.

In 1990, I heard a Japanese official on the news saying that the comfort women were prostitutes brought by private dealers. I flew into a rage. Why do they tell such outrageous lies? Next year I went to Tokyo and sued the Japanese government.

It hurts to recall the past. But facts must be told for the sake of history. What happened should not be repeated.'[44]

At the back of the wam museum, several women were working in front of computers. One of them, Yumiko Saito, came to welcome me. I owe her a lot because not only was she the one who invited me to the museum, she also introduced me to a few of the veterans I interviewed, since she herself had recorded their testimony for the museum archives. Yumiko had recently organised a special exhibition about Filipino comfort women here. She took me around, pointing to the photos on the wall: 'We went to the Philippines and met these ladies. They also came here and told their stories. They suffered for fifty years in silence, but finally they spoke out with enormous courage. They now live with dignity.'

Then she took me to Eriko Ikeda, the director of the museum, whose involvement with comfort women's issues goes back twelve years to her TV-producer days.

44 'The Comfort Women's Issue A-Z, wam, p. 33

Eriko Ikeda

'I worked at the NHK (National Broadcasting Company of Japan) as a director for thirty-seven years starting in 1973. We ran many programs on World War II, but before 1991 none of them had dealt with comfort women issues. During the War the Japanese military set up sex-slaves camps everywhere the soldiers were sent, but the fact had been kept secret back in Japan throughout the war, and the related documents had been burnt at its end. People gradually started to know about it through such books as an autobiography by Suzuko Shirota,[45] which came out in 1971, and a bestselling novel, *Comfort Woman*, by Kako Senda,[46] written in 1973. Japanese society, which had treated women as secondary citizens and kept brothels as public institutions not too long ago, did not condemn this shameful wartime system so severely. Male producers seemed to be reluctant to make a big issue about it. So I ran a programme about a Chinese comfort woman, Pe Pongi, who was abandoned in Okinawa after the war.

'In 1991, two months after this, Kim Hak-soon came forward to sue the Japanese government. Victims from the Philippines, Taiwan, Indonesia, Japan, Holland, North Korea, China and Malaysia followed suit. In 1993, Mr Yoichi Kono, representing the Japanese government, issued a statement of apology to comfort women. At the time, there was a heightened awareness all over the world about wartime violence against women. It became an important human rights issue. Between 1991 and 1996 I made eight programmes on the comfort women. Our staff had been eager to show on screen the painful memories and appeals of the women who had suffered so much. We were hoping to make such an impact that our government would apologise to and compensate the victims. But suddenly, no more proposals for comfort women programmes were accepted by our boss.

'Why? The political tide was changing. Revisionists formed a group to erase wartime atrocities from textbooks. The term "comfort woman" disappeared from them. The media, including NHK, instead

---

45 Shirota, Suzuko, *A Song in Praise of Maria*, Japan Christian Group, 1971
46 Senda, Kako, *Jugun Ianhu*, Futaba-sha, 1973

of investigating and arguing for truth, stopped reporting comfort women issues for fear of right-wing attacks. I was kicked upstairs to another department. In the meantime, former comfort women kept coming to Tokyo to sue the government. None of them won their case. I was angry. As a woman of the perpetrator country, I argued with my friends about what we should do for them.

'I'll tell you about a great lady, Yayori Matsui, an *Asahi* newspaper reporter. Sadly she passed away too young, but she did a great deal for comfort women. Born in Kyoto, a daughter of a minister, she went to America as an exchange student and to France to study at the Sorbonne. As a journalist, she believed that 'not knowing is a sin', and she exposed the truth about chemical hazards, pollution and human rights violations.

'About comfort woman, she argued passionately that systematic exploitation of women for sex is a violation of human rights and should be prosecuted as a war crime. "We have an obligation to help our fellow women victims. Since the Tokyo Tribunal did not deal with the sexual slave issue, let's hold our own international tribunal to judge their cases."

'Yayori spoke to lawyers and professors from Asia and the West and turned the idea into a reality. The Women's International War Crimes Tribunal on Japan's Military Sexual Slavery began in Tokyo on 8 December 2000, and lasted for four days. It was a deeply emotional event for me, as well as for the thousand people who came from all over the world to attend the trial. International legal experts, mostly women, acted as judges and prosecutors. Eight regional teams of prosecutors, including a team from North and South Korea, presented cases. Dozens of former comfort women testified. They hugged and cried, watching each other's testimony. Both Kim Hak-soon and Thomasa Salinog were there.

'The final verdict was given in the Hague. The Japanese men, including the Emperor and Tojo were convicted. Because the tribunal was organised by non-governmental organisations, it did not have the authority to enforce the judgment, and the defendants had been long dead anyway. But the verdict helped establish wartime sexual abuse as a crime against humanity, and it challenged the Emperor's exemption from responsibility for the war.

'Reporters came from all over the world, and the media in other countries covered this event widely. But in Japan it made hardly a ripple, with most newspapers giving the event only a few paragraphs in their back pages. Men wanted to keep the sex slave issue buried. The Women's Tribunal was largely treated as a non-event.

'A programme about this tribunal, "Wartime Violence Questioned," ran on NHK television on 30 January 2001. I wasn't involved in producing it because by this time I'd been transferred to another branch. But it was an utter disgrace. The facts were greatly distorted, and the show eliminated the testimony of the victims and the per-petrators as well as the final verdict. Instead, it featured right-wing scholars criticising the trial.

'Four years later, the chief producer, Akira Nagai, disclosed what had happened. It turned out that, shortly before the broadcast, the content of the programme had been changed under pressure from five MPs, including the future prime minister, Shinzo Abe.

'Yayori, the inspiration and passion behind the international tribunal, was diagnosed with liver cancer in 2002. She died only a few months later, but she used her remaining days to plan the founding of the Women's Active Museum on War and Peace. The museum was founded in 2005, using her assets as well as funds contributed by the public.

'I retired in 2010 from NHK and became the director of wam. Every month we organise special events. We invite speakers for lectures. We've been showing panel exhibitions like the one you see here in many cities in China, and they've been well received. I have plans to take the shows to other Chinese cities as well.

I was born in 1950, the year the Korean War started. I was a bookworm. I remember how excited I was when Mme de Beauvoir came with Sartre to Japan. I wrote novels until the Vietnam War transformed me into a peace activist. I've been interested in war issues since I was young because my mother always talked about the air raids in Tokyo. Many of her family were killed in them.

'My father went to war in China. I asked what he did there. He said that his commander was a major who belonged to the 731 Unit, which had engaged in biological warfare. So I thought my father might have done something terrible. "No, I worked at the Transport Corps and delivered food," he said. So I asked him if he had delivered steamed buns with poisoned bean filling, but he was poker-faced and said no.

After studying political science at Waseda University, I was hired by NHK as one of three women directors out of eighty. I was assigned to work on "Ohayo, Okusan!" (Good morning, Mrs Housewife) and ran 'today's menu'. You can tell what a long way I've come.

'I live alone and work even at home. I was married, but my husband and I didn't live together too long. But he didn't believe in divorce, It took thirty years before the divorce came through, He passed away five years later. After work I used to bicycle to visit my father, but he also passed away last summer.

We have a lot to do here. Can you believe that we have a Prime Minister who denies the Japanese military's involvement in coercing these women? He said that no records have been found in the government documents stating that comfort women were coerced. Such documents were found by Mr Yoshiaki Yoshimi [47] and others and have been published.

'In 2014, Abe raised doubts about the "Kono Statement" – an apology to comfort women for the Japanese military's involvement in coercing them. Abe asked the conservative historians to review the matter. He also directed his government in this regard to "step up a strategic campaign of international opinion so that Japan can receive a fair appraisal based on matters of objective fact."

The objective fact is that innocent young girls were abducted and deprived of their basic human rights, and were robbed of their futures and their dignity. When they returned home, they had trouble finding husbands, or their marriages suffered. Some could not conceive a child, and many became social outcasts, their suffering lasting all through their lives.

'Under pressure for his views about comfort women, Abe included the following paragraph in his statement on the 70th anniversary of

47 Yoshiaki Yoshimi, *Jugun-Ianhu* (Comfort Woman), Iwanami Shoten, 1995, pp. 3–7, 'Documents concerning "Comfort Woman"'

the war: "We must never forget that there were women behind the battlefields whose honour and dignity were severely injured."

'Abe did not apologise to the women, nor did he specify who the women were. But he acknowledged the fact that there were women who were deprived of their honour and dignity.

'People – journalists, students, and housewives – are coming to our museum to find out the truth. The staff members of wam and I are doing our best to teach them true history. We have to rush. The real witnesses – those comfort women – are dying away.

[Postscript: wam was awarded the Peace Prize, 2013, by the Japan Peace Academy, which is given annually to an individual or an organisation based in Japan that has contributed to peace.]

CHAPTER 14

The Nationalists Who Rewrite History

At a Burma Veterans Association

In October 2012, I was a guest at a monthly meeting of the Burma Veterans Association. Around an elongated table sat twenty veterans, two younger men, and an old lady. The president explained to me that the lady was a nurse who had worked on the battlefield in Burma. One young man, Mr A, was the son of a soldier who had been killed in Burma; the other, Mr B, was the son of a Navy pilot who had been a member of the Pearl Harbor team.

Until the 1990s, there were thousands of veterans associations all over Japan; affiliated members numbered more than a million. With so many veterans dead or very old, many of these organisations no longer exist, but some continue, their numbers bolstered by people from the post-war generation.

After the president introduced me to the group, he asked me to explain why I was there. 'In England, people are very kind to me,' I said. 'But a World War II veteran told me that he used to hate the Japanese. "The captors at my POW camp were very cruel." I also read the diary of my neighbour's father, a former POW in a Japanese camp, which described the prison guards in a similar way. I was ashamed that I had no knowledge of the plight of the POWs or even of their existence. I ended up meeting a dozen former British POWs and writing a book about them. After that, I wanted to meet Japanese veterans in order to know the other side of the story. I am grateful that many former Japanese soldiers were willing to share with me the stories of the war they had fought. Some talked frankly about the atrocities they had committed. Others were still sad about comrades who had died of starvation and diseases. The Japanese soldiers seemed to be victims as well as perpetrators . . . '

'Stop, Mrs Sherwin,' shouted Mr A. The blue veins on his temple were bulging and his voice shook with anger. 'I don't think you are in any position to judge or criticise the soldiers who fought that war. Listen. My father was taken to war leaving his young wife, me and my infant brother. He was among 34,000 troops who fought in the Imphal Campaign for two and a half months. He was sick and starving and died under enemy fire. But he was a patriotic young man. He was no victim. He was happy to die for the Emperor. Those who grew up after the war have no idea what the old soldiers were like.

'You live in England and look at the war from the Allies' point of view. I know your kind. You probably have the same ideas as those judges who condemned our leaders in the Tokyo Tribunal. You think that we were evil aggressors. I don't think you have a right to criticise us, or write a book about us . . .'

My heart started to pound and I could not even talk. I felt as if I had been run over by a train.

'In fact, the Western nations had been imperialists long before we were,' Mr A went on. 'The British colonised African countries, India and Burma. Americans took the Philippines, the Dutch, Indonesia. We Japanese tried to catch up with them, colonising Korea and invading China. They didn't like what we were doing because we weren't white. They didn't want their dominance to be threatened, and the balance of power tipped. They called us yellow monkeys and yellow swine. We never called them white monkeys.

'The judges of the Tokyo Tribunal punished our leaders for the atrocities we had committed, but in the wars of the Westerners, they also had a long history of committing atrocities. In this war, America wiped out our cities with carpet bombings. They dropped atomic bombs on Hiroshima and Nagasaki, incinerating 200,000 people and peeling their skin like potatoes. Wasn't this a crime against humanity? But they have not been judged in any tribunals . . . In the Tokyo Tribunal they said we were the aggressors in the war. But we fought in self-defense against the western nations. They ganged up on us . . .'
With his finger pointing at me, Mr A kept on talking.

'We invaded China,' I managed to interrupt. 'We were definitely the perpetrators in the case of China. We did not go there to fight in self-defense. Without Japan invading China, conquering Manchuria and starting to threaten Southern Indochina, America would not have imposed an oil embargo on Japan. We were the aggressor America wanted to contain. In the case of the Pacific War, was the surprise attack on Pearl Harbour self-defense?'

'We attacked Pearl Harbor for self-defense,' Mr A said, proudly.

Before I said anything, an old man shook his head and waved his hand in the air. 'Let's stop all this arguing. It was a terrible war indeed. But it's time to forget and look forward.'

Mr A wasn't about to stop, but before he continued, another voice cut in. 'Mrs Sherwin, are you writing a book to criticise Japan and their soldiers? I don't think you should.' It was Mr B, the son of a Pearl Harbor pilot. His voice was softer than Mr A's and his manner gentler, but he was just as adamant: 'Because we lost the war, we were criticised for everything we'd done,' he said. 'And we criticised ourselves for whatever we had been. Everything was wrong – our ethics, our education, our social system and our way of life. We developed a masochist mentality and inferiority complexes. Suddenly, we were a powerless and inferior nation.

'The real reason we lost the war was that America had more natural resources and military power than we did. We didn't have the oil or the steel to produce ships, airplanes and arms. It was a war between haves and have-nots, not a war of good against evil or right against wrong. For us it was a war for survival.

'Do you know that I'm a member of *Tsukuru-kai* – the famous group which created a new history textbook for children? People call us revisionists. But all that's different about our history book and others is what we choose to emphasise. We were a defeated nation and have had a negative view of our nation. But don't we want our children to grow up feeling proud and positive about being Japanese rather than guilty and inferior? They should know that Japan is a good country, and we try to make that possible by not exaggerating the negative aspects of our history.'

'There are lots of things we should be proud of in Japan,' I said, finally getting calm enough to speak out. 'For instance, of the peaceful, high-tech nation we have built after the war. We should be proud of that, but not of the war. Children should not be taught to be proud of the war and the way we fought it.'

Tired of the intense debate, the old veterans began talking to each other and left us alone. Mr B continued to talk – this time about himself.

'My father, a Pearl Harbour pilot, committed *seppuku* after the war and my brave mother who assisted him was arrested on a charge of murder. You know it was a tradition for someone to assist a samurai in performing hara-kiri. I had to be at a coroner's inquest although I was a young boy. The trauma of the family experience has never left me. I grew up in the shadow of the war as a son of a hero turned into a war-criminal.'

It was understandable Mr B wanted to do something to exorcise the dark images of war. I was genuinely sorry for him.

After the meeting was over, several veterans talked to me about their experiences in Burma. 'It was a reckless war we had no chance of winning. General Mutaguchi shouldn't have started such a campaign,' one said. Another said, 'Our food ran out in ten days. We walked across raging rivers. Half of us were swallowed in torrents. We still think of the comrades who lost their lives there. That's why we still come here and talk about them.'

A Memorial Service for the Battle of Kohima –
Akiko Macdonald and Yasuo Naito

In July 2013, I had a chance to be with some of the British veterans who had fought in the Burma Campaign. The occasion was a memorial service for those killed in the Battle of Kohima in 1943. The victory at Kohima in northeastern India had been a turning point in the Burma Campaign, and it meant a lot to the British. The service, which was held in the magnificent York Minster in the presence of HRH Prince Andrew, was impressive, as British rituals often are. I was there because Akiko Macdonald, the chairperson of the London-based Japanese Burma Society, had kindly invited me to attend.

Seventy years after the battle, officers and soldiers who had fought in Kohima were there with golden decorations on their uniforms. It was lovely to see these veterans smiling happily, but my thoughts kept drifting back to their counterparts – the Japanese ex-soldiers I had met at the Burma Association meeting, whose memories were sad and bitter. I remembered the Japanese veterans telling me that there was no chance of winning the Imphal-Kohima campaign. Then why did they even start it?

Japan was losing the war on all fronts by the end of 1943 and Prime Minister Tojo was looking desperately for any possibility of reversing this trend. The 15th Army Commander, Ren-ya Mutaguchi, was Tojo's protégé. He had a dream of conquering India, which sounded megalomaniacal to anyone else. But Tojo was attracted by the idea of fortifying Burma and blocking the route to China which the Allies had been building to send arms to Chiang Kai-shek. An Indian campaign would benefit from the support of Chandra Bose, a commander of the Indian National Army and a champion of India's independence from Britain who was enthusiastic about cooperating with the Japanese.

Mutaguch's plan was first to win Imphal, an isolated border town in North-East India. A 210 kilometre road wound north from Imphal to the hill town of Kohima before running on to the railhead at Dimapur, a gateway to central India. It was the only way to India. Therefore, it was important to occupy Kohima as well. Mutaguchi said he would win Imphal and Kohima in just three weeks before the monsoon season began in May. In order to cross over the 2,000 metre-high Arakan mountain ranges, the soldiers could not carry too much food and ammunition. So, borrowing the idea from Genghis Khan, he arranged that the troops would take bullocks along. 'They can carry the stores and munitions and when the animals are of no further use, you can have a feast by roasting them.'

But while Mutaguchi was preparing his plan, the Allies had been making a major effort to build up their strength in the region in order to regain Burma. Churchill had negotiated with Roosevelt to get assistance for this effort. In August 1943, the Allies created a new command responsible for the South East Asian Theatre under Admiral Mountbatten.

When the Japanese troops began marching west on 8 March 1944, it was as if they had jumped into the trap the enemy had set. Besides, the biggest failing of Mutaguchi's campaign was not to plan for an adequate food supply. Laden bullocks were not used to walking all day in difficult terrain. The first hurdle was the crossing of the Chindwin River. The animals were frightened of water. The soldiers dragged them on, but once they were in, they bellowed fiercely, cut themselves loose and were swallowed up by the river. Some soldiers were carried away with them. Half of the bullocks were lost. Some of the animals which had made it to the other side, sat down and wouldn't budge. Some stumbled as they walked on the bumpy road. Others collapsed in mountains and fell off cliffs. In the end none were left.

Akiko Macdonald's father had been a veterinary surgeon in the 31st Regiment Division. They had been fighting in the Kohima region. 'After all his cows and horses died,' she said, 'my father assumed that it was his time to go. His comrades were dying of diseases and of starvation. Roads were strewn with white bones.'

But to his utter surprise, his commander, Kotoku Sato, made a decision which no ordinary Japanese commander would have imagined. He disobeyed his Commanding General, Ren-ya Mutaguchi's order to advance to Dimapur and decided to pull his troops back to the nearest food and ammunition depot in order to save his men from starvation. As a result, the British-Indian Army regained the entire Naga area, which led to their victory in the Imphal Campaign.

Disobeying orders was almost unheard of in the Japanese military and it would surely have ended in a court martial handing down a death sentence. In this case Sato had been declared 'insane in extremely severe battlefield conditions' and was dismissed which was considered an extraordinarily lenient punishment. 'Naturally, I have great respect for Commander Sato,' Akiko says. 'Besides, I'm married to an Englishman. So I feel compelled to keep the legacy of the Burma campaign alive and promote peaceful relations between Japan and England. You know what? Some people call me a nationalist . . . maybe I am. I'm very patriotic. I am sympathetic to those Japanese soldiers – who went to Burma and died. They fought for their country just as the soldiers from the Allied countries did. I knew that in China and in the Philippines our soldiers did terrible things and no apologies are enough for the victims and their families, but in most of the other theatres of the war, our soldiers were just brave young men who dedicated their lives to their country and to the Emperor.'

At the ceremony in York I had a chance to meet Yasuo Naito, the London Bureau Chief of *Sankei Shimbun*, a conservative paper in Japan. He was there to cover the memorial service. Ever since my encounter with Mr A and Mr B, I had felt a little wary about talking to Japanese men with strong nationalist views. But Mr Naito looked like an amiable man with a civilised manner. Unlike some Japanese, he was not shy and was talking animatedly with British people at the service. I was curious to know what kind of views a journalist of a conservative Japanese paper had about World War II. After coming home, I wrote him an e-mail asking if he would write about his thoughts on the war. The following is the gist of what he wrote:

'I spent three of my high school years in the Soviet Union because my father was a Moscow correspondent for *Tokyo Shimbun* from 1977 to 1980. It was the height of the cold war. People were nice to me even though I was Asian, but I was upset when a history teacher said that Japan was an extremely militant and aggressive nation. I argued passionately with her in my poor Russian, pointing out that the Soviet Union was just as militant and aggressive as Japan. It was then that I realised that I loved my country very much.

'When I returned to Japan, I found Japanese teachers were arguing against raising our national flag at school and refusing to sing our anthem. If I ever said, "I am a patriot," I was likely to be labeled a dangerous boy. This struck me as wrong. Isn't it only natural to love the country where you were born and grew up? Don't we want to keep our good traditions and culture? For instance, the Japanese seem to have the spirit of harmony and cooperation. They helped each other and kept order during the recent earthquake and tsunami.

'Mrs Sherwin, I'm sorry that those men you met at a Burma Association were a little rude to you. But even those extreme nationalists are no terrorists. They would not explode bombs to hurt people. So don't worry.

'The pacifist education Japanese children received in the aftermath of the war made everyone tame. It produced a generation of vegetables who can only chant "anti-war" sutras. How to keep a moral high ground and not to be weak-kneed is a question the nationalists are facing. While at university I studied physics, but in the last year I changed my mind and applied for this newspaper job. As a journalist, I wanted to search for the answer to a question: what can we do to make Japan a strong nation and an advocate for justice?

'The Chinese and the Koreans' passionate loathing for Japan is creating dangerous tensions between us. No matter how often we apologise to them for our wartime atrocities, they never grant us even a sliver of forgiveness. They mass-produce anti-Japanese films and wartime dramas with the sole purpose of rubbing in the cruelty of the Japanese. Peaceful relationships cannot grow in such an environment.

'It is essential for Japan to cooperate with the countries with which we share the same values. We have to be able to defend ourselves and share responsibility for keeping peace in the world and stand firm against non-democratic countries.'

My Confrontation with Another Nationalist

I travelled to Berlin in July 2014. I wanted to visit there since I began working on this book project and particularly after I read Ian Buruma's *The Wages of Guilt – Memories of War in Germany and Japan*.[48] It took some time before I could persuade my American husband Jimmy to come with me. In the past he had refused to set foot in Germany.

The trip was a revelation for me. Until I was there, I did not realise how deeply the scars of the war and the memories of the Holocaust are etched into the daily life of the city.

On a street a few blocks from our hotel, four small brass plaques were laid among the cobblestones. The engraving on one plaque read: 'Here lived Otto Koppel, born in 1902, deported in 1941 and murdered in Auschwitz in 1942.' Reading the other three plaques made it clear that they were a family – parents and two young children who had the same fate.

These plaques are called *Stolperstein*, stumbling block, and are placed in front of the victim's former home. A man named Gunter Demnig

48 Farrar, Straus & Giroux, Inc., 1994

started this project to commemorate victims of the Holocaust and it extended beyond the boundaries of Germany to neighbouring countries. There are currently 40,000 of them, and the number is increasing. Suddenly, the Holocaust was no longer a statistic to me. I saw in my mind's eyes the young family being taken away from the spot on which I was standing.

Unlike Japanese cities, where all the mementos of the war are long gone, in Berlin there are constant reminders of the War and the Holocaust – a Nazi bunker with its bullet holes and rusted barbed wire blocking the windows, the remnants of the Berlin Wall, memorials and museums.

The 'Memorial to the Murdered Jews in Europe' is a huge block in the very centre of Berlin, with hundreds of coffin-shaped dark grey steles in memory of the six million Jews and others murdered by the Nazis. A woman journalist was the driving force behind this memorial. She and her supporters collected donations, and eventually the Bundes-tag passed a resolution in favour of the project. There were objections and it took seventeen years before it opened in 2006. But what a courageous decision it was for the Germans to set up a memorial for the worst crime their nation had committed in the centre of the city where no one can pass without seeing it.

'After the War the Germans did a great deal of soul searching,' I remember my German friend saying to me. 'During decades after the war, at times an impenitent mood prevailed, but we had brave leaders like Willy Brandt and Richard von Weizsacker who articulated the responsibility of the Germans and told us that remorse for the past was the duty of every German and should itself be a source of pride for the nation. We left the sites of concentration camps intact and created memorials and museums. All our children visit them from school to learn from our past mistakes.'

At the end of the trip Jimmy said, 'I cannot forgive what they did, but the efforts they have made to atone after the war are commendable. I was glad I came here.'

When I returned home, I wrote an opinion piece for the *Asahi* newspaper describing how the Germans had dealt with the wages of sin after the war – how the people and the government united in their efforts to preserve the memory of their negative history so that they would never forget what had happened.

After my article came out,[49] though drastically shortened, I received many favourable letters, but a severely critical one from one reader. The title of her letter was: 'Are the Japanese Perpetrators of Atrocities?' She accused me of weighing the Japanese war crimes on the same scale as the Holocaust. I insisted that any comparison of weights of sin with other countries should not influence the way we handle our own responsibility for the war. Reflecting on the war is a matter which should be dealt with in our own country. I wrote to her that it seemed to me that our nation did not mourn enough and did not teach children the true history of the war.

She wrote me again to say, 'The West had conquered weak nations and exploited their people and resources. They blamed Japan for doing the same in Korea and Manchuria.

'I don't say that all the things Japan did in Asia were great. But the wars in those days were savage and the Western people also fought brutal wars. Besides, our war did something great. All the Asian countries were liberated after the war. Could their independence have been achieved without the war? It was certainly expedited by the war.

'Victors may have almighty power, but power does not mean justice. Just because the West was the victor, they cannot blame us for everything. Sense of balance is essential in judging historical facts. Your argument lacks balance. You live in the West and look at things from the western point of view. I don't know if you are still a Japanese citizen, but it's deplorable that even genuine Japanese often talk like you – as if she or he belongs to America.'

I wrote her back saying that Japan had nothing to do with the liberation of the Asian countries. They were involved in the war to help the Allied countries and their independence was a precious reward after their tremendous sacrifice.

49 'Opinion Column', *koe*, *Asahi*, 17 August 2014

Mr Shinzo Abe and his grandfather Kishi's heritage

Under Prime Minister Shinzo Abe, Japanese nationalists have gathered strength. Who is Mr Abe? In order to understand him, it is a good idea to know about his maternal grandfather, former Prime Minister Nobusuke Kishi, who was Mr Abe's mentor.

Kishi was a senior official in Manchuria and the Commerce and Industry Minister in the Tojo Cabinet during the war. He spent three years in Sugamo Prison as a war-criminal suspect, but in 1953, five years after he was released from prison, he was elected an MP and in 1957 became Prime Minister.

As Thomas Berger writes in his illuminating book, *War, Guilt, and World Politics after World War II*,[50] compared with Germany where there were no prominent Nazi figures in the post-war political scene, in Japan the wartime men of power permeated the post-war political structure. That was because the US occupation faced shortages in finding elites to work with who were untainted by the old regime, since most Japanese had been part of the Imperial system. Aside from Kishi, former war criminals such as Mamoru Shigemitsu and Okinori Kaya had cabinet positions after the war.

Naturally, these men were not inclined to talk about their wartime past which would undermine their legitimacy. This was one of the reasons why post-war Japan was slow in showing remorse.

On the one hand, Kishi was a pragmatic politician who promoted post-war international peace in South East Asia; on the other he was an unrepentant imperialist who refused to see that his nation had committed war crimes. He explained why he returned to politics. 'I was a cabinet member at the start of the war and consider it my responsibility to explain to people that the war was not fought with wilful aggression, but out of absolute necessity. We were pushed into a corner and could not help beginning the war.'[51]

50 Berger, Thomas U, *War, Guilt, and World Politics after World War II*, Cambridge University Press, 2012, pp. 142–3

51 Nobusuke Kishi, Kazuo Yabuki, Takashi Ito, *Reflections of Nobusuke Kishi: Fragmentary Thoughts*, Bungei-Shunju, 1981

He did not like the new Constitution imposed on Japan by Mac-Arthur. He believed that the US occupation policies were aimed at weakening Japan, making it boneless so that it would not rise again. One of the reasons he returned to politics after the war was that he wanted to see the constitution amended.

Mr Kishi adored his grandson, Shinzo Abe. Mr Abe wrote in his bestselling book, *Toward a Beautiful Country*, that he was proud of how the roar of protesters failed to ruffle his grandfather.

Abe's father, Shintaro Abe, Kishi's son-in-law, was also a politician and could have been prime minister had he not died of a heart attack. Shintaro's view of the war was different from his father-in-law's, Shintaro's father, Kan Abe, was a liberal politician and Shintaro grew up to respect his father's political views. Shintaro went to war in China and it made him realize that the war was wrong. His views can be seen in this comment he made as foreign minister: 'World War II was a gravely mistaken war and this government is well aware of the international criticism of it as a war of aggression, and I will deal with [this criticism] sincerely.'[52] Although his son was working as his secretary then, Shinzo did not share his father's views, but his paternal grandfather Kishi's.

Shinzo Abe's cherished plan, inherited from Kishi, is to amend Article 9 of the Constitution: 'The Japanese people forever renounce war as a sovereign right of the nation and the threat or use of force as a means of settling international disputes.' Mr Abe knows that it is not easy to amend this article which the majority of Japanese are proud of. Therefore, he has been eroding its content without an amendment, as if rewriting a story with its title unchanged. He has passed several laws accelerating the build-up of the military, including an expansion in the role of the Self-Defense Forces.

In July 2015, the Japanese lower house of Parliament voted through a bill, after opposition lawmakers walked out in protest, which would give the armed forces limited power to engage in foreign combat for the first time since World War II. This was a significant victory for Mr Abe. But since then, many thousands of people have participated in

52 Shintaro Abe's talk in a Foreign Ministry Committee, 6 December 1985

demonstrations to oppose the bill. For example, on 30 August 2015, 120,000 demonstrators surrounded the Diet chanting opposition to the bill. Even so the Upper House passed the bill.

This reflects how deep-rooted anti-war feelings are amongst the Japanese. As a nation, Japan may not have expressed enough penitence, but its people are allergic to the word 'war'. Whether the constitution was given by MacArthur or not, Article 9 is so deeply embedded in the country's psyche that it is considered its own proud birthright.

Some Japanese may be nationalists, but most of them have learned hard lessons from the last war and are staunchly committed to peace and freedom.

CHAPTER 15

Ayako Kurahashi

A Pilgrimage to Fulfill Her Father's Dying Wish

In April 2012, I received a letter from Ayako Kurahashi, along with her three books. She sent them to me because she had read my book about the English POWs in Japan. She wrote that her father was a *Kempei*, a military policeman, who had been in China for ten years. On his deathbed he asked that his apology to the Chinese people be inscribed on his gravestone. It took twelve years for Ayako-san to carry out his wish. She retraced his footsteps, relived his life and grieved for what he might have done to the Chinese people. After that she went to the Chinese village where her father had been stationed and apologised to its residents.

Ayako-san inherited the burden of the war's unfinished business from her father. She studied the history of the war, and imagined what her father might have done. She could not take back the lives which had been lost or the damage done, but she did what a second generation could do. 'I learned so much through the process. I am a better person now. I cherish every living soul,' she wrote.

I met Ayako-san in Japan in October that year. She was a gentle and unassuming lady, but one could somehow feel that she was carrying enormous love and passion inside her. The following is the story I put together from what she told me and from her books: [53]

'It was March 1986. My father, Yukichi Osawa, was about to die

53 Kurahashi, Ayako, *What My Kempei Father Left for Me: A Journey of Two Generations – Father and Daughter*, Kobunken Publishers, 2002
— , *My Father's Dying Wish: Legacy of War Guilt in a Japanese Family*, translated by Philip Seaton, Paulownia Press, UK, 2009
— , *Nagai Kage: Long Shadow*, Hon-no-izumi-sha, Tokyo, Japan

after a long illness. I had been commuting to his hospital in Gunma from my job as a teacher at a junior high school in Tokyo. During one of my last visits, he stretched his shaking arm to his bedside drawer and took out a small piece of paper. He handed it to me and said, in a feeble voice, "When I die, I want you to engrave these words on my tombstone. Will you?"

I was so preoccupied with his deteriorating condition that I only glanced at the paper without really reading it. I said, "No problem." He looked relieved and dozed off. My father passed away four days later. He was seventy-one.

'Later when I read the message, I still did not fathom the full implications of his request. It said: "For ten of my twelve years and eight months of service in the former Japanese military, I worked as a warrant officer in the *Kempeitai* of the Imperial Japanese Army in China, based in Tianjin, Beijing, Shanxi province, Linfen, Yuncheng, Manchuria and Dongning. There I took part in Japan's war of aggression. I hereby offer my earnest apologies for the acts I committed against the people of China."

It turned out that both my brother and my uncle had also received the same message from my father written on a scrap of paper. When I asked my brother what to do about the will, he said, "You know, not only Dad, but also my kids and I will be buried in the same grave. You may not care since you won't go in there,[54] but we won't feel comfortable because we didn't do anything wrong in China."

' "Then what shall we do? Is it all right not to carry out his wish?" I asked. "Enough," he raised his voice, irritated. "We've already decided this between Uncle and me. Other old veterans in the village keep quiet about the war. They may take the engraving of wrong-doings in China on our dad's tombstone like a permanent scar on the village troops' record."

'My brother refused to talk any more about it. I put myself in his shoes. He had taken over my father's clothing shop and had to worry about the store's reputation. In a rural village where people make a big fuss about other people's business, an unusual message inscribed on a

54 A married woman is usually buried in her husband's grave.

gravestone might not sit well. The old veterans in particular wouldn't like it. I felt as if the case was closed and I couldn't bring up the subject any more.

'Four years later, in 1990, I retired from my teaching job because I wanted to do other things in life. All of a sudden, my father's dying wish came back to haunt me. It was surprising for me that my practical-minded father, whom I remembered for his dry humour, left a dying wish which revealed the agony he had suffered in secret. When I was young, my father's cries often woke me up in the middle of the night. Mother would say, "It's a dream about China again." But I'd never asked what he did in China to make him have bad dreams. Now I wished that I had questioned him about it. I thought I knew my father better than anybody else in the family, but that might not have been the case. How much did I really know him?

'He was born in 1915. Being the third son of a poor farmer, my father did not even go to junior high school. He took the exams to be a military policeman, a well-paid job in those days. He passed the exams and went to China. He married my mother who also went there as a military nurse in order to support her family. After Japan's defeat my mother returned on the last boat to Japan with my eldest brother, while my father was captured in China and destined to be sent to Siberia. But he managed to escape. On the desperate journey, he was caught again in Korea. He escaped again and a year later came home in rags, all skin and bones.

'He opened a clothing shop off the main street in his home town. He was a hard worker and the shop flourished. He organised the local traders' association and was its president for many years. On social occasions he told jokes and loved political debates, but in the family there was constant fighting. My parents didn't get on well. Mother was a beautiful lady. Her heart was with someone else and once she left home for a while. My father channeled his passion into the education of the children. My two brothers resented his Spartan discipline and became rebellious. I loved school and my grades were good. I was my father's favourite child.

'He never told me anything about his wartime experiences, but holding me on his lap, he taught me a few Chinese words and told me how his nose froze in the winters in Manchuria. As I grew older, he introduced me to his favourite films and novels, most of which involved war stories. They are the reason I abhor war. My father had strong words for Emperor Hirohito. Out of duty to the Emperor, he spent ten years in China. The Emperor did not utter a word of apology to the nation. As a modern woman I find it hard to imagine that people were so easily manipulated into believing that the Emperor was a god. But then I realised that, without textbooks, we too, are prevented from learning the real history of the war. It was my responsibility to find out the truth. If my father hurt innocent Chinese people, it was my job to apologise.

'In my quest to learn more about my father, I visited his older brother in Tokyo. Unlike my father, Uncle was a gentle soul. He became a *Kempei* as my father did and went to China. But he did not like atrocities, determined to quit the military police, and somehow he did so. Whether he knew more about what his younger brother had done in China or not, Uncle did not tell me. No other relatives I visited told me anything either.

'In the meantime, I read stories about the war criminals who had returned from a Chinese retention camp and formed a group called *Chu-ki-ren*. You know about it, don't you? They were genuinely sorry for what they had done in China and publicly testified to it. I went to one of their meetings and it made a strong impression on me. I contacted one of their members, Yoshio Tsuchiya, who was a *Kempei*. He visited the surviving family of the Chinese guerillas he had executed, and apologised, kneeling down on the floor, tears running down on his cheeks.

'I was determined to retrace my father's footsteps. In Nagoya, I visited the former commander of the Dongning *Kempeitai* detachment that my father had belonged to. Dongning was on the border where the former Soviet Union and North Korea met. The commander said that the main role of his police was intelligence gathering about the Soviets. He did not tell me much about my father. His wife spoke with nostalgia about how the area was covered with lilies of the valley in the early summer, and how well my father played the accordion.

'I had the good fortune of meeting a clinical psychologist, Professor

Noda Masaaki. It so happened that NHK ran a television programme of his interviews with members of the post-war generation and he wanted to talk with me about my father's dying wish. In the programme, Professor Noda said, "Your relatives opposed carrying out your father's wish. You went along with their decision. This may be a way Japanese people compromise. But on the other hand, doesn't your respect for your father and the desire to carry out his wish override a collective family decision?"

'Professor Noda's words struck me like an electric shock. Until then I hadn't thought of my father's wish from the perspective of the individual. He also suggested, "Treat the war as the one he fought himself rather than the war that was forced on him. Let him take full responsibility as a man." Professor Noda was right. In his will my father did not write a collective apology. He did not blame the authorities for his actions. He apologised for "the actions I committed against the people of China." After all, he had chosen the path of a career soldier and was trained to kill people. I should respect my father as an individual and fulfill his dying wish, even against what our family desired.

'When the documentary was broadcast, several friends called. One of them said, "When I was a kid, we were burnt out by the Great Tokyo Air Raid. My family did nothing wrong. We were victims of that war. There is no need for you to feel guilty. It was the responsibility of the Emperor and the wartime leaders." This colleague has been involved in a peace movement and is passionate about it. Our views had much in common, but he had not known about Japanese aggression.

'Around that time my brother died suddenly. It turned out that he took his own life because of a worsening heart condition and problems at work. It was a terrible shock to me. Every morning I lit incense and read sutras. I was in deep mourning. But I had to go on. I decided to deal with my father's will by myself.

'It was a happy surprise that my father's siblings responded to my request, saying that they had no objection to my carrying out his dying wish. Further good news came when I wrote to my nephew M, who had inherited my brother's household. He said, "You can go ahead with your obligation to your father about the inscription." M gave two reasons why he agreed. The first was that Grandfather had apologised to the Chinese people and that itself was a good thing. The second was that M had no objection because "if I had not been able to carry out my own father's dying wishes, it would have been painful."

'My brother's suicide saddened M and his family. Having experienced the loss of his father, M understood my feeling. His straightforward answer made me happy. I invited a stonemason along with M to the grave. We wanted the memorial stone to be a proper one, even if it was beyond our modest budget. We picked a black granite stone just over a metre tall. In several months it was done. The stone stood tranquil under the autumn sun. I patted it and said in a whisper, "Father. I hope you are glad." It was only a stone, but with the words engraved on it, it shone with a dignity befitting my father. I was proud I had finally carried out his dying wish.

'It had taken twelve years to fulfil his wish, but I should say that I needed just as long a time to come to terms with what my father had done. I have done research on the war, read about *Kempeitai*, attended lectures and meetings and have gone through counseling. I've also written three novels based on what I imagined my father had done in China. They were written based on the testimony of those who had committed war crimes.

'I had illusions about my father. In the first two stories I portrayed my father as an idealised figure. After that I happened to read a story of a *Kempei* in a *manga* comic book. He had the face of a demon and acted as a devil incarnate. As I looked at the image carefully, I saw my father's face. Suddenly my stubborn belief in my father as a saint shattered. My father must have tortured and killed Chinese just as the other *Kempeis* had done. I found myself crying, but the tears washed away many of my illusions. At last it had sunk in. I wrote the last story facing reality, although I still cried as I wrote.

'A friend said to me once, "My father was a soldier, but he was such a good man I cannot imagine him having done any terrible things." That was how I used to think, too. But even a good man could do something terrible in some circumstances. Many people do not want to delve into what their fathers did. You don't stir the pot because you don't want to find a devil hiding at the bottom. But it is part of bearing the responsibility for the terrible suffering in Asia inflicted by our fathers' generation.

'In the 1990s Korean women who had been made to work as sex slaves of the Japanese army gathered the courage to come forward. The Japanese were becoming more aware of wartime issues. I went to hear a talk by a former comfort woman and was mesmerised by her testimony which was given in beautiful Japanese. After that I joined a comfort women support group. I found out that these women came forward under assumed names. Confucian ethics are still observed in Korean society and if their identities were exposed, it would harm not only them but also their relatives. How many of these women suffered in silence? To do nothing about them would be a disgrace.

'I met former perpetrators as well as victims. I discovered that quite a few old men who had been repentant for their war actions were now involved in activism. I formed a small group with friends called the "Post-war Generation Joining Hands". We invited speakers to talk. Sometimes we just met for discussion.

'Once I was at a meeting of the "No More Nanjing Society" and met a Christian man named Nozaki Tadao. He talked to me enthusiastically about a group tour he had made to China and suggested that I should join the tour in the following year. So I did and visited China with the group. It was made up of people from the "China-Japan Association" and the "Delegation to Plant Trees for the Victims of the Nanjing Massacre". Ever since 1986 they have visited Nanjing and planted trees as an act of atonement. All thirty-two members of the group were friendly and I felt comfortable right away.

'At the Memorial Hall of the Victims of the Nanjing Massacre Museum, a large number of skeletons were piled up in a big glass building. Some had their mouths open and bodies contorted in pain. There was a small body near one of them. They may have been parent and child.

'This was only the first trip of three I made to China. Soon after I returned to Japan, Professor Noda told me that he'd visit China for the book launch of his translated book, *War and Guilt*. He wanted me to go with him and give a talk about my father's memorial at a museum in Beijing.

'This second trip to China led me to yet another chance to visit China. At a dinner during the symposium I happened to sit next to a freelance journalist Ban Zhongyi. We were just chatting and at some point I mentioned that my father's last posting was Shimenzi near Dongning. Ban got all excited. "In the autumn I'm going there to see an old lady who was forced to be a comfort woman. Why don't you come with me?"

'I almost jumped out of my chair. "Yes, please," I said eagerly. It was only later that I began to get nervous. Come to think of it, we were total strangers. All I knew about Ban was that he wrote books and produced documentary films. He didn't know me at all, except for my father's memorial stone. Later I found out that Ban had been employed by a Japanese grassroots activist group called Society to Support Former Chinese Comfort Women and went all over China looking after them. I knew he must be a good man.

'I flew to Beijing with a rucksack on my back. Ban's pretty new bride, Keiko, travelled with me. We stayed at a small family-run hotel in Beijing and met up with Ban the next evening. The following day we flew to Harbin in the rain. From Harbin, it took eight hours to reach Dongning, a forlorn town close to the border with North Korea. For dinner we had cold Korean noodles sprinkled with a frightening amount of chili powder. The next day it was cold and rainy again. After an hour's taxi ride, we finally arrived at a hamlet where a Korean woman, Ri Bongwoon, lived. A few years earlier, when she had been ill, Ban had arranged for her hospitalisation. Ever since then she had been waiting for Ban's visit.

'Seventy years ago Ri had been taken away from Korea on a Japanese truck to Shimenzi where she was forced to work as a comfort woman. When the war ended, she was abandoned there. She married a Chinese man, but was unable to bear children. For this reason, her husband was often violent towards her. After he died, her husband's family was generous enough to let her stay in their house.

'We had lunch with Bongwoon at a café in the village. She was so very happy to see Ban, but hardly touched her food. Ban said, "Come on, eat something, Ri." He picked up some food with his chopsticks and put it on Bongwoon's plate. Toward the end of the lunch, Bong–

woon suddenly burst out crying. She said: "For a long time, I was treated like a dog, but Chinese people took care of me and even helped me live in an old people's home. I wish I could do something to show my thanks, but I'm too old to work and am good for nothing." I was sitting next to her. I put my arm around her shoulder and held her tight.

'We visited another comfort woman Yi Kwanja in the village of Gaoan. Unlike Bongwoon, she did not recognise Ban. She just stared at me when Ban explained the purpose of my visit. Her icy response made me shudder, although being a perpetrator's daughter I didn't expect a warm welcome. This was a woman whose life was ruined by the Japanese. Eventually, perhaps finally recalling who Ban was, she suddenly smiled. As Ban spoke about me, she nodded. When it was time to leave, I hugged her and wished her well.

'The next day, again in the rain, we drove further south. The roads had turned into muddy streams, but the driver pushed on until we finally reached Shimenzi, where my parents had stayed the last two and half years of the war. Ban went to the house of the village elder, eighty-one-year-old Guo Qingshi. When Ban told him the purpose of my visit, Guo called in all the neighbours. I showed the pictures of my father in a *Kempei* uniform. How happy I would be if someone said they actually knew him. But if they spelled out all the terrible things he had done to them or their families, could I bear it? Anyhow, I came here to convey my father's apology to them. Now was the opportunity to make his wish a reality.

'Everyone spoke up, but none of them remembered my father. But within a few minutes they came up with the names of family and friends who had been killed by the *Kempeitai*. This place was so close to the Soviet border that lots of them had been suspected of being Soviet spies. "But don't you remember Mr B? He was a very kind *Kempei*," a man said. "Once I had forgotten my identity card. He let me pass." "Yes, Mr B mingled with us in the village rather than staying in the barracks."

'I had the wishful thought that Mr B was my father. I repeated my father's name and showed his picture again. I was dejected when they shook their heads. They went on to say that the commander was not a nice man. A man said, "He hit me a lot for no reason." I told them that the commander was ninety-one and still alive in Nagoya. One man clucked his tongue and others cursed. I took out a photo of my father's memorial and showed it to them. "I apologise to you all. Thanks to Mr Ban, I'm here and I'm happy to have an opportunity at long last to convey my father's apology." I broke down in tears.

'People took turns to console me. "Thank you for having come here from so far away. Your father was a lucky man to have a nice daughter like you." "It wasn't your father. It was the leaders of the war who were to blame." Why are the Chinese people so big-hearted and kind? We said our farewells to Guo and the group. After that, we visited the area where the military barracks used to stand. It looked unreal because there was only a small hill looking down on a river. The military police station where my father was stationed was now used as an elementary school.

'We got into the car of a young man named O who had come and picked us up. Now we would be traveling a long way home. In the car I thought I would never come back here again and suddenly had an urge to turn back. I had a feeling that Guo might have known my father, but did not say so. He had remembered all the other four *Kempeis* well. So it is unlikely that he didn't know my father. After all, my father had been there for two and a half years and Guo used to be a cook at a restaurant which was frequented by officers. It's possible that Guo pretended he did not remember because he did not want to say bad things about my father.

'When they said that B was kind, but B turned out not to be my father, I was sad. It must have shown in my face. Guo saw it and did not want to tell me that he knew my father. After all, my father had done something bad enough to repent and make him write an apology. I wished I could see Guo one more time to check on it. But I had to swallow my words to ask driver O to turn back to Shimenzi.

'I've never learned what my father did as a *Kempei*. But the best thing about this trip was that I met many people in China, particularly those who had gone through the war and still talked to me kindly. On the way back, through the car window, I again looked at this remote region where only rice, beans, weeds and trees grew. The area had military importance only because it was where the Chinese, Russian and Korean borders meet.

'At midnight on 8 August 1945, the huge Soviet First Far East Army attacked. My father, following orders, remained at the site of the killings and tragedies. Then he escaped and returned home a year later, but he carried with him a heavy burden of guilt until the day of his death. Now almost seventy years later, this site at least looked peaceful, trees and plants having absorbed the blood and tears people had shed on the land.'

Postscript

On my last trip to Japan, I visited Yasukuni Jinja, a Shinto shrine that is at the centrer of an international controversy. For this trip to the shrine, my cousin Takuya Inoue came along with me. I seldom see Takuya-san because of my long absence from my country, but I know from my sixth sense that he is a kindred spirit. For one of his charity works, he is a volunteer treasurer of Bridge for Peace, a group founded by a young Japanese woman, Naoko Jin, which works for reconciliation with Filipinos.

Aside from being larger than any other Japanese shrines I had visited, Yasukuni Jinja was a typical square wooden structure with a traditional slanted tiled roof. From outside, it was nothing special, but I heard that the interior was awe-inspiring. It was noon on an ordinary weekday. The shrine was not crowded, only dotted with old women dressed in black kimonos and men in dark suits. I knew they must be members of Izokukai, a group of the families of the war dead who gather here for memorial services.

From the quiet environment, there is nothing to indicate that this shrine is the subject of an international controversy. Shinto is an indigenous spirituality and not even a religion in the sense that there is no canon except for a miscellany of folklore and mythology. Shinto became politically important between 1868 and 1945 when mythology was incorporated into the Emperor's family history to legitimise his deity. During World War II the government utilised Shinto shrine worship as a force for mobilising imperial loyalties. Yasukuni became a place where the war dead were enshrined.

What made this shrine an affront to other countries was that in October 1979, its newly appointed chief priest, Nagayoshi Matsudaira, ordered that the fourteen A-class war-criminals be enshrined here. He later declared, 'When I looked through the document and found out that enshrining of the war-time leaders into Yasukuni had already been decided and that the timing was up to the chief priest, I quickly made it happen.' The war-criminals were deified as Showa Martyrs.

Soon the news that the war-criminals had been secretly enshrined in Yasukuni was covered by Kyodo News. But most Japanese were only reminded of the fact in 1985, when China and other Asian countries opposed Prime Minister Nakasone's official Yasukuni visit.

In the face of criticism by Asian nations, Nakasone canceled a second Yasukuni visit. But even after that Prime Minister Koizumi visited several times. The current Prime Minister Abe has visited Yasukuni and provoked anger not only from neighbours, but also drawn criticism from Ambassador Caroline Kennedy.

We did not stop at the altar to put our hands together because neither of us wanted to pray for the A-class war-criminals, but I bowed in my mind for the soldiers who had lost their lives in the war.

I went straight to the Yushu-kan war museum attached to the shrine. As soon as I entered the museum, I felt as if I had flown back to the time of the war. An A6M Zero fighter was parked on the ground and the imposing model C56 locomotive No. 31, which served on the Thai-Burma Railway, was standing in front of me. It is the machine Railway Man, Eric Lomax, saw puffing along the new railway he had helped to build and was excited about even if it was an enemy machine.

As I walked through its rooms with panels, pictures and objects, explaining the glory of the nation and of its war, I noticed that the museum presented a heavily revisionist interpretation of history. Japan's conquest of East Asia during the pre-World War II period was explained as an effort to save the region from the imperial advances of the Western powers. Japan's goal in World War II was to liberate Asia from Western imperialism; its attack on Pearl Harbor a necessary move undertaken in self-defense.

Nowhere in the museum was there any mention of atrocities committed by the Japanese. One of the panels stated that after the invasion of Nanjing, 'residents were once again able to live their lives in peace.'

I wanted to walk out and looked for an exit when we suddenly emerged into a large area with a see-through ceiling where a *Kaiten* human torpedo was sitting like a huge black coffin. The image of

Minoru Wada sitting inside this monster ship in pitch dark silence at the bottom of the sea stopped my breath and I felt choked as he must have for the long days and hours of waiting for rescue and death.

In the last room before the exit there was a wall full of small black and white photos of Japanese young men – more like boys – in buttoned-up black school uniforms. Although some of them wore smiles, believing in the cause of the war, they all had been deprived of the chance to live a full life.

In my mind, behind the pictures of these boys, loomed the faces of tens of thousands of soldiers from the other ends of the world – sailors, pilots, army men and POWs who did not live full lives, and also women, children and Chinese peasants.

The fact that Japan was allowing this museum to present a revisionist view of history was in marked contrast to the Berlin museums which presented the cold hard facts about the Jewish Holocaust.

Professor Carol Gluck of Columbia University says[55] that we live in the age in which the 'politics of apology' are the international norm. This has developed over the past half-century as Europe came to terms with the Holocaust. Nations are expected to acknowledge their past actions and crimes.

Professor Thomas Berger of Boston University also writes that 'we live in an age of apology and recrimination.'[56] Germany has been the 'model penitent'; Japan, the 'model impenitent'.

Indeed the Japanese were slow to face the truth of the war. They did not mourn or atone sufficiently for the enormous harm their war had brought to the world – particularly in Asia and the pacific. Over the years, they were gradually coming to grips with the truth, but one cannot say that the nation represented by the current government has made much progress.

However in the course of writing this book I have met many people in the post-war generations who did painful soul-searching about the war. Not only peace activists, but also historians, artists, journalists and

55 Interview with Carol Gluck, 'Change in Japan is a Long-distance Run', *Asahi*, 17 September 2013
56 Berger, Thomas, op. cit., pp. 8–10

housewives all grappled with the war's legacy, each in their own fashion. Many are building bridges to former enemy countries, and turning former foes into friends.

I have also met veterans who feel deep shame and regret about their own conduct and mourned the death of their comrades and foes. I hope that the powerful voices of these old soldiers who spoke here in the name of peace and truth will be long remembered even after they are gone from this earth, and that they help guide Japan to a better future.

Bibliography

Reference Books

PART ONE

Preface to Part One

Yosano, Akiko, 'Kimi Shinitamou Kotonakare' (Don't Lay Down Your Life), published in *Famous Japanaese Poems Shine in English*, Misuzu Shobo, Tokyo, Japan, pp. 76–9

Chapter 1

Kumagai, Shin-ichiro, *Kaneko-san's War: Reality of the Chinese War-front*, Little More, Tokyo, 2005
Chu-Ki-Ren Quarterly 49, January 2012
Sone, Kazuo, *Private Record of Nanjing Massacre*. Sairyu-sha, Tokyo, 1984

Chapter 2

Iwai, Tadamasa and Tadakuma, *Tokko: Testimony by the Brothers Who Became Suicide Bombers*, Shin-nippon, 2002

Chapter 3

Wada, Minoru, *Voice of Sea God Does Not Die Down: Diary of a Kaiten Tokko Student*, Kadokawa, 1972
Takeda, Goro, *Kaiten Tokko Student Force: Kaiten was No Superb Weapon*, Kojin-sha, 2008
Iwai, Tadamasa and Tadakuma, ibid., pp. 126–7
Taya, Haruko and Cook, Theodore F., *Japan at War: An Oral History*, New Press, 1992
Kozu Naoji, *Human Torpedo, Kaiten*, Asahi Sonorama, 1995
Kike Wadatsumi no Koe, *Writings of the Fallen Japanese Students*, Wadatsumi-kai, Kobun-sha, 1959

Listen to the Voices from the Sea, translated by Midori Yamanouchi and Joseph L. Quinn, University of Scranton Press, Scranton, 2000

Chapter 5

Iida, Susumu, *Japanese Soldiers in Hell: Truth about the New Guinea Front Line*, Shincho, 2008

—, *The Long Road to Atonement*, Iwanami, 2009

—, *Unfinished-War*, Oshi-sha, 1987

—, *Letters from Sugamo Prison*, Togo-sha, 1990

—, *Blue Bird Was Not There*, Fuji, 2003

—, *Even if the World Perishes Tomorrow: A BC Class War Criminal's Last Words to the Young*, Nashinoki-sha, 2014

Chapter 6

Mitsuhashi, Kunitami, *Poems of Birds: Return from a Death Island*. 'Ants', was translated by Susan Gaulter from 'Ari', p. 16 et seq., Kadokawa, 2005

Chapter 7

Utsumi, Aiko, *Why Was Kim Indicted?*, Asahi Shimbun Publications, 2008

—, *Sugamo Prison: Peace Movement by War Criminals*, Yoshikawa Koubunkan, Tokyo, 2004

Oomori, Junro and Watanabe, Ko, *BC Class War Criminals: Voices from Prison*, NHK Publications, 2009

Dunlop, E. E., *The War Diaries of Weary Dunlop: Java and the Burma–Thailand Railway, 1942–1945*, Thomas Nelson, Australia, 1986

Chapter 8

Kumai, Toshimi. *Blood and Mud in the Philippines: The Worst Guerrilla War in the Pacific War*, Jiji-Tsushin-sha, Tokyo, 1977

Walker, Scott, *The Edge of Terror*, Thomas Dunne Books, St Martin's Press, New York, 1950

Kumai, Toshimi, *An Essay, US–Japan Dialogue on POWs, January 2012* http://www.kumaibuki.com/Kumai_memoir.pdf

Tenny, Lester I., *My Hitch in Hell: The Bataan Death March*, Brassey's Inc., 1995

Chapter 9

Kurihara, Toshio, *Siberia Internment*, Iwanami, 2009
Takasugi, Ichiro, *In the Shadow of Auroras*, Iwanami, 1991
Henmmi, Jun, *A Will from the Lagel*, Bunshun Bunko, 1992

PART TWO

Preface to Part Two

Gomikawa, Jumpei, *Ningen-no-Joken, Human Conditions*, Bunshun Bunko, 1966
Noda, Masaaki, *War and Guilt*, Iwanami, Tokyo, 1998
Ienaga Saburo, *Japan's Past, Japan's Future: One Historian's Odyssey*, Roman and Littlefield, New York, 2001
Kersten, Rikki, *Neo-Nationalism and Liberal School of History*, Japan Forum, Vol. 11, No. 2, 1999, pp. 191–203
Masalski, Kathleen Woods, *Examining the Japanese History Textbook Controversies*, Internet
Bix, Herbert P., *Hirohito and the Making of Modern Japan*, HarperCollins Inc., 2000
Jomaru, Yoichi, 'An Essay on Passing on the Recollections of the Battlefield', *Chu-ki-Ren Quarterly*, No. 49, January. 2012

Chapter 10

Kumagai, Shinichiro, *Why Talk about Aggression: Postwar History of Chu-ki-ren, China Returnees' Link*, Iwanami Booklet, no. 659, Tokyo, 1982
Yoshikai, Natsuko, *Memory that Cannot be Erased: Confessions of a Former Doctor*, Nitchu Shuppan, 1981
Kobayashi, Setsuko, Mio-san Who Went back to Sky in Fushan, Suginaini-Keyaki Shuppan, 1999
Kobayashi, Setsuko, *Memory of Vivisection: A Former Military Doctor, Ken Yuasa's Postwar Activities*, Nashinoki-sha, 2010
Komori, Yoichi, *Senso e no Sozoryoku: Imagination for War*, Shin-Nippon Shuppan-sha, Tokyo, 2008

Chapter 11

Lomax, Eric, *Railway Man*, Vintage, 1995
Mitsuda, Yasuhiro, *Rainbow Over the River Kwai*, Nashinoki-sha, 2011

Chapter 12

Sasamoto, Taeko, *The Allied POWs' Epitaphs*, Kusa-no-Ne, 2004
Holmes, Keiko, *Agape: A Journey of Healing and Reconciliation*, Inochi-no-kotoba, 2003

Chapter 13

Yoshimi, Yoshiaki. *Jugun Ianhu* (Comfort Woman), Iwanami Shoten, 1995
Shirota, Suzuko, *A Song in Praise of Maria*, Japan Christian Group, 1971
Senda, Kako. *Jugun Ianhu*, Futaba-sha, 1973
Ikeda, Eriko, et al., *NHK is in Danger*, Akebi Shobo, 2014
What Are You Afraid of?, compiled by Hisako Matsui, Iwanami Shoten, 2014
Testimonies of Comfort Women: Breaking 50 Years of Silence, compiled by Asia Forum, Kokusei-sha

Chapter 14

Jomaru, Yoichi, *Study on 'Shokun' and 'Seiron': How Conservative Opinions Have Changed*, Iwanami, 2011

Chapter 15

Kurahashi, Ayako, *What My Kempei Father Left for Me: A Journey of Two Generations – Father and Daughter*, Kobunken, 2002
—, *My Father's Dying Wish: Legacy of War Guilt in a Japanese Family*, translated by Philip Seaton, Paulownia Press, UK, 2009
—, *Nagai Kage: Long Shadow*, Hon-no-izumi-sha, Tokyo, Japan

Bibliography

SECONDARY SOURCES

Baruma, Ian, *Wages of Guilt: Memories of War in Germany and Japan*, Atlantic Books, 1994

Berger, Thomas U., *War, Guilt and World Politics after World War II*, Cambridge Uuniversity Press, 2012

Bix, Herbert P., *Hirohito and the Making of Modern Japan*, HarperCollins, 2000

Buruma, Ian, *A Year Zero: A History of 1945*, 2012

Dower, John W., *War without Mercy: Race and Power in the Pacific War*, Pantheon, 1986

—, *Embracing the Defeat*, Norton, 1999

Fujisawa, Akira, *Nihon Gunji-shi, Japanese Military History, I and II*, Shakai Hihyo-sha, Tokyo, 2006

Gordon, Andrew, *A Modern History of Japan: From Tokugawa Times to the Present*, 2003

Hanto, Kazutoshi, *Showa-shi: History of Showa,1926-1945*, Iwanami-Shoten, Tokyo, 2004

Hastings, Max, *Nemesis: The Battle for Japan,1944–45*, HarperPress, 2007

Hotta, Eri, *Japan 1941: Countdown to Infamy*, Knopf, 2013

Mitter, Rana, *China's War with Japan, 1937-1945: The Struggle for Survival*, 2013

Tobe, Ryoichi, *Japanese Army in China: Dream and Setbacks of the China Specialists*, Kodansha Metier Selected Books, 1999

Yoshida, Yutaka, *Japanese Views of War*, Iwanami, 2005

—, *Japanese Soldiers*, Iwanami, 2002

—, *Heishi-tachi-no Sengo-shi: Soldiers' Postwar History.* Iwanami Shoten, Tokyo, 2011

A Soldier's Two Battlefields, China and Okinawa, compiled by Utsumi, Ishida and Kato, Shakai-Hyoron-sha, 2005

229

Acknowledgments

I will spend the rest of my life thanking my husband, Jimmy, for his unflagging support and editorial advice.

Many thanks to my daughter, Mako Yoshikawa for her literary advice and enthusiasm for my project. Her constant reassurance that I'm working for a good cause sustained my morale. I appreciate the perceptive comments and technical assistance of her husband, Rob Sabal. They accompanied me on several interviews and eased and lightened my travels.

My cousin, Takuya Inoue, is a retired banker, but should have been a historian. He read each chapter three times and frequently visited the National Diet Library (Japan's equivalent of the Library of Congress) to check and verify the facts in this manuscript. I do not know how to thank him enough.

I am very grateful to the rest of my family: Yoko, Peter, Aiko, Eric, Miranda, Ali, Galen and Jon. My nephew, Kenjo Inoue, an avid reader of history, helped me understand the younger generation's views about the war. My sister, Aiko Moroto, provided invaluable support whenever I was in Japan.

I deeply appreciate the help of my distinguished friend, the phiolosopher and historian of ideas, John Gray, who kindly read my manuscript at an early stage and helped it on its journey. I am enormously grateful to his wife, my dear friend Mieko, who has been very supportive all the way through the ups and downs of working on this book.

My heartfelt thanks to Professor Martin Collcutt, formerly the Chair of Princeton University's East Asian Studies Department, for his constructive critique and encouragement. The historian, Yutaka Yoshida, kindly met me and shared with me his vast knowledge of WWII. I am grateful to another historian, Aiko Utsumi, for telling me about her forty-year study of the status of minorities in Japan.

Acknowledgments

I owe Trevor Bedeman whose father was a POW for his support and encouragement for my project. Tim Baddeley, Piers and Fiona Bizony read chapters and gave insightful comments. Susan Gaulter translated Kunitami Mitsuhashi's story, 'Ants'. I am grateful to Angelina Jenkins for her help with Chinese words. Nualla Lawrence and Liz Harding helped me in multiple ways.

The two books by Shin-ichiro Kumagai, *Kaneko-san's War* and *Why Talk about Aggression*, were invaluable references in connection with Chapter 1 and Chapter 10. Fujio Kurata kindly arranged my meeting with Yasuji Kaneko.

I would also like to thank Yukako Ibuki, Miyuki Endo, Yumiko Saito, Yoichi Jomaru, Kotaro Itabashi, Satoshi Sonobe and Fusako Watanabe for their invaluable help and advice. I'd like to express my appreciation again to both the veterans and the members of the post-war generation who shared their experiences and hard-earned wisdom with me.

It was a great regret for me not to be able to include in this book all the wonderful people I met and their precious life stories. Let me at least introduce just a few of them briefly here.

I was determined to meet Hayashi Inouye when I read his book on his wartime experiences. He thought the war was evil, but did not lose his humanity even in the most savage situations. He had the heart to lament his enemies' deaths and treated POWs with compassion. In his book he wrote that when the war was over, he raised his arm and waved to the enemy' – no, they were no longer the 'enemy' – whom he saw over the broken iron bridge in a village of Burma. To his joy, they also raised their arms to him. He wanted to run to them, say hello and pat them on the shoulder . . .

After a long search, I finally located him. He was a genuinely lovely man as I had expected, but at ninety-six he was deaf and I had difficulty communicating with him.

His comrade in the same regiment, Toshimi Nakamura, lives in a fancy house in Nagasaki thanks to the successful cinema house he ran after the war. Although over ninety, he has the brains and body of a fifty year old and wrote an amazingly detailed day-to-day battlefield record based on the diary he had kept throughout the war. He said he knew Japan would lose the war, but fought dutifully and bravely. He almost died countless times. After the war, he organised his company's veterans' association. With its members, he went back to Burma ten times to gather the bones of his comrades and give donations to the schools in the villages which the war had ruined.

Miyuki Endo was a flight attendant, but meeting with a former captain of the Japanese air-transportation unit, Mr Kobayashi, on a flight to New York led her to a career as a historian. He gave her an old cardboard box containing his diary and those of the soldiers who had died in the campaign with the British and Chinese allied forces in north Burma and bordering Lameng in the west of China's Yunan province. Ms Endo spent seven years interviewing the surviving witnesses of the campaign and obtaining related materials from Britain, the US and China. Her thesis and the book based on it was critically acclaimed as 'history seen through the soldiers' eyes.' She still does research on the war, attends veterans' association meetings and makes good friends with the old soldiers.

Naoko Jin made a trip to the Philippines in 2000 as a university student. The tour was organised by a professor who taught a seminar about the legacy of World War II. At a gathering in a village, a woman rose to her feet. 'I never want to see a damn Japanese ever again. What the hell have you come here for?' she cried out. Her husband had been taken away by the Japanese army on spy charges in 1943, the year after they got married. He never came home.

Back in Japan a Buddhist monk told Naoko about a former soldier who, just before his death, deliriously muttered his regrets for the atrocities he had committed in the Philippines. Naoko wanted to help heal the deep sorrow of those affected by the war and set up a 'Bridge for Peace'. Its members frequently visit the Philippines.